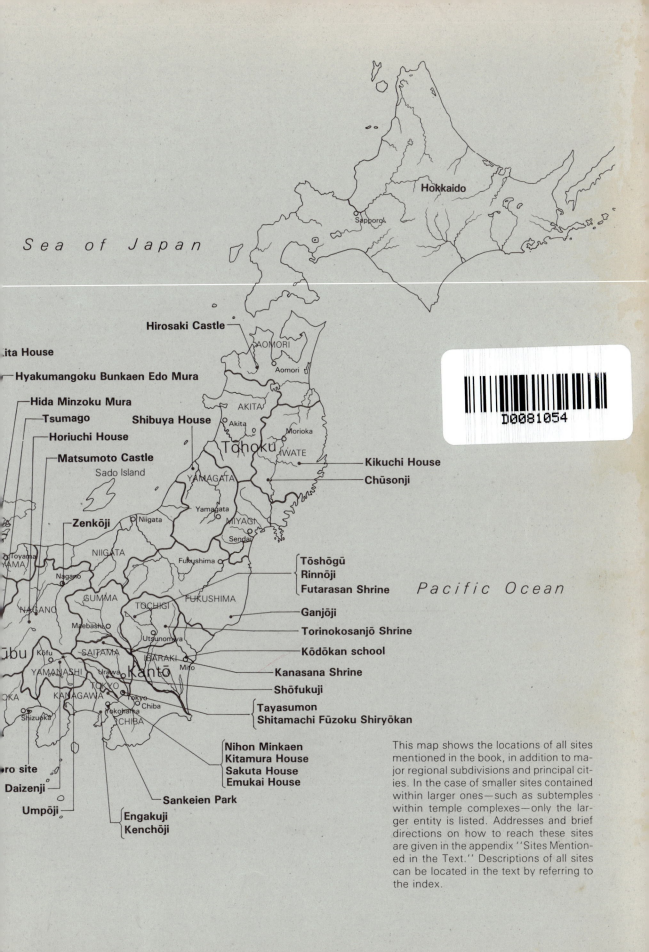

Hokkaido

Sapporo

Sea of Japan

Hirosaki Castle

AOMORI

Aomori

ita House

Hyakumangoku Bunkaen Edo Mura

AKITA

Hida Minzoku Mura

Akita

Morioka

Tsumago

Shibuya House

IWATE

Horiuchi House

Tōhoku

Matsumoto Castle

Sado Island

YAMAGATA

Kikuchi House

Chūsonji

Yamagata

Zenkōji

Niigata

MIYAGI

Sendai

NIIGATA

Toyama

YAMA

Fukushima

Nagano

Tōshōgū
Rinnōji
Futarasan Shrine

Pacific Ocean

GUMMA

TOCHIGI

FUKUSHIMA

Ganjōji

NAGANO

Maebashi

Torinokosanjō Shrine

Utsunomiya

Kōdōkan school

ubu

Kōfu

SAITAMA

IBARAKI

Mito

Kanasana Shrine

YAMANASHI

Urawa

Kantō

Shōfukuji

OKA

KANAGAWA

TOKYO

Tokyo

Tayasumon

Shitamachi Fūzoku Shiryōkan

Shizuoka

Yokohama

Chiba

CHIBA

Nihon Minkaen
Kitamura House
Sakuta House
Emukai House

ro site

Daizenji

Sankeien Park

Umpōji

Engakuji
Kenchōji

This map shows the locations of all sites mentioned in the book, in addition to major regional subdivisions and principal cities. In the case of smaller sites contained within larger ones—such as subtemples within temple complexes—only the larger entity is listed. Addresses and brief directions on how to reach these sites are given in the appendix "Sites Mentioned in the Text." Descriptions of all sites can be located in the text by referring to the index.

D0081054

What is **JAPANESE ARCHITECTURE ?**

What is JAPANESE ARCHITECTURE?

Kazuo Nishi and Kazuo Hozumi

translated, adapted, and with an introduction by
H. Mack Horton

KODANSHA INTERNATIONAL LTD.
Tokyo, New York, and San Francisco

Distributed in the United States by Kodansha International/USA Ltd., through Harper & Row, Publishers, Inc., 10 East 53rd Street, New York, New York 10022. Published by Kodansha International Ltd., 12-21, Otowa 2-chome, Bunkyo-ku, Tokyo 112 and Kodansha International/USA Ltd., with offices at 10 East 53rd Street, New York, New York 10022 and the Hearst Building, 5 Third Street, Suite No. 430, San Francisco, California 94103.

Originally published under the title *Nihon kenchiku no katachi: seikatsu to kenchiku-zōkei no rekishi* by Shōkokusha Publishing Co., Ltd.
  LCC 84-48695
  ISBN 0-87011-711-4
  ISBN 4-7700-1211-x (in Japan)
First English edition, 1985

CONTENTS

INTRODUCTION

Ruth Benedict, in her early but influential introduction to Japanese culture, *The Chrysanthemum and the Sword*, spoke of the tendency to see Japan and its people in terms of "but also's"—pacific but also at times warlike, conservative but also given to innovation. She might have made reference to their architecture as well, for the Japanese through the ages have evolved a building art that seems to delight in opposites and contradictions. In reading through this overview of Japan's secular and sacred architecture, from it origins to the end of the Edo period in the nineteenth century, one is struck again and again by the extremes that seem to characterize the country's traditional building arts.

Perhaps size is the most obvious case in point. In the realm of religious architecture, there is the Great Buddha Hall of Tōdaiji temple, the largest wooden structure on earth after having been rebuilt at only two-thirds of its eighth-century dimensions. Nearly fifty meters in height, it houses a bronze Buddha large enough to hold a person in the palm of its hand. But also there is Kasuga, the shrine of the great Fujiwara family, which is centered on four main structures each only two meters wide by less than three meters deep. There are even miniature shrines that fit on a shelf in a corner of a private residence or in a niche in a roadside wall. In residential architecture, the spacious Imperial Palace complex of the Heijō Capital in Nara once contained more than five hundred buildings on grounds over a square kilometer in area, and the Palace of the Heian Capital was even larger in size. Consider, too, the sprawling castle and palace of the Tokugawa shōguns in Edo, whose acres of grounds still define the center of modern Tōkyō and house the present palace of the imperial family. Standing against this expansiveness, there are the rows of simple and unassuming townhouses that were the norm for medieval city dwellers. And at the lower end of the scale is the teahouse, whose influence on Japanese architecture has been inversely proportionate to its tiny size. The Konnichian Teahouse, for instance, has a plan containing only one and three-quarters *tatami* mats (one mat is about one by two meters in size), yet it has been viewed since its creation in the seventeenth century as one of the monuments of tea taste.

Gardens, too, seem almost infinitely variable, from the tiny, enclosed courtyards in such temples as the Daisen'in of Daitokuji to the gracious parks of Katsura and Shugakuin Detached Palaces, which include winding paths for leisurely walks as well as ponds large enough for boating. Thus, on the one hand, the garden can be reduced to an almost incorporeal entity, as in the single flower in the decorative alcove of a teahouse or the raked sand of a Zen-style "dry landscape." On the other, it can be expanded nearly infinitely by means of "borrowed scenery," as at the Shugakuin Palace or at Entsūji temple in Kyōto, whose gardens incorporate distant mountains into their designs.

No less extreme are differences in height, from the pair of seven-story pagodas at Tōdaiji that once soared one hundred meters above the temple precinct—nearly twice the height of the tallest pagoda left today—to a teahouse door so low one must crouch to pass through it. To be sure, most Japanese architecture is only one story in height, but that one story is surprisingly elastic: the Great Buddha Hall of Tōdaiji contains only one story, though the pent roof on the exterior makes it appear from the outside to have two.

Then again there are extremes in plans, from the Sinitic ideal of bilateral symmetry seen at Asukadera or Shitennōji temples to the almost random layouts of mountain temples of the Esoteric Buddhist sects, which are influenced by the exigencies of their terrain. Residential plans include both the relative symmetry of the ideal Shinden complex and the rambling mansions of the later courtly and warrior elites, which meander through their grounds with as little regard for symmetry as has a mountain brook.

A more profound set of extremes is seen in the Japanese treatment of architectural surfaces. At one pole is the Sukiya style with its simplicity and understatement, its refined sense of design and exploitation of natural, unadorned materials. At the other is the Tōshōgū Shrine at Nikkō, a riot of polychromy and sculpture that covers nearly every inch of available surface. The taste for ornament, moreover, is not an isolated phenomenon—the seventeenth-century Tōshōgū was foreshadowed in the twelfth century by the Golden Hall of Chūsonji with its gold-leaf walls and its interior of lacquer and mother-of-pearl, and in the fourteenth century by the Golden Pavilion of Rokuonji, its two upper stories likewise finished in sheets of gold. A mixture of the two tastes is seen at Nishi Honganji temple, where a huge audience hall lavishly fitted with intricately carved transoms and polychromed screens with gold backgrounds is connected by a few meters of corridor to a cozy set of private rooms that are the epitome of understatement, incorporating as they do subdued ink paintings, plain paper screens, rough-hewn posts, and unpainted woodwork. This bipolarity in the treatment of surfaces hints at underlying extremes of attitude toward artifice itself. The teahouse de-emphasizes the hand of the builder; the Tōshōgū flaunts it.

The "but also" theme holds true in the matter of age and time—Japan is known both for the oldest extant wooden buildings in the world, the Golden Hall, Pagoda, and Inner Gate of Hōryūji, which are thought to date to the end of the seventh century, and for the regularity with which great parts of cities and temple compounds have been laid waste by fire. One is struck too by the irony that buildings devoted to Buddhism, a religion that stresses the evanescence of all things, are the oldest in the country, whereas only a handful of the hundreds of castles built for impregnability and permanence now survive as originally built. Then there is the case of Shintō shrines, ancient in history and design but traditionally dismantled and rebuilt of fresh materials at set intervals to ensure ritual purity. The structures at Ise Shrine have been rebuilt sixty times, the last occurring in 1973, making them not only very old, but also very new. Among residential structures there is on the one extreme Katsura Palace, which was expanded and redesigned for decades under its successive princely owners, and on the other Kamo no Chōmei's "ten foot square hut," which the owner could dismantle and reassemble elsewhere as the spirit moved him.

From one perspective, the entire course of Japanese architectural development through the ages can be characterized in terms of two poles, the native and the foreign. Buddhist architecture was, of course, introduced from China, and subsequent developments on the Asian continent were imported into Japan by Chinese émigrés or Japanese traveling monks, often with little lapse in time. Chinese architectural styles from the Six Dynasties to the Qing thus have their Japanese representations, with the added irony that Japan is often the only place where examples of those Chinese forms still remain.

But the heavy influence of Chinese culture and the determination of the Japanese to stay abreast of Continental stylistic change were continually tempered by indigenous developments. An outstanding example of this tendency is the invention by native builders of the hidden roof, an innovation which gives a characteristic Japanese cast to the structures using it. And not long after the Great Buddha and Zen styles of architecture were introduced, Japanese carpenters were already combining elements from them with those of earlier architecture to new, eclectic effect. Indeed, the constant dialectic between the native and the foreign has engaged the Japanese throughout their written history (a history itself first recorded in Chinese) and inspired continual efforts to isolate, or create, a purely Japanese cultural counterpart to that which was imported. In the case of architecture, the problem of self-definition has been complicated by the fact that even Ise Shrine, considered the touchstone of native architectural attitudes, reached its present form only after the introduction of Chinese styles into the country and itself shows some Chinese influence.

The reader can, if he or she wishes, expand the list of opposing architectural elements. There remains, however, one last ''but also'' that should be mentioned here, perhaps the most important of all. This is the fact that despite extremes in size, plan, decoration, age, and historical development in various examples of Japanese architecture, there is a bedrock of basic similarities that, if not universal, still apply in a great majority of cases. It is this core of shared traits that allows us to speak of ''Japanese architecture'' in general, instead of isolated Japanese buildings. These fundamental consistencies are particularly remarkable considering the variety of climates that characterize the Japanese archipelago and the millennium and more that separates the earliest and latest examples of the nation's traditional architecture. The authors of *What is Japanese Architecture?* assume a basic familiarity with many of these shared characteristics, and it is accordingly worthwhile to consider some of them here.

Perhaps the most fundamental point of commonality between buildings both magnificent and humble, secular and sacred, is the choice of materials. Though treated in different ways and with varying degrees of skill, nearly all structures are made primarily of wood, with paper for screens, straw for mats, plaster and clay for fixed walls, and reeds, wood shingles or planks, or tile for roofs. The main point of departure from Western architecture, and indeed some Chinese structures as well, is that stone is largely avoided, save in temple podia, castle foundations, miniature pagodas, and the like.

In addition, the basic structure of most buildings is the same, being based on the post and lintel system, with thin, non-bearing walls, either movable or fixed, in the intercolumnar bays. The only major variations are the thick, protective walls of wood, usually covered with plaster, in storehouses and castles.

In most cases, the posts also support a raised floor.

Resting on the post and lintel skeleton is a great roof, which is usually the most arresting aspect of the exterior design. It often accounts for half the height of the exterior elevation. The eaves, supported by complex brackets in most temples but by simpler constructions in domestic structures, extend out well beyond the sides of the building to protect verandas beneath. The inner format of most buildings is centered on an interior core, from which secondary spaces may radiate.

It is perhaps because of the reliance on wood as the primary material and the post and lintel system as the basic structural technique that Japanese architecture usually favors the rectilinear over curves and arches. Though one does see curvilinear forms in coved ceilings, cusped windows, and such, these are decorative details of otherwise planar constructions, and the curves that grace the gables or tips of the eaves on many Japanese buildings are, with few exceptions, much more gentle than examples found in China. Barrel vaults are absent, and the entasis (convexity) on posts of early temples diminishes in later styles.

The deep eave overhang, aside from its exterior visual effect, lends a characteristic dimness to interiors. The quality of inside illumination does vary, it is true, according to the season and the location of each room in the structure, and it also changes to some extent over the centuries, as exterior partitions develop from wooden shutters or screens to paper partitions. Nonetheless, a diffused, mellow light, darkening toward the ceiling, remains almost universal. In his essay "In Praise of Shadows" (*In'ei raisan*), the modern novelist Tanizaki Jun'ichirō emphasizes the importance of this characteristic in the formation and maintenance of all aspects of traditional Japanese culture.

Fluidity of interior partitioning, another outstanding feature of Japanese architecture, is perhaps derived from its reliance on the post and lintel system. Large spaces can be subdivided by not only fixed walls, but also by either free-standing screens or removable ones set on built-in rails. And vice versa, a small space such as the Taian Teahouse can be enlarged to accommodate extra guests by the simple expedient of removing one of its interior partitions. In temple architecture, while fluidity is not universal, it is present in large enough measure to be noteworthy. It is particularly apparent in many temple buildings in and after the medieval period, in which a number of different functions, such as ritual observances and sermonizing, are carried out in a single main hall that accordingly requires spaces that can be selectively opened and closed off. The abbot's quarters too, which may serve as a residence and lecture hall for the abbot during his lifetime and as a temple to his memory after his death, is characterized by this same internal fluidity.

There is, moreover, a fluidity in Japanese architecture between inside and out. Though fixed walls are frequently used, the distinction between wall and door is very elastic, and whole facades in both temples and residences can be opened to the elements at will by folding open or swinging up the panels between the posts or by sliding open, or even removing entirely, the wooden or paper screens. The veranda therefore serves as a transitional space, regarded as part of the building when viewed from the exterior, and as part of the outside world when viewed from within. In this way Japanese buildings usually demonstrate a highly attuned concern for integration with their natural environment. Not only are these wooden structures made of the same natural material that form their surroundings, but they are set out on their grounds to take best advantage of the immediate terrain. Where a scenic vista is not available, as with a city dwelling or some urban temple compounds, care is taken to incorporate a reminder of the natural world in the form of a garden, no matter how small. The authors point out that even the row houses of the common people in medieval towns often included gardens in the rear to provide both culinary and aesthetic refreshment. In the case of temples, even Kenchōji, with its highly unnatural axial plan, has a pond at its north end and junipers to both sides of its central walk. Likewise, the shrines at Nikkō, for all their effusive decoration, are laid out among rows of cedar trees and contain mountain paths designed to take artistic advantage of the natural terrain. Though such do exist, the building or complex that makes no nod to the natural environment is rare, indeed.

One element in most Japanese architecture that keeps the fluidity of design and concern for natural integration from playing havoc with artistic unity of expression is the system of proportional design developed over the centuries. The authors devote ample space to the manner in which each structural member is related by formula to the others through the use of modules, thereby ensuring a structural harmony within single buildings and from one building to another in a complex.

Another quality that keeps the design of even the most heavily ornamented buildings from completely losing artistic integrity is the fact that decoration tends to embellish rather than disguise basic construction. This is most apparent in the spare, naturalistic buildings influenced by tea taste. But even at Nikkō, which seems to have been decorated wherever humanly possible, the basic structure is unmistakably evident despite the ornament. The shrine does not use massive false fronts promising a completely different style from that which one actually finds upon entering, nor does it attempt to deny the presence or the function of the structure beneath the appliqué.

These various features shared by most Japanese architecture allow in turn a fluidity of yet a different sort—that between the secular and the sacred. Particularly in the Nara and Heian periods (the eighth through twelfth centuries), private buildings and complexes were turned into temple structures with little difficulty. In that way Lady Tachibana's mansion was incorporated as a religious building into Hōryūji temple, and Fujiwara no Tamemitsu's complex became a temple compound in its own right. Even the eastern of the two Imperial Assembly Halls of the Heijō Palace was later transformed into the Lecture Hall at Tōshōdaiji temple. This characteristic recalls the close relationship between Buddhist structures and palace architecture in China. In even earlier times there was a corresponding similarity between Shintō shrines and the palaces of Japan's emperors, as the rulers were themselves considered Shintō deities. Echoes of this bond still exist, intermingled with later Buddhist influences, in the present Imperial Palace in Kyōto.

All these shared characteristics lend an underlying unity to Japanese architecture despite the extreme variations we have outlined. They constitute in sum a continuing tradition that builders have turned to different social, religious, and artistic purposes through the ages, and that continue to exert a powerful influence on Japanese architects today.

H. Mack Horton

WORSHIP
The Architecture of Buddhist Temples and Shintō Shrines

The Shōun Pagoda of Kannōji temple stood at long last in completed splendor. As each course of scaffolding was removed another of the pagoda's five stories appeared, until finally it stood revealed in all its lofty glory.

The novel from which this passage is quoted (*The Five-story Pagoda* by Kōda Rohan) takes as its theme the imperishability of artistic inspiration. The choice of a pagoda to symbolize this message is particularly acute, as this structure has been the central identifying element of the temple complex ever since the introduction of Buddhism into Japan over fourteen hundred years ago.

Japan's religious architecture centers on Buddhist temples and Shintō shrines. Temple architecture was imported very soon after the introduction of the basic doctrines of the faith in the mid sixth century from the Korean Kingdom of Paekche. For the early Japanese, the Buddhist creed represented not only a new and immensely profound world view, but also one of the most impressive expressions of highly developed culture from the Asian continent. The Buddhist religion and its attendant art and architecture was for the early Japanese a route to higher civilization and international prestige. By the end of the sixteenth century Japan was building impressive monasteries on the Continental model, and by the mid eighth century a national system of provincial temples had been established with a well-developed ecclesiastical organization to maintain it.

Together with sculptural and painted images, the pagoda and the other buildings in the temple complex have served as the tangible correlatives of the idea of faith. Indeed, throughout Japanese history much of the best of the country's human and economic resources has been lavished on their construction. Especially in the classical period (eighth through twelfth centuries) and the medieval period (thirteenth through sixteenth centuries), Buddhist architecture took the lead in introducing new structural and ornamental features. Buddhist buildings are thus of critical importance not only to all other Japanese architecture but to the entire corpus of Japanese art.

Shintō, "the Way of the Gods," is Japan's indigenous religion. Not surprisingly, the roots of Shintō architecture go back to the very beginnings of Japanese civilization, and Shintō shrines have their own unique forms. The configuration of the Grand Shrine at Ise, for example, hearkens back to the granaries of the preliterary age, and its simple grandeur excites the same admiration as the best of the Buddhist tradition. The designs of most of the shrine types we know today, however, took their mature forms only in the eighth century, at which time Japan had already been heavily influenced by Buddhism. The history of the architecture of these two faiths is thus tightly interwoven. For example, the Tōshōgū shrine at Nikkō, the mausoleum of the first Tokugawa shōgun, looks at first glance to be more of a Buddhist temple than a Shintō shrine, and in sheer opulence and display it rivals or surpasses any Buddhist structure in Japan (figs. 77–79). The German architect Bruno Taut praised the purity and simplicity of Ise Shrine, but condemned Nikkō's ornamentation as artificial. His criticism is by no means incontestable, but it does suggests the range and richness of the body of Shintō architecture.

Religious architecture, particularly that of Buddhist temples, is a fitting place to begin our discussion, for many of the basic concepts introduced will apply to other Japanese building types. The temple, constructed by and large of wood but often resting on a podium faced with stone, is generally designed on the post and lintel principle, with non-bearing walls in the bays (*ken*) between each pair of posts. Resting above is a grand roof, originally of tile but later with variations such as wood shingle, whose eaves are cantilevered far out over the verandas by means of a system of brackets. The brackets rest on the posts beneath and sometimes in the intercolumnar spaces as well. The core of the temple, the *moya*, is usually one, three, five, or some other odd number of bays in width by two in depth. Surrounding this central core on most structures are peripheral sections called *hisashi*, usually one bay in width. Hisashi with separate pent roofs beneath the main roof are called *mokoshi*, and they may surround the moya directly or, as is more frequently the case, serve as tertiary spaces and border the hisashi that are under the main roof (figs. 1, 16). A building with a moya three bays wide will thus usually have a five-bay facade (in the absence of mokoshi or other additions) as it includes the hisashi widths on both sides.

We will begin our discussion with the oldest extant temple in Japan, Hōryūji, and use it as a starting point for an introduction to the temple complex and its main structures—the pagoda and image hall—together with the corridor and inner gate that enclose them, and the subsidiary structures outside that corridor (figs. 1–2). Thereafter we will trace the changes that affected the temple plan and the styles of the constituent structures as religious and engineering innovations occurred at home or were introduced from China. These include the rise of the so-called Esoteric mountain sects and the concurrent breakdown of the regular temple plan, the growth of elegant private temple complexes for Kyōto aristocrats, then the introduction of the Zen and the Great Buddha styles from Sung-dynasty China and the inevitable eclecticism that resulted in the medieval era. We will end the chapter with a look at the origins and developments of Shintō architecture, paying special attention to both its unique features and those that show the influence of Buddhist building concepts.

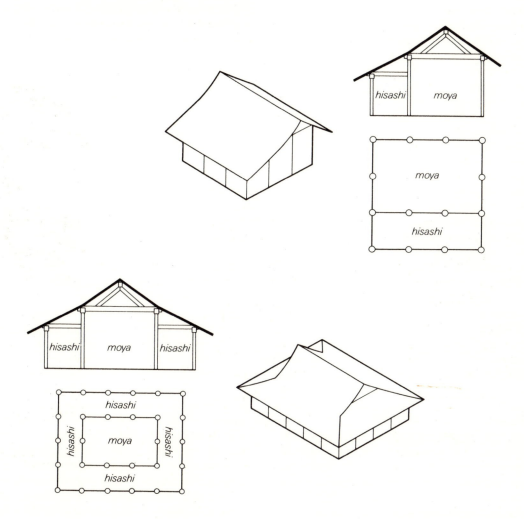

HŌRYŪJI TEMPLE AND ITS SYMBOL, THE PAGODA

Japan's Oldest Extant Temple Complex   On the plain of Ikaruga, just outside the ancient capital of Nara, Hōryūji temple stands in serene silence. Backed by gentle hills, the temple presents an image of beauty and strength synonymous with the best in Japanese Buddhist architecture. Hōryūji's Five-story Pagoda (Gojū no Tō; figs. 1–2) together with the Golden Hall (Kondō) next to it, the Inner Gate (Chūmon), and most of the surrounding Corridor (Kairō; fig. 2) are the oldest surviving wooden buildings in the world and a logical starting point for a discussion of Buddhist architecture in Japan.

The history of Hōryūji began in A.D. 587, when the Emperor Yōmei, suffering from an illness, set about to construct a temple for the worship of Buddhist images. His piety proved fruitless and he died in the same year, but the Empress Suiko and her regent, Prince Shōtoku, carried out his wishes and saw the temple project through to completion in 607.

The Hōryūji they built, however, was consumed by fire in 670, and it is the rebuilt version that stands today.

The Asuka Style   The exact years of the reconstruction of Hōryūji remain conjectural, with some suggesting a date as late as the Nara period (710–84). But the style of the extant structures is different from most other Nara works and shows a number of features that clearly belong to the Asuka era (552–710). These include marked entasis (a slight convexity) on the columns as well as cloud-pattern bracket arms supporting the eaves (fig. 2). The style also incorporates a thin block plate (*sarato*) between the tops of the columns and the main bearing block (*daito*) supporting the bracketing (visible in the corridor in the foreground of fig. 2). Also indicative of the "Asuka style" are the stylized Buddhist swastika pattern in the ornamental railings (fig. 2) and the inverted V-shaped struts beneath them (see fig. 65).

The four oldest Hōryūji structures mentioned above incorporate these Asuka-period elements. Though the present corridor connects the Sutra Repository (Kyōzō), Belfry (Shurō), and Lecture Hall (Kōdō) at the north of the Golden Hall and pagoda, these three structures were originally outside

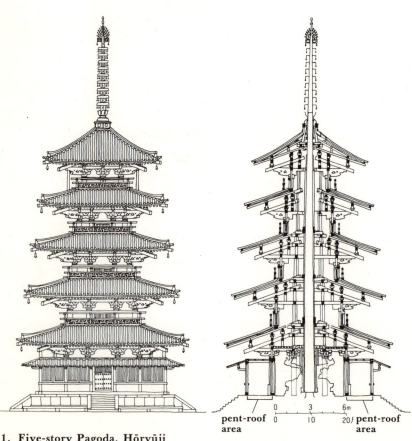

pent-roof area   0   3   6m
                   0   10   20ʃ pent-roof area

1. Five-story Pagoda, Hōryūji

of what was then a perfectly rectangular enclosure (see fig. 7).

Origins of the Pagoda The pagoda enshrines symbolic relics of the Buddha, and the golden hall houses his image. Running through the center of the pagoda from uppermost roof to base is a single massive column that rests on a foundation stone, beneath which are interred the relics which represent the bones of the historical Buddha.

The prototype of the Japanese pagoda is the Indian stupa, a hemisphere of stone and earth with an umbrella-shaped spire above, built for the same purpose of venerating the relics of the Buddha. These relics and the stupa housing them were the only monuments allowed by the early Indian Buddhist church; Buddhist anthropomorphic images did not begin to appear until centuries later. The pagodas of China and Japan are said to have developed from the Indian stupa spire.

The Pagoda as Symbol As pointed out in the introduction, the pagoda is the symbol of the Buddhist sacred precinct. Its lofty height and distinctive shape are entirely in keeping with this role. The five stories of the Hōryūji pagoda gradually decrease in size toward the top, though later pagodas show less diminution, with some seeming nearly straight from top to bottom. Indeed, the Hōryūji pagoda has the most marked diminution of any extant example, giving it a sense of great stability.

But though the pagoda, as reliquary, was the central structure of the monastic compound in the early years of Japanese Buddhism, it gradually relinquished its primary position as Buddhist images and the golden hall housing them gained in importance. The pagoda became in consequence more ornamental than functional, as suggested by the appearance of temples such as Yakushiji and Tōdaiji, where two pagodas were built in front of a central image hall (see figs. 3, 8, 10).

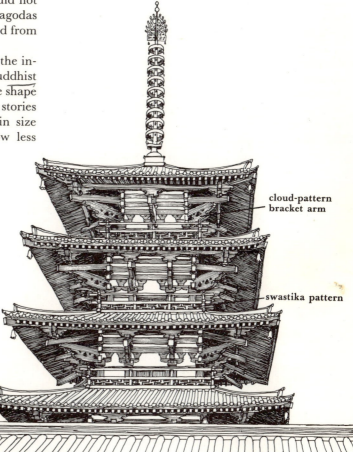

cloud-pattern
bracket arm

swastika pattern

2. **Five-story Pagoda from Corridor, Hōryūji**

block plate
bearing block

From One Pagoda to Two

From One Pagoda to Two From its introduction in the mid sixth century, Japanese Buddhism received the support of the central government. Thus when sculptors and carpenters arrived in Japan in 577, temple construction proceeded at a fast pace. Asukadera, generally thought to have been the first temple complex constructed in Japan (no longer extant), was begun in 588 and completed in 596. The pagoda was located in the center of the compound, with golden halls surrounding it on three sides and a corridor enclosing the whole (fig. 4).

The pagoda is still located in a position of preeminence at Shitennōji (early seventh century; fig. 5) in front of a single golden hall, but at Kawaradera (mid seventh century; fig. 6) it stands *beside* the southern of two golden halls. At Hōryūji (built in 607 on a different plan, burned, then rebuilt on the present plan from 670; fig. 7) a single pagoda flanks a single golden hall. By the latter part of the seventh

century, then, multiple golden halls have in general disappeared, but the single hall has achieved a position of parity with the pagoda. This configuration was standard thereafter, until the capital, which was traditionally relocated for reasons of ritual purity on the death of each sovereign, was moved to the Fujiwara Capital in 694 (see p. 56). There, as we have seen, Yakushiji temple was built with not one but two pagodas in the inner precinct (fig. 8). When the first truly permanent capital, Heijō, was established in 710 at Nara, Yakushiji was rebuilt there according to the same plan. Where multiple golden halls, then, had surrounded a central pagoda in the late sixth century at Asukadera, multiple pagodas now framed a more important central golden hall a century later.

The pagoda further declined in importance at Kōfukuji, a temple thought to have been moved to its present location in the second decade of the eighth

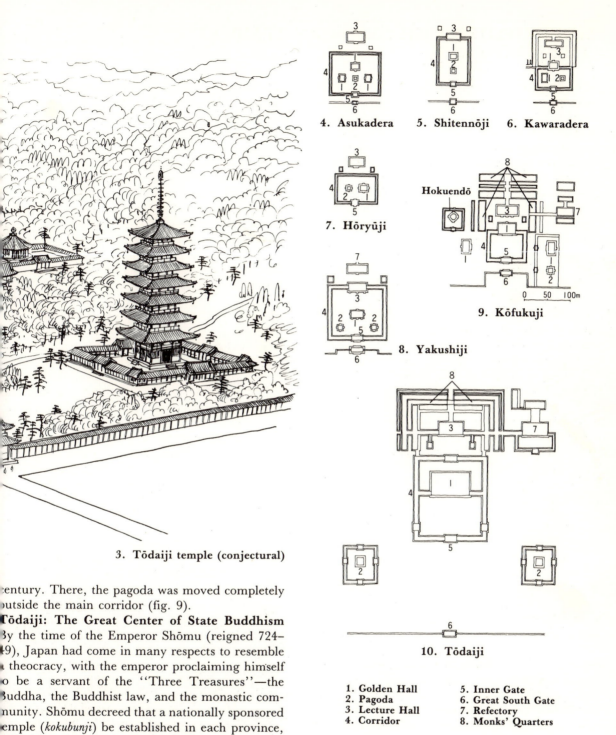

4. Asukadera 5. Shitennōji 6. Kawaradera

7. Hōryūji

Hokuendō

9. Kōfukuji

8. Yakushiji

0   50   100m

3. Tōdaiji temple (conjectural)

10. Tōdaiji

1. Golden Hall
2. Pagoda
3. Lecture Hall
4. Corridor
5. Inner Gate
6. Great South Gate
7. Refectory
8. Monks' Quarters

century. There, the pagoda was moved completely outside the main corridor (fig. 9).

Tōdaiji: The Great Center of State Buddhism
By the time of the Emperor Shōmu (reigned 724–49), Japan had come in many respects to resemble a theocracy, with the emperor proclaiming himself to be a servant of the "Three Treasures"—the Buddha, the Buddhist law, and the monastic community. Shōmu decreed that a nationally sponsored temple (*kokubunji*) be established in each province, and that a great central temple be raised in the capital to oversee them. Tōdaiji temple was begun accordingly, and in 760 the Lecture Hall (Kōdō) and Great Buddha Hall (Daibutsuden) were completed (figs. 3, 10). The latter structure was of truly monumental proportions, and housed a huge gilt bronze image of Vairocana, the Cosmic Buddha, that took two years to cast and three more to polish and gild. (Today, rebuilt at only two-thirds the size of the original, the Great Buddha Hall is still the largest wooden structure on earth.) Several decades thereafter, two seven-story pagodas, each one-hundred meters tall, were built to either side of the front of the main precinct. The Great Buddha Hall stands at the center of the compound, with the Lecture Hall and Monks' Quarters (Sōbō) to the north and the Refectory (Jikidō) to the east.

ARCHITECTURE OF THE PURE LAND

The World of Heian Buddhism In 794 the capital was moved to Heian, present-day Kyōto. It would remain there for the next thousand years and more and witness the efflorescence of classical Japanese culture. Appropriately enough, this epoch is called the Heian period (784–1185), after the name of the capital. Soon after the Heian Capital was founded, two brilliant clerics, Saichō (767–822) and Kūkai (774–835), introduced new Buddhist teachings that rivalled the old "Six Sects" of the former Nara capital. Saichō's sect, Tendai, was founded atop Mt. Hiei to the northeast of the Heian Capital, and its first temple was named Hieizanji (later renamed Enryakuji). Kūkai founded his new sect, Shingon, atop Mt. Kōya in present-day Wakayama Prefecture, calling his temple Kongōbuji. Temples of these two sects, which together are now grouped under the rubric of Esoteric Buddhism (Mikkyō), were frequently located in mountain regions, in keeping with their rigorous, ascetic doctrines. These Esoteric temples often abandoned the symmetrical temple plan owing to the uneven terrain of their mountain settings. They also adopted a new type of pagoda, the "jewelled pagoda" (hōtō), characterized by a roughly hemispherical body with a pyramidal roof and spire atop it. Later the central hemispherical area was enclosed by subsidiary sections with pent roofs (mokoshi) on the four sides, creating the "many jewelled pagoda" (tahōtō; fig. 12). Thereafter the hemispherical portion was removed save for a rounded vestige above the pent roof and below the main roof.

The Phoenix Hall of the Byōdōin It was also in the Heian period that Pure Land (Jōdo) Buddhism first achieved popularity. Originally closely tied to the Tendai sect in Japan, it captured the imagination of aristocrats and, later, of commoners as well with its simple doctrine of salvation and rebirth in the "Pure Land" through prayer to the Amida Buddha. Court nobles took to building private Buddha halls (jibutsudō) on their manors so as to have an image of Amida near at all times and encourage pious meditation.

In the latter half of the Heian period, the imperial family and the high nobility began building entire temple complexes around a garden and pond, following the same practice used at their private villas (see pp. 64–67). The villa-temples were still Esoteric in orientation, as Pure Land doctrines had yet to give rise to independent sects, but they were designed to reproduce on earth Amida's paradise, and fortunes were lavished on them in pursuit of this ideal.

One of the finest extant examples of this Pure Land villa architecture is the Byōdōin. Located in Uji, just to the south of Kyōto, it was originally the villa of Yorimichi (990–1074), head of the most powerful of all Heian noble clans, the Fujiwara. The fact that a villa could be changed into a place of private family worship with only a few monks in attendance suggests how different was this type of faith from the

11. Phoenix Hall, Byōdōin

state-sponsored monasticism of the older Nara sects, which continued to survive concurrently.

The most famous of the Byōdōin structures is the Phoenix Hall (Hōōdō), completed in 1053 (fig. 11). Inside is housed a gilded statue of Amida on a lotus throne, backed by a swirling gilt mandorla (fig. 14). Above hangs an opulent canopy, and carvings of heavenly musicians are in attendance on the surrounding walls. Members of the Fujiwara family would sit across the pond to the east and look west at the seated Buddha, imagining themselves reborn in Amida's "Western Paradise." The structure housing the statue is designed as a stylized phoenix, with winglike raised corridors to both sides and a tail to the rear (fig. 13). The building is as elegant and light as its appointments, the overall effect providing a fine example of the elegant "Fujiwara style."

Amida Halls and the "Latter Days of the Law"
The year 1051 was believed to be the fifteen-hundredth anniversary of the death of the Buddha and the beginning of the final decline of the Buddha's teachings. At that time, it was believed, only the Amida Buddha had the power to save mankind, and halls dedicated to Amida flourished in consequence. The Phoenix Hall is one example of this trend, as is the Golden Hall (Konjikidō) of Chūsonji, a temple built in 1126 by a wealthy provincial clan in northern Japan. The gilded exterior and the lacquerwork and mother-of-pearl appointments make the Golden Hall equal to the most magnificent Kyōto monuments and show how far into the hinterlands Pure Land belief had penetrated.

12. Tahōtō, Ishiyamadera

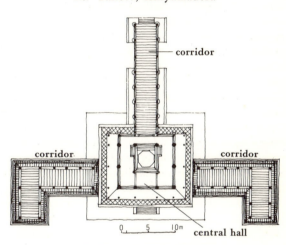

13. Phoenix Hall, Byōdōin

strut and block

14. Statue of Amida, Phoenix Hall, Byōdōin

NEW MEDIEVAL FORMS—
THE GREAT BUDDHA STYLE

The Rebuilding of Tōdaiji   The Heian period came to an end when two great military houses, the Taira and the Minamoto, contended with each other to wrest power from the court aristocracy. The ensuing struggle, known as the Gempei War (1180–85), ended in victory for Minamoto no Yoritomo (1147–99). Yoritomo received imperial appointment as *shōgun* (generalissimo) in 1192 and established his administration in Kamakura, far to the north of Kyōto. Thereafter the emperor and his court in the capital would reign, but the shogunate would wield actual power. The change put an end to Japan's classical period and ushered in the medieval age.

Tōdaiji, the greatest temple of the old Nara sects, had been destroyed early in the Gempei conflict in 1180. Reconstruction was begun the next year, though, by the great prelate Shunjōbō Chōgen (?–1195). Chōgen had made the perilous crossing to Sung China a remarkable three times to bring back new Buddhist thought as well as the latest developments in Chinese culture. He thus chose a Sung architectural style for the Tōdaiji rebuilding. Chōgen was thereafter supported in his innovative choice by the equally daring shōgun Yoritomo. The priest made use not only of such native carpenters as Mononobe no Tamesato and Sakurajima Kunimune, but of the Chinese sculptor and carpenter Chen Heqing, which suggests the close contact he maintained with the Continent.

The Great Buddha Style (Daibutsuyō)   The Great South Gate (Nandaimon; fig. 15), through which one enters the Tōdaiji complex, was completed in 1199 as part of Chōgen's reconstruction. Two other structures at the complex remain from Chōgen's time, the Founder's Hall (Kaizandō) and the worship section (*raidō*) of the Lotus Hall (Hokkedō), but the Great South Gate is the best example of Chōgen's architectural style at Tōdaiji. The gate's most immediately apparent characteristic is the multiple tiers of brackets sunk directly into the great columns and stabilized primarily by lateral ties extending the entire length of the facade (figs. 15, 20–21). The style is simple yet dignified and well suited to rebuilding on a quick and massive scale, since many of the structural members are of the same size and thus easily mass-produced. The Great South Gate was rebuilt on the

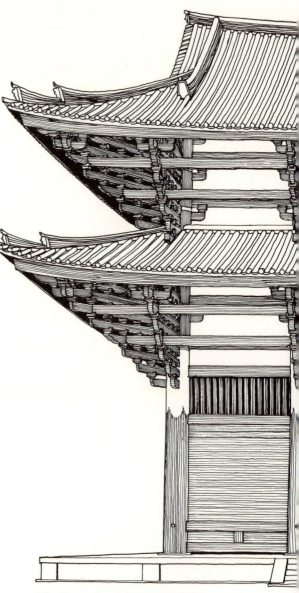

15. Great South Gate, Tōdaiji

same location and plan as the original, and despite its innovative design it was perfectly in keeping with the grandiose style of its predecessor. The Great Buddha Hall was also rebuilt in the new manner and gave its name to the style as a whole. It was again burned in 1567 and rebuilt in the same style in about 1700. This mode also used to be referred to as the "Indian Style" (Tenjikuyō), though it has no connection with that country.

Besides Tōdaiji, Chōgen built a number of other temples in the Great Buddha style near the capital and to the west. One fine extant example is the Pure Land Hall (Jōdodō) of Jōdoji temple (Ono City, Hyōgo Prefecture), which Chōgen built in 1192 (see fig

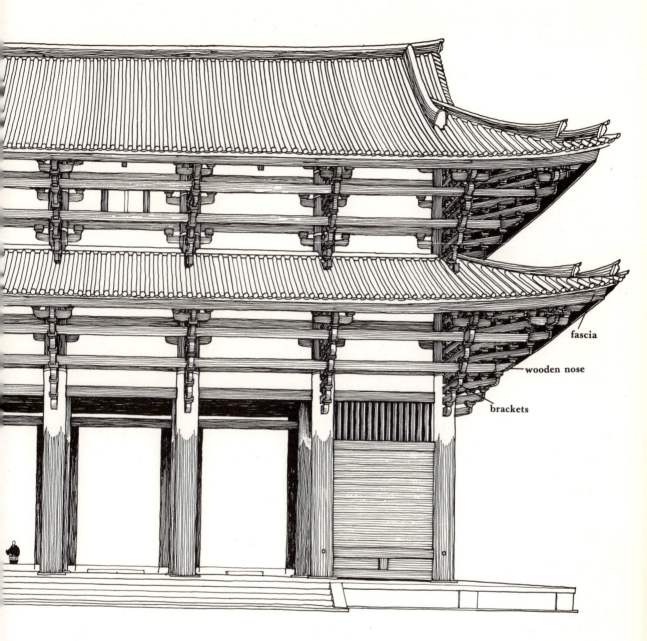

fascia

wooden nose

brackets

19). It is a square structure with three six-meter-wide bays per side and a central altar area one bay square. The low, pyramidal roof has no curve, and the rafter ends are hidden by long fascia (rafter-end covering boards, *hanakakushiita*; for other examples, see figs. 15, 20), which obviate the necessity of finishing each rafter-end separately and thereby increase construction efficiency. Inside there is no ceiling, in order that the complex pattern of columns, "rainbow" beams (*kōryō*), and struts may be displayed (see fig. 18). In the center of the structure stand three gilt images, which strikingly contrast with the vermilion color of the wooden structural members. The boldness and vitality of the building may give a more complete idea

of the effect of the Great Buddha style than even the Great South Gate.

Decline of the Great Buddha Style The Great Buddha style did not long survive its chief advocate, Chōgen. Possibly it was linked too strongly in people's minds with the regime of the shōgun and its policies. More importantly, its severity apparently did not harmonize with Japanese tastes. But elements of the style, such as its very rational structural program and its characteristic detailing, were absorbed into other building styles and were long-lived and influential.

NEW MEDIEVAL FORMS—
THE ZEN STYLE

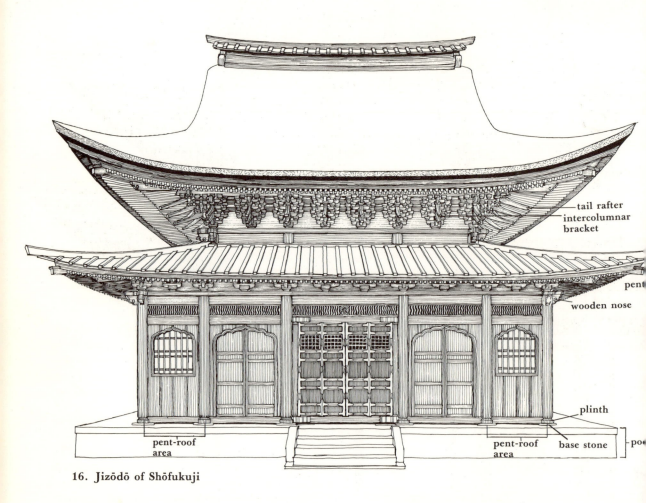

tail rafter
intercolumnar
bracket

pent

wooden nose

plinth

pent-roof
area

base stone

po

pent-roof
area

16. Jizōdō of Shōfukuji

The Architecture of the Zen Sect (Zenshūyō) At the same time that Chōgen was rebuilding Tōdaiji, another monk, Myōan Eisai (1141–1215), was introducing the Rinzai sect of Zen Buddhism to Japan from China. Soon thereafter, a second Zen sect, Sōtō, was brought to Japan by Eihei Dōgen (1200–1253). Eisai received the patronage of the second Kamakura shōgun, Yoritomo's son Yoriie, and was able to establish temples in Kamakura and in Kyōto. But Dōgen declined the invitation of the shogunal regent, Hōjō Tokiyori, and went instead deep into the mountains of present-day Fukui Prefecture, where he built the temple Eiheiji, the Sōtō headquarters. Both sects were able to expand, partly because their stern self-discipline and respect for intuitive understanding appealed to the warrior mind, and partly because the new Zen organization had deep ties with Chinese culture and learning and was

not monopolized by the court, which the shogunal regime viewed with suspicion.

Together with new doctrines, the Zen sect also introduced a new architectural style into Japan, one that, like the Great Buddha style, was developed in Sung China, but which is quite different in design. The Zen complex is in general axial in plan and roughly bilaterally symmetrical. This reflects the regimentation of the Zen monk's daily life, in which each act is expected to contribute to an overall attitude of religious discipline. The Zen sect sets out rules for not only the shape and appointments of each structure, but also the scale and placement of each building in the complex.

It is, however, in the structure and ornamentation of the individual buildings that the identifying characteristics of the Zen style are most apparent. Each hall is set on a stone podium (fig. 16), and each

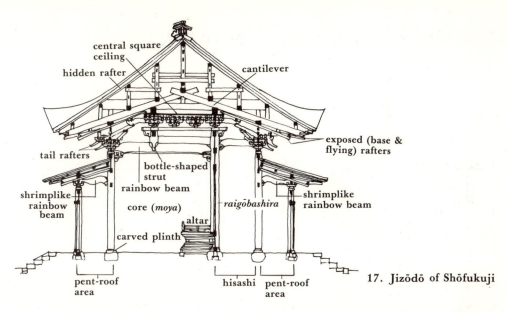

central square ceiling

hidden rafter

cantilever

exposed (base & flying) rafters

tail rafters

bottle-shaped strut

rainbow beam

shrimplike rainbow beam

core (*moya*)

raigōbashira

shrimplike rainbow beam

altar

carved plinth

pent-roof area

hisashi

pent-roof area

17. Jizōdō of Shōfukuji

has a stone floor. The posts sit on carved stone blocks, or plinths (*soban*), rather than directly on base stones, and are beveled at both top and bottom. The brackets rest not only above each post, as in the Great Buddha style, but in the intercolumnar spaces as well (compare figs. 15, 16).

Though Sennyūji, a Ritsu-sect temple in Kyōto, also uses the Zen style, the mode was by and large limited to Zen temple complexes, from which it takes its name. It is also known as the "Chinese style" (Karayō) in contradistinction to the earlier style of Buddhist architecture, which by the twelfth century had come to be thought of as indigenous and accordingly called the "Japanese style" (Wayō). Like the Great Buddha style of Chōgen, many of its innovations were adopted piecemeal into the buildings of other sects, but unlike Chōgen's style, the Zen type thrived on its own as well.

The Shōfukuji Jizōdō According to an inked inscription on one of its bracket members, the Jizōdō of Shōfukuji temple dates to 1407 and is thus the oldest Zen temple in eastern Japan to which an exact date can be affixed. The structure is three bays wide by three deep and is one story tall, but the surrounding area with pent roof (*mokoshi*; fig. 16) gives it the appearance of a five-by-five-bay, two-story building. Atop rests a hip-and-gable (*irimoya*) roof. At the core of the Jizōdō is a one-bay-square section within which stands the altar.

In comparison to the Great Buddha style and the earlier so-called Japanese style, the Zen-style members are proportionately thinner and give the exterior an attenuated appearance. This entails no sacrifice in stability, however, thanks to a more efficient use of the tie beams (*nuki*) that pierced the columns they connected. (For further discussion of details of the Zen style, see pp. 26–27.)

The Shariden of Enkakuji temple in Kamakura is very similar in appearance to the Jizōdō, and is likewise famous. The original burned in 1563, and the present structure is believed to have been moved from Taiheiji, one of the five Kamakura nunneries. But the history of Taiheiji is unclear, and a precise date cannot be fixed to the Shariden.

Naturalized Design Though the Zen style was imported from Sung China, it would be a mistake to assume that Japan's extant Zen structures are perfect replicas of Chinese prototypes. Over the years Japanese carpenters altered the original designs to suit native preferences. One obvious example is the roof, which in Japan is often covered with wood shingles rather than the more Chinese-style tiles and is supported by a double-tiered system of rafters (fig. 17). The lower layer of rafters (*keshōdaruki*) is exposed, and the second layer (*nodaruki*), which actually supports the roof above, is hidden and set at a steeper pitch than the exposed rafters beneath. Later, the construction was further strengthened by the addition of a cantilever (*hanegi*) between the two rafter sets.

Until this "hidden" or "double" roof system was developed in the tenth century, it had been impossible to build wide spaces without having a steep drop in the angle of the rafters over the peripheral sections (*hisashi*) of a building that surrounded the core (*moya*). The hidden roof made it possible for the pitch of the underside of the roof to be set independently of that of the exterior, thus allowing gently inclined exposed rafters over the periphery. This eliminated heavy shadows and gave a feeling of horizontality and calmness to the outlying spaces. The hidden roof was a Japanese innovation and its use made Japanese temple spaces quite different in feeling from their Chinese antecedents.

23

DETAILS OF THE GREAT BUDDHA STYLE

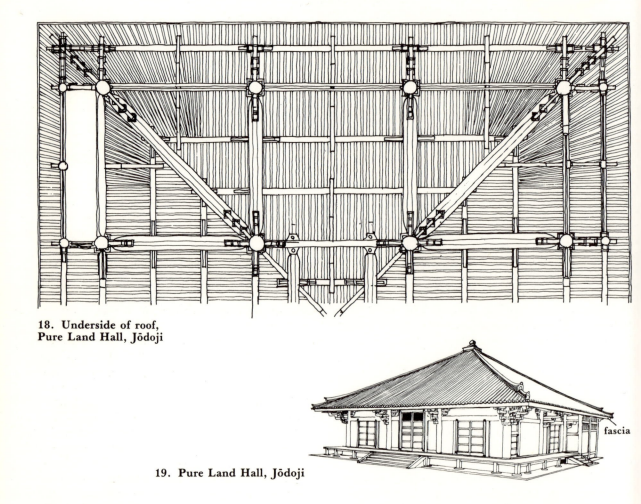

**18. Underside of roof,
Pure Land Hall, Jōdoji**

19. Pure Land Hall, Jōdoji

fascia

Structural Characteristics As mentioned earlier, the Great South Gate of Tōdaiji and the Pure Land Hall of Jōdoji are the two finest extant examples of the Great Buddha style. Figures 20 and 21 show how the bracketing system is arranged. The bracket arms (called *sashi hijiki*) are set directly into the posts (fig. 21), making them quite different from the conventional brackets which were simply placed atop the posts (see fig. 48 for comparison). The posts are laterally stabilized by penetrating tie beams (*nuki*) which pierce the center of the posts (fig. 21). These beams provide stronger structural support than the common non-penetrating tie beams (*nageshi*), which are pinned to the posts' sides. The posts are strengthened back to front by more penetrating beams tied into the posts at the core of the structure.

By and large, the brackets themselves face only front to back, and lateral arms are in general eschewed in favor of unbroken bracket ties (*tōrihijiki*) that provide the necessary lateral support (compare figs. 20, 23).

Further structural simplification is seen in the single layer of rafters that carry the roof but are masked at the ends by the fascia mentioned previously (figs. 15, 20). Nor is the more complex double roof system in evidence. Economy is exercised too in the rafter placement, unique to the Great Buddha style, which is in fan pattern (*ōgidaruki*) on the corners (fig. 18)—thus providing more corner support than the parallel style (*heikōdaruki*) of standard "Japanese-style" roofs—but is parallel in the center of each side (compare this arrangement with figs. 22, 28). As indicated earlier, the complex roof construction is visi-

24

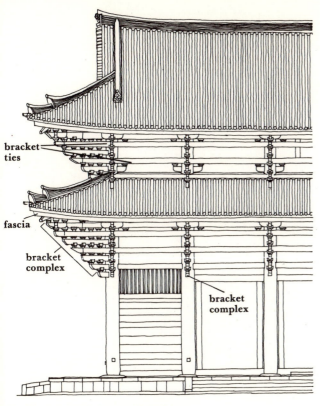

bracket
ties

fascia

bracket
complex

bracket
complex

20. Great South Gate, Tōdaiji

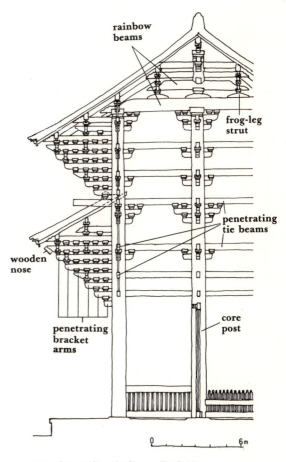

rainbow
beams

frog-leg
strut

penetrating
tie beams

wooden
nose

penetrating
bracket
arms

core
post

0   6 m

21. Great South Gate, Tōdaiji

ble from the interior as there is no ceiling, and the structural members thus take on an added ornamental function. The interior "rainbow" tie beams (fig. 21), referred to as such because they are slightly curved and tapered at the ends, have a configuration unique to the Great Buddha style, being nearly round in section and bearing a groove on the underside in the shape of a monk's staff (*shakujō*).

Decorative Details The Great Buddha style uses structural members that are proportionately much thicker than those used in Zen buildings. Moreover, the Great Buddha design demands main columns that run the entire height of the structure. Obtaining the requisite lumber for the building campaign at Tōdaiji was a challenging process as a result, and Chōgen's laborers went deep into the mountains

before finding trees tall and thick enough to serve.

The Great Buddha style also uses a unique french-curved design at the beam tips (called *kibana* or "wooden noses"; barely visible in figs. 15, 20–21) as well as in the "frog-leg" struts (the curve not visible in fig. 21); for "wooden noses" in Zen-style structures, see figures 23–24, and for other frog-leg struts, see page 39. Paneled doors of simple design are used as well, and they are hung from large wooden hinges (*waraza*) attached to penetrating tie beams at top and bottom. Similar doors, but more ornamented, are used in Zen-style structures (see fig. 25).

DETAILS OF THE ZEN STYLE

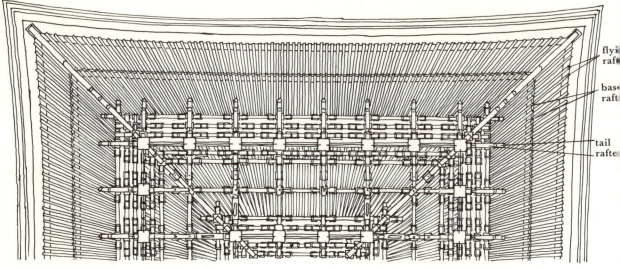

flyi[ng]
raft[er]

bas[e]
raft[er]

tail
rafte[r]

22. Underside of roof, Jizōdō, Shōfukuji

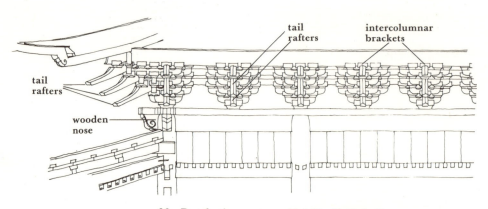

tail
rafters

intercolumnar
brackets

tail
rafters

wooden
nose

23. Bracketing system, Jizōdō, Shōfukuji

The Typical Zen Monastic Plan We have already seen that the Zen complex employs a characteristic axial layout. One fine example is that found in an extant plan of Kenchōji dated 1331, showing the temple as it was rebuilt after a fire in 1315 (fig. 26). One enters the temple ground over an arched bridge. Then, once through the Main Gate (Sōmon), one passes between rows of junipers that stand before the Enlightenment Gate (Sammon), which corresponds to the inner gate (*chūmon*) of other sects. To the east are the bathing facilities (Yokushitsu); to the west, the latrine (Seichin). Beyond is the corridor-bordered central court, planted again with junipers, with the Buddha Hall (Butsuden) at the north. To the east of the Buddha Hall is the Tochidō (hall for the worship of local deities) and to the west is the Founder's Hall (Soshidō). Outside the central court to the east are the temple kitchens (Kuri), and to the west the

Monks' Quarters (called Sōdō in Zen complexes). North again is the Dharma Hall (Hattō), originally for lectures on doctrine. At the northern extremity of the compound is the Guest Hall (Kyakuden) for the entertainment of important personages. It overlooks an elegant pond. In other Zen complexes this space is occupied by a *hōjō*, the residence of the abbot and a second area for lectures and doctrinal discussion.

Structural and Ornamental Details The Jizōdō of Shōfukuji (see fig. 16) is a fine specimen of Zen-style detail. The windows are cusped (*katōmado*; fig. 24), and the paneled and ornamented doors (*sankarado*) are, like those of the Great Buddha style, fixed to the penetrating tie beams by hinges (*waraza*; fig. 25). Above both windows and doors runs the transom that admits light through its "bow-shaped" members. Beam ends are carved in a french-curved design

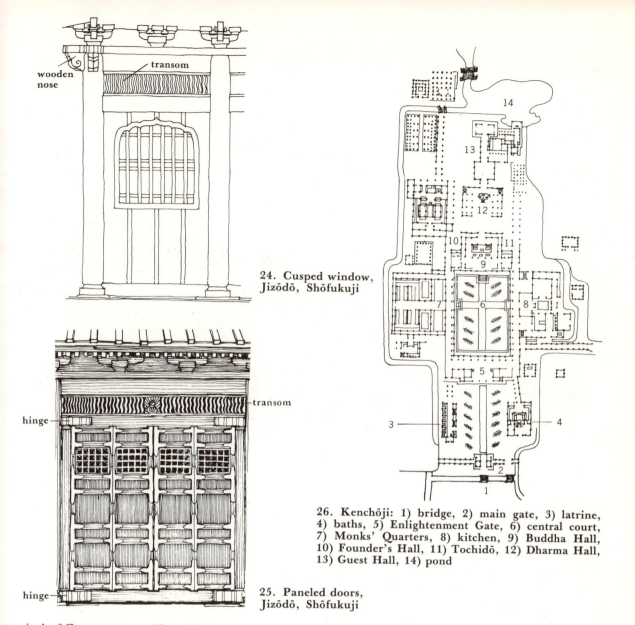

24. Cusped window,
Jizōdō, Shōfukuji

26. Kenchōji: 1) bridge, 2) main gate, 3) latrine,
4) baths, 5) Enlightenment Gate, 6) central court,
7) Monks' Quarters, 8) kitchen, 9) Buddha Hall,
10) Founder's Hall, 11) Tochidō, 12) Dharma Hall,
13) Guest Hall, 14) pond

25. Paneled doors,
Jizōdō, Shōfukuji

typical of Zen structures (figs. 23–24).

The roofing system is a marvel of complex engineering. Inside, it visually radiates from a central square ceiling (*kagamitenjō*) that hangs above the one-bay-square central section of the structure where the altar stands (see fig. 17). The rear end of the ceiling is supported by two posts (*raigōbashira*) that reach up from the back of the altar beneath, but the two posts one would suppose to be necessary to hold up the ceiling front are cut out, to provide an unblocked view of the altar from the entrance. Instead, the front end of the ceiling is supported by two short "bottle-shaped struts" (*taiheizuka*) that rest on two giant transverse beams. These beams span two bays front to back, from the two rear *raigōbashira* posts out to where the front of the building proper meets the peripheral pent-roof section. The rafters radiate from above this central square ceiling (fig. 22), fanning out around the entire structure, not simply at the corners as in the Great Buddha style. At the periphery of the underside of the roof are two types of exposed rafters, the base rafters (*jidaruki*) and flying rafters (*hiendaruki*) beyond them (figs. 17, 22). Together they form the visible lower roof and mask the hidden roof pitched at a steeper angle above them. A third type of rafter, the "tail rafter" (*odaruki*), is cantilevered into the brackets themselves (figs. 17, 22–23; for an example of a tail rafter in a Japanese-style temple, see fig. 55). The carved noses of these rafters contribute to the visual complexity of the bracket system (figs. 16, 23). The rafters of the pent roof do not radiate, but are instead parallel, as in the Japanese style.

27. Main Hall, Chōjuji

Chōjuji Despite the introduction of the newer Great Buddha and Zen styles in the Kamakura period (1185–1333), the older so-called Japanese style continued to be used. One particularly fine example of the medieval Japanese style is the Main Hall (Hondō) of Chōjuji temple (Kōka District, Shiga Prefecture; fig. 27). A temple of the Tendai sect, it is composed of an Inner Sanctum (Naijin) and an Outer Sanctuary (Gejin; figs. 29–30), separated by lattice doors with a diamond-pattern transom above.

The cross-section illustration shows how each of the two areas has its own exposed roof (keshōyaneura) above it, with a single hidden roof (noyane) built over both, visually unifying the structure from the exterior. This shows that originally the building was composed of two more-or-less separate structures, the rear one called the Principal Hall (Shōdō) and the front one, the Worship Hall (Raidō). The Main Hall of Chōjuji has a calm appearance, thanks to the thick structural members, simple bracketing, and low roof. The traditional paralleled rafter system (fig. 28) clearly contrasts with the fan raftering used in the Great Buddha and Zen styles.

The Rebuilding of Kōfukuji The Japanese style was also used in the project to rebuild the Fujiwara temple of Kōfukuji, which was destroyed along with

Tōdaiji in 1180. Kōfukuji was not rebuilt in Chōgen's new Great Buddha style because the aristocratic Fujiwara family, creators of the Phoenix Hall, was by this time a venerable and conservative house, and they favored traditional design. Some structural improvements were incorporated, however.

Today, only two buildings at Kōfukuji remain from the post–1180 reconstruction campaign. They are the North Octagonal Hall (Hokuendō) and the Three-story Pagoda. The former was rebuilt by Nara-area carpenters associated with the temple, and they used the original Nara-period foundation stones. The design of the North Octagonal Hall consequently bears a great debt to the eighth-century prototype. The pagoda was rebuilt by Kyōto carpenters trained under the influence of Heian courtly taste and is accordingly more delicate and refined.

The Eclectic Style Toward the end of the Kamakura period, the Japanese style began adopting elements from the two newer building types. The wooden noses of beams and bracket arms might adopt the Great Buddha style, or the posts supporting the porch roof (kōhai) might stand on Zen-style carved plinths or be connected to the building proper by the bulbous S-shaped "shrimplike rainbow beams" (ebi kōryō) that often connect the pent-roof

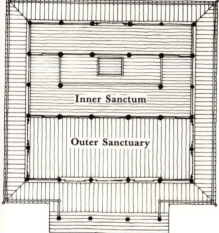

28. Underside of roof, Main Hall, Chōjuji

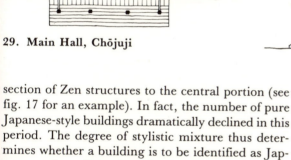

29. Main Hall, Chōjuji

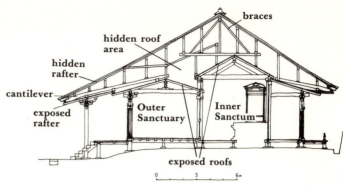

braces

hidden roof area

hidden rafter

cantilever

exposed rafter

Outer Sanctuary

Inner Sanctum

exposed roofs

0   3   6m

30. Main Hall, Chōjuji

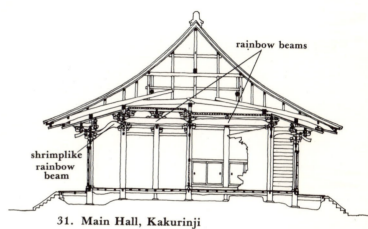

rainbow beams

shrimplike rainbow beam

31. Main Hall, Kakurinji

section of Zen structures to the central portion (see fig. 17 for an example). In fact, the number of pure Japanese-style buildings dramatically declined in this period. The degree of stylistic mixture thus determines whether a building is to be identified as Japanese style or Eclectic style (Settchūyō).

An Example of the Eclectic Style The Main Hall (Hondō) of Kakurinji temple (Kakogawa City, Hyōgo Prefecture) is a particularly well-known Eclectic style structure (fig. 31). The hall, thought to have been built in 1397, is basically of the Japanese style, with details of the Great Buddha style selectively added, such as the nearly round Great-Buddha-style "rainbow" beams. The combination of these two styles occurs so frequently that some architectural historians refer to it as the New Japanese style (Shin Wayō). In the case of the Kakurinji Main Hall, however, Zen-style elements were also blended into the design, as in the above-mentioned "shrimplike rainbow beams" (fig. 31). The Main Hall (Hondō) of the Myōōin temple (Fukuyama City, Hiroshima Prefecture), built in 1321, is another example where all three main medieval styles are used in combination.

A small number of pure Japanese-style buildings did continue to be built even in the Muromachi peri-

od (1338–1573). One such structure is the Golden Hall (Kondō) of Kōfukuji, dated 1415. As was the case with the North Octagonal Hall and Three-story Pagoda discussed earlier that survive from the early Kamakura rebuilding of the temple, the style was deliberately chosen because of the temple's ancient history and its location in the old Nara Capital. All in all, however, the introduction of the Great Buddha and Zen styles made a profound impact on medieval builders and influenced the development of a variety of new architectural effects. Kamakura-period architecture was therefore much more stylistically varied than that of earlier periods. In succeeding centuries Buddhist architectural types settled into more or less fixed forms.

A large number of impressive medieval buildings still survive, including the thirty-three-bay Main Hall (Hondō) of the Rengeōin (also called the Sanjū-sangendō; Kyōto, 1266), which is constructed in the Japanese style with some details in the Great Buddha style. Also notable is the Five-story Pagoda of Kōfukuji (Nara, 1442), a separate structure from the even older Three-story Pagoda of the same complex, mentioned earlier.

THE GOLDEN AND
SILVER PAVILIONS

Kitayama Culture and the Golden Pavilion
Following the first military government (shogunate) founded by Yoritomo in the late twelfth century, a second such administration was established by the Ashikaga family in 1338, and the two centuries and more of its existence are known as the Muromachi period (1338–1573). One of the finest examples of the architecture of the Ashikaga is the Golden Pavilion (Kinkaku), built in 1398 by the third Ashikaga shōgun, Yoshimitsu (fig. 32). It was part of a sumptuous villa complex located in Kyōto's Northern Hills (Kitayama), and that area gave its name to the Kitayama culture of Yoshimitsu and his circle. The villa later became Rokuonji temple, and the pavilion is formally known as the Relic Hall (Shariden).

A three-story structure, the Golden Pavilion is built over the villa's spacious pond and casts its reflection in the water before it, to startlingly beautiful effect. The first floor of the building (fig. 33), named the Chamber of Dharma Waters (Hōsuiin), is built in residential style. Above it, designed as a Buddha hall in the Japanese style, the Tower of the Sound of Waves (Chōonkaku) houses an image of the Bodhisattva Kannon. The third story, the Cupola of the Ultimate (Kukyōchō), is in the Zen style of architecture and holds an Amida triad and twenty-five Bodhisattvas.

The Golden Pavilion, the sole survivor of Yoshi-mitsu's villa complex, was destroyed by arson in 1950. It was rebuilt in 1955, however, and is a near-perfect re-creation of the original.

Higashiyama Culture and the Silver Pavilion   In 1484, nearly a century after the construction of the Golden Pavilion, the eighth Ashikaga shōgun, Yoshimasa, began work on his own villa in the Eastern Hills (Higashiyama) of Kyōto. Consciously basing his villa concept on the Kitayama complex of his predecessor, Yoshimasa continued work on his mansion and garden until his death in 1490, at which time it was converted into a temple and renamed Jishōji. Two of its structures remain today, the Silver Pavilion (formally called the Kannon Hall, or Kannonden; fig. 34) and a building for private worship, the Hall of the Eastern Quest (Tōgudō or Tōgūdō). As is the case with the Golden Pavilion, the first floor of the Silver Pavilion, called the Hall of Emptied Mind (Shinkūden), is in residential style (fig. 35), and the top floor, the second, called as at the Golden Pavilion the Tower of the Sound of Waves (Chō-onkaku), is influenced by the Zen style. Though Yoshimasa may have planned to cover his pavilion in silver leaf, there is no evidence that it was ever applied, and the building remains today of unpainted wood.

During the century that separated the Golden and Silver Pavilions, there were developments in residential spaces (to be discussed in Chapter 2) that are reflected in these two structures. This is particularly evident when the lower floors of the two structures are compared. The first story of the Golden Pavilion is based on the Shinden style of domestic architecture that first took shape in the mansions of the Heian-period nobility (see pp. 64–67). Such Shinden structures are planned around a large cen-

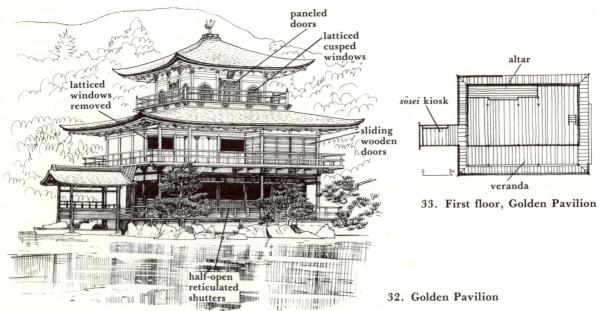

paneled doors

latticed cusped windows

latticed windows removed

sliding wooden doors

half-open reticulated shutters

altar

sōsei kiosk

veranda

33. First floor, Golden Pavilion

32. Golden Pavilion

cusped windows with paper screens

34. Silver Pavilion

paper-covered screens with wainscoting

35. First floor, Silver Pavilion

tral open area surrounded by peripheral rooms and verandas under the eaves. Walls are composed primarily of *shitomido*—large, two-part reticulated shutters. In the illustration of the Golden Pavilion (fig. 32), the upper halves of the shitomido have been raised parallel to the floor and hooked to the soffit above to let in light, but the bottom halves (which are removable) have been left in place between the posts. The second floor contains newer *mairado* sliding wooden doors as well as latticed windows. At the Silver Pavilion, though (fig. 34), the shitomido have been entirely replaced by sliding paper-covered screens (*shōji*) with high wooden wainscoting, a design which appears to have been developed in the latter part of the fifteenth century. It is not known whether the Silver Pavilion used these wainscoted shōji originally or whether it was fit with shōji and mairado in combination and then, later, redesigned with wainscoted shōji. But in either case, the absence of shitomido clearly reflects a later design. The plan, too, has abandoned the single open room for a combination of smaller spaces (compare figs. 33, 35), and this configuration continues in use hereafter.

Despite these differences, in overall conception both pavilions are based on that of the Saihōji temple and "moss garden" complex designed in 1339 by Musō Soseki (1275–1351). Working on the site of an older Pure Land temple, Musō constructed a dry landscape garden at the north and added Chinese elements to the original garden and pond to the south. His design revolutionized garden art and is believed to have been inspired by the famous Sung-dynasty Zen text, *The Blue Cliff Record* (*Bi yan lu*). Its Lapis Lazuli Pavilion (Ruriden), which is no longer extant, was the model for both the Golden and the Silver Pavilions, and its Hall of the Western Arrival (Sairaidō) served as the inspiration for Yoshimasa's Hall of the Eastern Quest. Yoshimasa's garden pond is said to have once been large enough for pleasure boating, but the garden and temple grounds were reduced to their present dimensions in the Edo period (1600–1867).

The Kitayama (1367–1408) and Higashiyama (1443–90) periods, symbolized respectively by the Golden and Silver Pavilions, mark the two cultural high points of the Muromachi era. The culture of the periods was strongly based on Chinese taste, much of which was introduced through the agency of Zen monks. It was informed as well, though, by native ideals, and much of what we think of today as the quintessence of the Japanese artistic experience, for example, the tea ceremony, ink painting, and the Nō drama, reached fruition during these years. It was also the time in which some of Japan's most famous landscape gardens were made, including not only that at Saihōji but also the rock gardens of Ryōanji and the Daisen'in of Daitokuji and the pond garden of Tenryūji, the last another creation of Musō Soseki.

The basic concept of a multistoried garden pavilion overlooking a pond continued to be influential even after the Muromachi period. One of the finest extant later examples is the Hiunkaku Pavilion in the garden of Nishi Honganji in Kyōto, now thought to have probably been built some time between 1615 and 1624.

36. Picture Scroll of the Legends of Ishiyamadera Temple

37. Picture Scroll of the Kasuga Gongen Miracles

Classical versus Medieval Building   Most major building projects of Japan's classical era (the eighth through twelfth centuries) were sponsored by the court. But with the decline in the power of the aristocracy and the approach of the medieval era (thirteenth through sixteenth centuries), court-supported building projects became far fewer, and the initiative passed to the individual estate owners, warriors, and temples.

Construction techniques changed as well over the ages. Lumber, for example, was split with a wedge and then smoothed with an adze (*chōna*) and a long-bladed plane (*yarikanna*) rather than sawed as in the Heian centuries. It was therefore easier in the medieval period to make thin planks or delicate wooden components.

The Two-Man Saw and the Bench Plane   As the medieval period wore on, it became progressively more challenging to obtain the massive lumber used in earlier structures. The scarcity necessitated the use

of smaller trees, which in turn contributed to the development of new tools and methodologies. Two important advances in this area were the inventions of the two-man saw (*oga*; close to a bucksaw in appearance) and the bench plane (*daikanna*). The two-man saw, operated vertically (fig. 40), allowed the manufacture of much thinner planks, and the bench plane, essentially an angled blade ("plane iron") projecting a fraction of an inch from a flat block of wood, greatly improved the smoothness of the planks. It is not known exactly when these two tools began to appear, but they are not seen in the picture scrolls of the Kamakura and early Muromachi periods.

Construction Scenes in Picture Scrolls   *The Picture Scroll of the Legends of Ishiyamadera Temple* (*Ishiyamadera engi*; fig. 36) dates from about the early fourteenth century and shows a great deal about contemporary construction methods. In the foreground, lumber is being brought to the site in ox carts. A more unwieldy slab is being pulled in after it on

38. *Picture Scroll of the Legends of Matsuzaki Tenjin Shrine*

39. *Picture Scroll of the Legends of Matsuzaki Tenjin Shrine*

40. *Thirty-Two Round Poem Competition of Trades*

rollers. In the hut behind, workers at the right are smoothing planks with adzes in front and with long-handled planes behind. At the left, other men are using saws in the foreground and, again, adzes behind. At front center in the hut, two men split a block with wedges.

Another valuable illustration is provided by the *Picture Scroll of the Kasuga Gongen Miracles* (*Kasuga Gongen kenki e*) painted in the late Kamakura period (fig. 37). At the far right of the picture, men pound in foundation stones where the alignment lines intersect. The man carrying the measuring stick on his shoulder and pointing is probably the master carpenter. To the left of this scene, in the foreground, two men mark off a post with carpenter's squares and ink brushes. Behind them two more workers inscribe a straight line on a plank by snapping a taut, ink-covered string to it. Another pair of workers behind them use wedges to split a plank. In the hut in the background more carpenters saw and notch wood.

A third instructive illustrated source is the *Picture Scroll of the Legends of Matsuzaki Tenjin Shrine* (*Matsuzaki Tenjin engi*), which comes down to us from about 1311 (figs. 38–39). In figure 38 workers have constructed a scaffold of thin, round posts with planks set on top. The master carpenter, his left hand holding a measuring stick, uses a string weighted by a carpenter's ink pot to check whether a post is plumb. An aristocrat, perhaps a patron of the project, sits behind and watches the work progress. In figure 39 wedges, adzes, and long-handled blades are shown, but the two-man saw has yet to appear. One depiction of such a tool is found with the caption "two-man saw" in the *Thirty-Two Round Poem Competition on Trades* (*Sanjūniban shokunin utaawase*), shown here in figure 40. The poem accompanying it uses the word *nokogiri* for "saw," and the same word is used today.

TEMPLE ARCHITECTURE IN THE EARLY MODERN PERIOD

41. View from Middle Sanctuary toward Sanctum Sanctorum, Main Hall, Zenkōji

The Popularization of Architecture After a century of civil war that racked the entire country, Japan was reunited in the late sixteenth century by three great generals—Oda Nobunaga (1534–82), Toyotomi Hideyoshi (1536/7–98), and Tokugawa Ieyasu (1542–1616). The latter established the Tokugawa shogunate, Japan's third military government. Under the Tokugawa the country was closed off from most Western intercourse until the arrival of the naval squadron of Commodore Matthew C. Perry in 1853.

Although Japan was largely isolated from the outside world during the Edo period (1600–1868), travel within the country increased due to the long-standing peaceful conditions established under the shogunate. Much of this travel took the form of pilgrimages by the general public to temples and shrines, and the military government encouraged ties between the people and various places of worship. As a result, temples began to cater to the less-refined tastes of the common folk and adopted effusive color schemes and ostentatious sculpture.

The Main Hall of Zenkōji One of the most popular pilgrimage spots in the north of Japan was, and still is, Zenkōji temple (Nagano City, Nagano Prefecture). Rebuilt in 1707, the Main Hall (Hondō) boasts a complex plan (fig. 43) composed of an Outer Sanctuary (Gejin), Middle Sanctuary (Chūjin), Inner Sanctum (Naijin), and Sanctum Sanctorum (Nainaijin). The pilgrim could enter the Outer Sanctuary while still wearing his footwear, and then after removing it rest on the elevated *tatami*-mat floor of the Middle Sanctuary. But the most famous attraction of the Zenkōji Main Hall is the pitch-dark tunnel beneath the Sanctum Sanctorum, through which pilgrims are encouraged to grope their way to earn religious merit.

The facade of the Main Hall is massive in appearance, but like the Jizōdō of Shōfukuji (see fig. 16), what looks to be a two-story design is actually one story plus a huge subsidiary area with a pent roof (fig. 42). The Main Hall was constructed on a grand scale to inspire the thousands of pilgrims who made the trip to pray for health, domestic tranquility, com

42. Mai

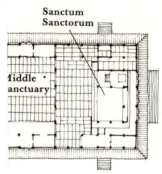

44. Sammon gate, Sōfukuji.

mercial
cerns. In a word, Zenkōji was built as a popular attraction, and it suits its purpose perfectly (fig. 41).
Kiyomizu Temple Another temple with great popular appeal is Kiyomizudera, located in southeast Kyōto. The Main Hall (Hondō) is built on the side of a low but steep mountain, and it boasts a large stage area supported by complex and impressive scaffolding that reaches far below. This mountainside *kakezukuri* foundation has been popular in temples of the Esoteric sect since the Heian period, but seldom employed to such arresting effect. Much of the city of Kyōto is visible from the temple, and the view has pleased thousands of pilgrims since the Edo period. The intricate system of roofs over the various structures and connecting corridors in the complex is also well known.

Architecture of the Ōbaku Sect The Ōbaku sect of Zen was first introduced into Japan in the mid seventeenth century from China. Together with the new sect came another style of religious architecture, that of the Ming and Qing dynasties. One of the examples of the Ōbaku style is Mampukuji temple in Uji , south of Kyōto, which was established by the Ming emigré Yin-yuan Long-qi (1592–1673). The main structure, the Daiyūhōden, dates from 1668.

Another impressive Ōbaku temple, Sōfukuji, was built in Nagasaki by Chinese immigrants from Fuzhou in Fujian Province. The Daiippōmon gate was rebuilt in 1694 from materials constructed in China and transported to Japan. Its vivid polychromy and extremely intricate four-tiered bracket system are touchstones of the Ōbaku style.

The introduction of the Ōbaku-sect style did not, of course, preclude continued building in the other building types theretofore in use. For the rebuilding of the Great Buddha Hall at Tōdaiji, for example, the Great Buddha style was readopted, though the facade of the structure was reduced from eleven bays to seven. The project, which lasted from 1688 to 1709, was undertaken by the monk Kōkei (1648–1705), who was awarded the elevated Buddhist title *shōnin* for his work.

BUDDHIST ARCHITECTURE—
STRUCTURE AND DETAIL

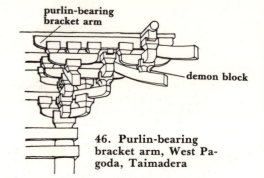

purlin-bearing
bracket arm

demon block

45. Demon block, West Pagoda, Taimadera

46. Purlin-bearing bracket arm, West Pagoda, Taimadera

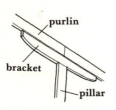

purlin

bracket

pillar

47. Boat-shaped bracket arm, Main Hall, Dai-sen'in, Daitokuji

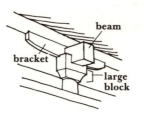

beam

bracket

large block

48. Large block and bracket arm, Dempōdō, Hōryūji

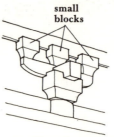

small blocks

49. Flat three block, Great Lecture Hall, Hōryūji

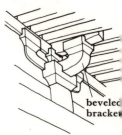

beveled bracket

50. Projecting three block, Main Hall, Chōkyūji

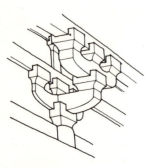

51. Projecting complex, Hokkedō, Tōdaiji

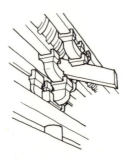

52. Two-step complex, Five-story Pagoda, Kaijūsenji

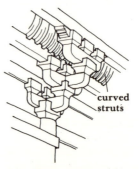

curved struts

53. Two-step complex, Main Hall, Daizenji

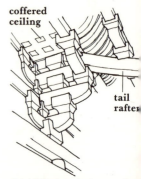

coffered ceiling

tail rafter

54. Three-step complex, West Pagoda, Taima-dera

Bracketing The Buddhist temple has manifold uses —besides housing one or more images, it serves as a place for ritual and worship, and as a symbol of the Buddhist faith. To serve these purposes, it requires imposing and permanent structures. The grandeur of the temple is in large part created by the deep eave overhang of the dignified roof, and the course of bracketing that supports it beneath. The bracket system is thus one of the keys to both the structure and the ornament of the temple, and it has undergone a long series of refinements in consequence.

The bracket complex (*kumimono* or *tokyō*) consists of two basic parts, the bearing block (*masu*) and the bracket arm (*hijiki*; fig. 48). The bearing block is basically a square or rectangular cube beveled at the bottom (the "block tail" or *tojiri*). When set directly on a column, this component is known as a "large block" (*daito*; fig. 48); on a bracket arm, it is called a "small block" (*makito*; fig. 49). Bearing blocks set on corner posts have more intricate bevel carving at the block tails and are called "demon blocks" (*onito* in consequence (fig. 45).

The outward support of the bracket complex is provided by bracket arms. They too are beveled at their projecting ends, making them resemble human

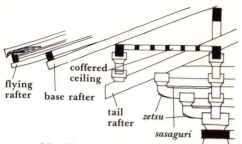

flying rafter
base rafter
coffered ceiling
tail rafter *zetsu*
sasaguri

55. Three-step complex, Three-story Pagoda, Yakushi-ji (730)

Development of the Three-Stepped Bracket

The three-step bracket is still at an early stage in its development at the Three-story Pagoda of Yakushiji (730; fig. 55). The design has not reached the point where all blocks are used in vertical rows of twos or threes. Bracket arms still retain the slight tonguelike protuberance (*zetsu*) on their lower corners and the understated concavity on their upper surfaces (*sasaguri*; fig. 55), both features of brackets at such early sites as Hōryūji. Later the zetsu and sasaguri cease to be used.

By the tenth century, all the blocks at the Daigoji pagoda appear in vertical groups (fig. 56), and curved struts (*shirin*) are fit between the second and third steps of the bracket complex. A final development occurs in the fourteenth and fifteenth centuries, when each of the uppermost three-block bracket arms has exactly six rafters above it, two per block (fig. 58). Though impossible to tell from figure 57, this is the case at the Three-story Pagoda at Jōrakuji. The system, called "six-branch placement" (*rokushigake*), effects a more organic relationship between the brackets and rafters.

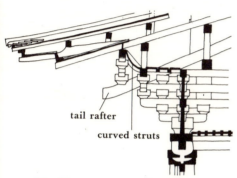

tail rafter

curved struts

56. Three-step complex, Five-story Pagoda, Daigoji (952)

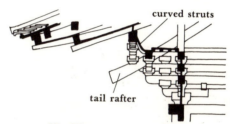

curved struts

tail rafter

57. Three-step complex, Three-story Pagoda, Jōrakuji (1400)

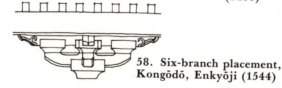

58. Six-branch placement, Kongōdō, Enkyōji (1544)

elbows (*hiji*), whence comes their Japanese name "elbow wood" (*hijiki*; fig. 50). When the uppermost bracket arm rests on the small blocks beneath and directly supports the purlin above without the agency of more small bearing blocks of its own, it is called a purlin-bearing bracket arm (*sane hijiki*; fig. 6).

Though the bracket complexes used in the Japanese, Great Buddha, and Zen styles are all different in configuration, that of the Japanese style is the most basic, and its general characteristics apply to the other two as well. We will therefore concentrate here on the Japanese-style bracket complex. The

simplest of these is the "boat-shaped bracket arm" (*funahijiki*), which directly supports the beam above (fig. 47). When it rests on a large bearing block, it is called a "large block and bracket arm" complex (*daito hijiki*; fig. 48). Mounting three small blocks atop the bracket arm makes it a "flat three block" complex (*hiramitsudo*; *mitsudo* meaning "three blocks;" fig. 49). When a second bracket arm projects from this assembly perpendicular to the wall to support a rafter by means of a single bearing block, it is called a "projecting three-block" complex (*demitsudo*; fig. 50). Adding to that single block a second three-block unit under a purlin creates the "projecting com-

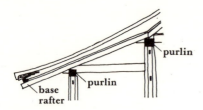

59. Single eave, Higashimuro, Hōryūji (late 7th cen., with later remodeling)

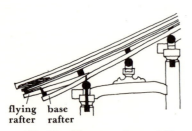

60. Double eave, Dempōdō, Hōryūji (739)

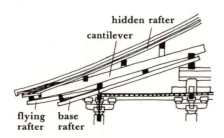

61. Double eave, Worship Hall, East Precinct, Hōryūji (rebuilt 1231)

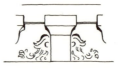

62. Strut and block with filigree, North Octagonal Hall, Kōfukuji (1210)

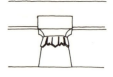

63. Collared strut, Mai Hall, Umpōji (mid 15th to mid 16th cen.)

Eave Construction

Eaves are supported by rafters (*taruki*), which rest on purlins (*keta*) and are cantilevered over the bracket complexes. In early structures the load of the roof is supported directly by posts beneath. This is the case at the Higashimuro of Hōryūji (fig. 59) and the Dempōdō of Hōryūji (fig. 60), both dating from the Nara period (710–84). Later, however, the burden of supporting the roof was assumed primarily by a huge cantilever (*hanegi*) hidden from view. One example is the Worship Hall (Raidō) of the East Precinct (Tōin) of Hōryūji, rebuilt in 1231 (fig. 61). The Worship Hall uses two sets of rafters, the exposed base rafters (*keshōdaruki*) below and the hidden rafters (*nodaruki*) above them, carrying the roof materials. The weight-bearing cantilever in between enables the rafters to be made thinner and extended out further. The two sets of rafters allow the underside of the eave to have a more gentle pitch.

Note too the single-eave raftering (*hitonoki*) of the Higashimuro, which uses only base rafters (*jidaruki*; fig. 59), and the double-eave raftering (*futanoki*) of the Dempōdō and Worship Hall, both of which have base rafters and flying rafters (*hiendaruki*) projecting beyond them (figs. 60–61). Flying rafters increase the curve of the eave ends. It is interesting as well that the Higashimuro uses no bracketing at all (fig. 59). The Dempōdō has simple boat-shaped brackets not visible in the cross section.

plex" (*degumi*) or "one-step complex" (*hitotesaki*; fig. 51). A bracket complex with a second such assembly projecting a second step outward to support a second purlin is called a "two-step complex" (*futatesaki*; figs. 52–53); with a third, a "three-step complex" (*mitesaki*; figs. 54–57), and so on. In the case of the three-step complex, the third three-block assembly is usually supported by a "tail rafter" (*odaruki*) cantilevered out over another bracket arm beneath (figs. 54–57). A comparison of the illustrated examples of the three-step bracket complex shows the refinement the design underwent over time, from the Three-story Pagoda at Yakushiji (Nara City, 730; fig. 55), to the Five-story Pagoda at Daigoji (Kyōto City, 952;

fig. 56), to the Three-story Pagoda at Jōrakuji (Shiga Prefecture, 1400; fig. 57).

Intercolumnar Supports Additional support for the wall purlin is provided by intercolumnar support (*nakazonae*) placed in the intervals between the bracket complexes that have posts supporting them. In Zen-style structures, entire bracket complexes are used in these intercolumnar spaces as well as above the posts themselves (see fig. 23), but in other styles simpler members are used. The most basic of these simpler elements is the "strut and block" (*kentozuka*) seen, for example, on the Phoenix Hall of the Byō-dōin (see fig. 11). Ornamental variations of this include the strut and block with filigree (*oigata*; fig. 62

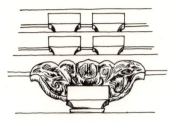

64. Floriate bracket arm,
Two-story Gate, Enjōji
(1468)

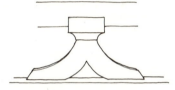

65. Split strut, Golden
Hall, Hōryūji (c.
680–94)

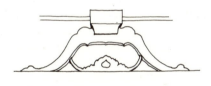

66. Open frog-leg strut,
Main Hall, Ujigami
Shrine (late 11th to ear-
ly 12th cen.)

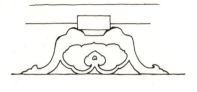

67. Open frog-leg strut,
Jizōdō, Shin Yakushiji
(1266)

68. Open frog-leg strut,
Jizōdō, Hōryūji (1372)

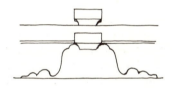

69. Closed frog-leg strut,
Second Main Hall,
Udamikumari Shrine
(1320)

and the "collared strut," named *minozuka* in Japanese for the collar's resemblance to the traditional straw raincoat (*mino*; fig. 63). Strut and block assemblies are sometimes used in vertical and/or horizontal pairs (fig. 64, top).

The second general type of intercolumnar member is the "floriate bracket arm" (*hanahijiki*), where a standard flat bracket arm with blocks has been stylized through floral carving (fig. 64, bottom). The third type is the "split strut" (*warizuka*), found either with straight or with slightly curved legs (fig. 65). The design, resembling the diagonal braces (*sasu*) supporting the roof ridge (see fig. 30), may have been the forerunner of the last main type of intercolum-

nar member, the "frog-leg" strut (*kaerumata*), though the origins of the latter are not precisely known (figs. 66–69). First appearing in about the twelfth century, the frog-leg strut became progressively more decorative, incorporating intricate carvings of flora and fauna. In the Edo period in particular the strut often nearly disappeared beneath coiling dragons or other sumptuous ornamentation. There are two basic types of frog-leg struts, the "open" (*hon kaerumata* or *sukashi kaerumata*), where the space between the legs is either empty or filled to varying degrees with carving (figs. 66–68), and the "closed" (*ita kaerumata*), a solid piece bearing only the characteristic frog-leg outline (fig. 69).

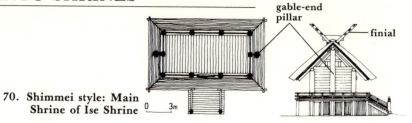

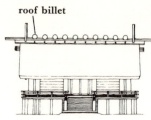

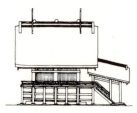

70. Shimmei style: Main Shrine of Ise Shrine

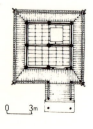

71. Taisha style: Main Shrine of Izumo Shrine

72. Sumiyoshi style: one of Main Shrines of Sumiyoshi Shrine

Nature Worship   Shintō, "the Way of the Gods," is Japan's indigenous religion. Animistic in nature, it worships not only anthropomorphic deities, but also the spirits of awe-inspiring elements of nature, especially certain mountains and trees. Early shrines used none of the monumental architecture of later Shintō structures. Some, like Miwa Shrine (Nara Prefecture) and Kanasana Shrine (Saitama Prefecture) have as their central object of worship the mountain behind them, and thus even today have no central building corresponding to the "main hall" (*honden*) used in other Shintō complexes. Instead, in the case of Miwa Shrine, a massive rock called a *yorishiro* atop Mt. Miwa is the focus of the sacred precinct. At the base of the mountain is a small worship hall (*haiden*) and a *torii*, the characteristic post and lintel gate that indicates a Shintō sanctuary (see fig. 83 for an illustration of a torii).

The Shrine Prototype   Actual shrine structures were probably built in response to the need to summon a deity in order to offer prayers for a bountiful crop or express thanks for a good harvest. These early structures, the prototypes of the shrines we know today, are found either in a central location in a village or before mountains, boulders, and other places where the gods were thought to dwell. These original constructions were most likely temporary in nature.

The configuration of the early shrines is unknown, but possibly resembled the portable shrines (*mikoshi*) still carried on poles during festivals today. Indeed, the arrangement of the foundation stones at Kasuga Shrine (see fig. 74b-d) and Kamo Shrine (see fig. 75) suggest that their principal structures were originally movable.

The Oldest Shintō Shrine Styles   The main types of Shintō shrines in use today took their final forms after the introduction of Buddhist architecture. Though influenced to varying degrees by Buddhist temple forms, they nevertheless remain stylistically separate and distinct. The three most venerable Shintō shrine styles are the Shimmei (fig. 70), Taisha (fig. 71), and Sumiyoshi (fig. 72). Each is primarily identified with one famous complex—Ise Shrine (Ise City, Mie Prefecture) for the Shimmei, Izumo Shrine (Hikawa District, Shimane Prefecture) for the Taisha, and Sumiyoshi Shrine (Ōsaka City) for the Sumiyoshi.

Ise Shrine actually consists of two shrine complexes, the Outer (Gekū) and Inner (Naikū; fig. 73). The most important structure is the Main Shrine (Shōden; figs. 70, 73) of the Naikū. Located in the center of the complex, it has an entrance portico projecting from its south side. Shrines (and other types of buildings as well) with entrances in the side

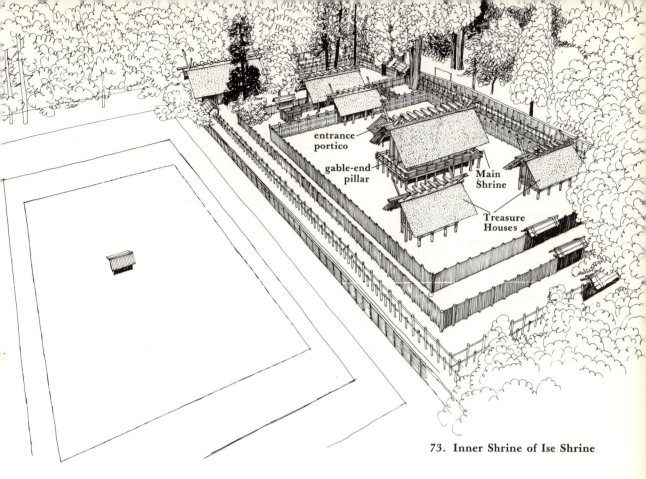

entrance
portico

gable-end
pillar

Main
Shrine

Treasure
Houses

73. Inner Shrine of Ise Shrine

parallel to the roof ridge are called *hirairi*, "side-entered," as opposed to those entered at the gable end (*tsumairi*). Visual support for the roof ridge is provided by two massive pillars, called *munamochibashira*, that stand independently beyond the gable sides of the structure and lean slightly inward. Above the plank walls is a miscanthus (*kaya*) roof topped by ten roof billets (*katsuogi*) and, at either end, forked finials (*chigi*) that are extensions of the bargeboards. The floor is elevated on posts. Surrounding the Main Shrine and the two Treasure Houses (Hōden) to the north are concentric fences, the Mizugaki, Uchi (Inner) Tamagaki, Tono (Outer) Tamagaki, and, surrounding the whole, the Itagaki.

To the east of the shrine complex in figure 73 stands a second lot with a small structure at the center. As a rule, the shrine buildings are rebuilt on the contiguous lot every twenty years in order to ensure ritual purity for this, the shrine to the goddess of the sun, Amaterasu, primary in the Shintō pantheon. The sixtieth rebuilding took place in 1973. Once the new shrine complex is completed, the older one is dismantled, and a small structure is built over the short "heart pillar" (*shin no mihashira*) over which the Main Hall used to stand. The rebuilding process, beginning with the cutting of special lumber far in the mountains, takes years to accomplish and is enor-

mously costly. Ise, therefore, is the only shrine today that is regularly rebuilt, though the practice was common at many shrine sites in the past.

Izumo Shrine, built for the worship of Ōkuninushi and four lesser gods, has a similarly ancient heritage and was rebuilt twenty-five times. The Main Shrine (Honden; fig. 71) is a gable-entrance structure of impressive size, hence the name Taisha, "Great Shrine." Originally it may have been even larger—shrine legends say the prototype stood nearly one hundred meters tall and was reached by a grand staircase. In plan, the present Main Shrine resembles that of the Daijōe Shōden, built for the accession of each new emperor. The Main Shrine at Izumo is thought, therefore, to preserve a floor plan characteristic of ancient domestic architecture.

The third of these particularly ancient shrines, Sumiyoshi, consists of four nearly identical gable-entrance structures that originally overlooked the sea, as befit a place of worship of gods of sea voyages (fig. 72). Today, though, the site is surrounded by a modern urban neighborhood. Whereas the Ise and Izumo Shrines are left unpainted, the Sumiyoshi buildings are finished in brilliant red and white.

COMMON SHRINE STYLES

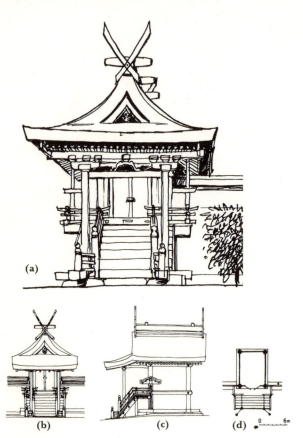

(a)

(b)   (c)   (d)

75. Nagare style: one of two Main Shrines at Kamo Mioya Shrine (Shimogamo Shrine)

74a-d. Kasuga style: exterior of Kasugadō, Enjōji; front, side, and plan of a Main Shrine, Kasuga Shrine

The Influence of Buddhist Architecture Shintō structures began very early in their development to adopt Buddhist temple characteristics. For example, the straight eaves, such as those at Sumiyoshi Shrine (see fig. 72), which are thought to have been the norm for early Shintō roofs, gradually adopted the gentle curve of Buddhist buildings. But Buddhist influence was not overbearing—the hip roofs and tiles common in Buddhist structures were not generally adopted by Shintō builders, and neither was the wattle-and-daub temple wall construction.

Further Buddhist influence entered in the Heian period with the development of the *honji suijaku* doctrine, which holds that Shintō deities are actually avatars of Buddhas and Bodhisattvas. This sectarian blending caused subsidiary Buddhist temples (*jingū-ji*) to be built on Shintō properties, and vice versa, Shintō shrines (*chinjusha*) to be constructed in temple complexes.

The Nagare and Kasuga Styles The Nagare style is the most widely used shrine type (fig. 75) and is characterized by a gable roof that slopes out over the entrance on the non-gable side of the structure. The design suggests a Shimmei-style building (see fig. 70)

with a roof extended at one side and lacking roof billets and forked finials. Its best examples are the two Main Halls (Honden) at the Kamo Mioya Shrine and the Main Hall and Provisional Hall (Gonden) at the Kamo Wakeikazuchi Shrine (both shrines in Kyōto City), which were last rebuilt in 1863.

The Kasuga style (fig. 74) is one bay in plan, with the entrance and stairs on the gable side and protected by a long porch roof. Kasuga Shrine (figs. 74b-d), from which the style takes its name, is thought to have been first built in the 730s at the foot of Mt. Mikasa east of the Heijō Capital, now Nara City (see p. 56). The present configuration of four identical one-bay Main Shrines (Honden) in a line is believed to go back to at least the Heian period. The shrine was rebuilt every twenty years until modern times, and the present main structures date from 1863. They resemble the Sumiyoshi style (see fig. 72) in their red and white color scheme, gable entry, and use of roof billets and forked finials, but differ in their smaller size and hip-and-gable roof with long porch overhang.

Two other fine examples of the Kasuga style are the Kasugadō (fig. 74a) and Hakusandō of Enjōji

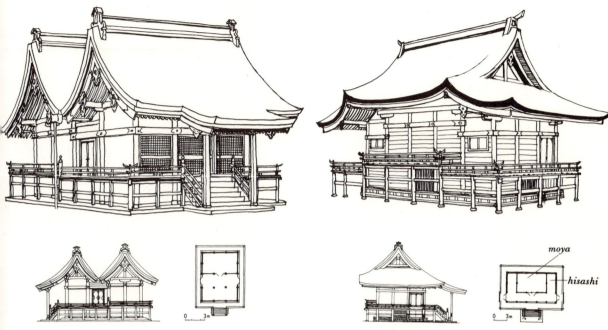

76. Hachiman style: Main Shrine of Usa Shrine

77. Hie style: Main Shrine of East Precinct, Hie Shrine

moya

hisashi

temple (Ninnikusenchō, Nara City), built between 1197 and 1228. They are the oldest Kasuga-style shrines extant and are thought to have been built originally as part of Kasuga Shrine, then moved to their present location when Kasuga was rebuilt. The Kasuga style is the second most commonly used shrine type.

Further Developments in Shintō Shrine Architecture The Hachiman style (fig. 76) was created by linking two Nagare-type shrines (fig. 75) back to front. The practice was first used in Buddhist structures to provide a separate space for worshippers. Another well-known shrine configuration is the Hie style (fig. 77), a hip-and-gable variant of the Nagare style, with a truncated rear roof. The design is the result of adding subsidiary spaces (*hisashi*) around all but the rear side of the central core (*moya*) and extending the roof further over those additions. Hie Shrine (Ōtsu City, Shiga Prefecture), after which the style is named, contains two nearly identical main structures, one each in its east and west precincts.

Other Buddhist architectural elements continued to be gradually incorporated as well. These included corridors, two-story gates, and even pagodas. One

superb example of fine design coupled with tastefully added Buddhist concepts is Itsukushima Shrine. First built on its present scale in 1168 by the great warrior Taira no Kiyomori (1118–81), Itsukushima Shrine (Hiroshima Prefecture) is built out over the water (see fig. 244). At high tide its main buildings and connecting corridors seem to float, their vermilion members reflecting on the shallow waves. The use of connecting corridors is reminiscent of the Shinden style of aristocratic domestic architecture (see pp. 64–67).

By the end of the Heian period in the twelfth century the major shrine styles had reached maturity. Further developments were limited to minor variations in configuration or style of ornamentation. Kibitsu Shrine (Okayama City), built in 1425, combines its Main Hall (Honden) and Worship Hall (Haiden) under one hip-and-gable roof, but with the gables doubled to indicate the two spaces beneath. Examples of the increasing use of ornamentation include the Shinra Zenshindō of Onjōji temple (Shiga Prefecture, late fourteenth century) and most notably the Tōshōgū at Nikkō (Nikkō City, Tochigi Prefecture; see pp. 44–47).

43

THE YŌMEIMON GATE, NIKKŌ TŌSHŌGŪ SHRINE

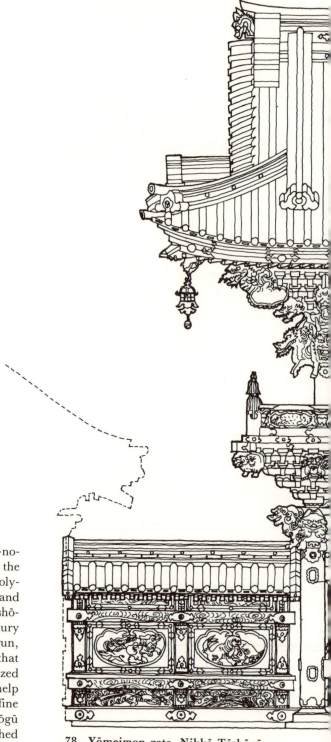

The Yōmeimon gate is nicknamed Higurashi-no-mon, or "Livelong-Day Gate," in reference to the time one could spend in staring at its brilliant polychromy and menagerie of sculptured dragons and lions. It serves as the main entrance to the Tōshō-gū, which was built in the early seventeenth century both as a mausoleum for the first Tokugawa shōgun, Ieyasu, and as a place of worship (*reibyō*) for that deified Tokugawa patriarch. Some have criticized the Tōshōgū's lack of restraint, but one cannot help admiring the workmanship it reflects. Another fine example of the extreme ornament at the Tōshōgū is the Karamon, a gate with cusped gables, reached after passing through the Yōmeimon (see fig. 79).

78. Yōmeimon gate, Nikkō Tōshōgū

JAPANESE BAROQUE

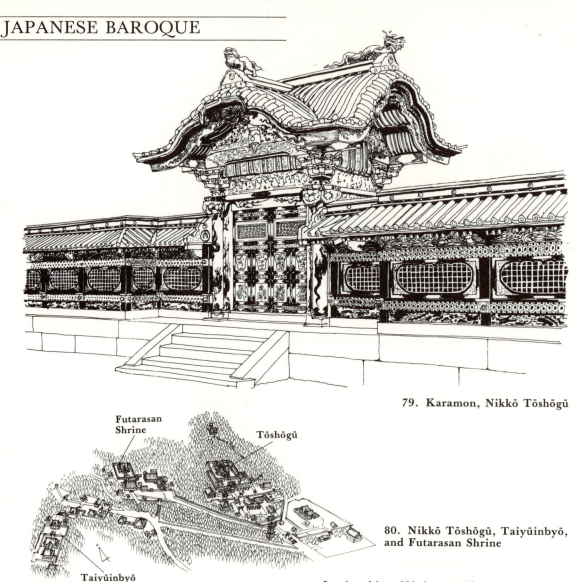

79. Karamon, Nikkō Tōshōgū

80. Nikkō Tōshōgū, Taiyūinbyō, and Futarasan Shrine

Nikkō Tōshōgū On the seventeenth of the fourth month of 1616, Tokugawa Ieyasu, victor of the last great battles for national hegemony, died at his castle at Sumpu (Shizuoka Prefecture). His remains were first interred at Kunōzan in Shizuoka Prefecture, then moved in the next year and enshrined at Nikkō, deep in the mountains of Tochigi Prefecture, where a rededication was held on the first anniversary of his death.

The present appearance of the Tōshōgū shrine, however, is primarily the result of the far-reaching renovation project of Ieyasu's grandson, Iemitsu (1604–51). Begun in 1634, the project was far enough along for another rededication ceremony of surpassing splendor to be held in 1636, again on the anniversary of Ieyasu's death.

Iemitsu himself is interred in a second complex at Nikkō, the Taiyūinbyō, which, though smaller than Ieyasu's, is quite marvelous in its own right. Built in 1653, it is situated on a hill to the west of the Tōshōgū (fig. 80). Both are artfully integrated into the contour of the land. The approaches leading to both have been cleverly laid out so that at each bend in the path the viewer is surprised by a totally new vista. The steps too have been set at strategic locations so that as one climbs them different buildings come into view, as if vying with one another to impress the onlooker with their *gesamtkunstwerk* of color and carving. The placement of the individual structures thus contributes to a dynamic of truly Baroque effect. The two mausolea are accompanied by a variety of other establishments, such as Futarasan Shrine, set halfway between the Tōshōgū and the Taiyūinbyō (fig. 80). **Increasing Ornamentation in Shrine Architecture** The splendor and display seen at Nikkō be-

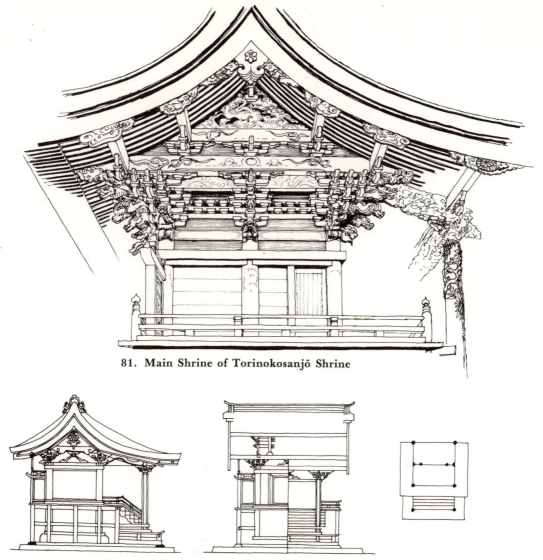

81. Main Shrine of Torinokosanjō Shrine

82. Illustrations from book of proportions (*kiwarisho*)

gan, soon after its completion to be imitated by shrines across the country. A case in point is the Main Hall (Honden) of the Torinokosanjō Shrine (Nasu District, Tochigi Prefecture), built in 1783 (fig. 81). There the tips of the tail rafters have been carved with extremely lifelike dragons, and the porch-roof supports and beams have been covered with carving as well.

The trend toward decoration continued to spread as the Edo period progressed. The frog-leg struts that had been only lightly ornamented in earlier structures came by the late Edo to be entirely filled with sculptural flora and fauna. The same tendency to elaborate was exercised on most other visible parts of the buildings.

Modular Design System (*Kiwarijutsu*) While concentrating increasingly on detailed ornamentation, builders produced few really innovative building designs. One reason for this was the gradual development at this time of a new system, called *kiwarijutsu*, of building according to set proportions and modules. By virtue of this system, the dimension of any one member related to those of all the other parts of the design. These proportions were set down in books called *kiwarisho*, and if a builder simply followed those directions, he was assured of producing a serviceable structure. The example illustrated in figure 82 shows a kiwarisho illustration of the proportions for a Nagare-style shrine. The shrine could be built in any size and be successful as long as the proportions of the constituent members related to each other as set forth in the diagrams.

Clearly the kiwarijutsu system was a boon to carpenters, but there is no denying that it militated against originality of overall design. Builders therefore channeled their creativity into the ornamentation of detail. Further description of kiwarijutsu can be found on pages 76–77.

THE NEIGHBORHOOD SHRINE

83. The shrine precinct—focus of neighborhood life

A Place for Worship and Recreation   In days gone by, nearly every town or farming village had at least one shrine which served, along with the Buddhist temple, not only as a center of religious life but as a playground for children, a place of rest and relaxation for adults, and a focus of neighborhood interaction. Behind it stood the grove of thickly growing trees so characteristic of shrine compounds. Though these patches of green are slowly bowing to urban sprawl, those that remain are a precious legacy.

The shrine compound is marked by the characteristic *torii* gate, whose simple yet striking design long ago became one of the symbols of Japanese culture (fig. 83). Beyond it, one passes between the statues of a pair of ''Korean dogs'' (*koma inu*), put there to fend off evil influences. Imported centuries ago from the Asian continent, they were once used even in the Imperial Palace. To the left, at the top

of the stairs, is the ablution basin (*chōzuya*) under its own roof, where one washes the hands and purifies oneself before prayer. The cool water is especially pleasant and refreshing in the heat of summer.

Across from the ablution basin is the stage where dances are performed on festival days for the delectation of gods and men alike. The compound also often has a storage building for the sacred palanquin (*mikoshi*) to parade the tutelary deity during shrine celebrations.

Most shrines are arranged in more or less this way, though some, like the Nikkō Tōshōgū, are built on a grand scale, and others are nothing but a miniature shrine set into a nook in a roadside wall. Shrine precincts are designed to take advantage of the natural features of the surrounding area and each reflects the care and consideration that generations of parishioners have lavished on it.

THE WORLD OF
THE CRAFTSMEN

84. Roofers (*Scenes In and Around the Capital* [*Rakuchū rakugai zu*]; reproduction in the Tōkyō National Museum)

85. Roofers (*Kuwakata Keisai's Pictures of Tradesmen* [*Kuwakata Keisai shokunin zukushi e*])

86. Carpenters (*Kitain Pictures of Tradesmen* [*Kitain shokunin zukushi e*])

The Age of Craftsmen The craftsmen who built the temples and shrines of the premodern era were grouped into a number of discrete specialties, including carpenters, plasterers, stone masons, and sawyers. In fact, the early modern period of Japanese history, from the end of the era of the country at war in the late sixteenth century until the end of the Tokugawa shogunate and advent of the Meiji Restoration in 1868, might be called the ''age of craftsmen.'' The Japanese word for craftsman, *shokunin*, had a wider meaning in the medieval period and applied to physicians and tradesmen as well, but gradually it narrowed to denote those who worked with their hands. It was used especially frequently in reference to those in the building trades.

Depictions of Craftsmen Illustrations on folding screens, picture scrolls, and woodblock prints provide fascinating glimpses into the activities of craftsmen in the early modern era. In figure 86, carpenters (*daiku*) are apparently at work building a shrine, to judge from the elevation drawing propped in the background. One worker, stripped to the waist, uses an adze to chip away at a square beam. In front of him another beam is being marked with a straight line by snapping an inked string. In figures 84 and 85, roofers (*yanefuki*) are at work setting shingles. The black dots represent rocks set on the shingles to help keep them in place. In figure 92 a stone mason (*ishiku*) chisels a rock, and in figure 91 sawyers (*kobiki*) cut long planks, with Mt. Fuji in the distance. In fig-

87. Tatami makers (*Kuwakata Keisai's Pictures of Tradesmen*)

89. Metalworkers (*Kitain Pictures of Tradesmen*)

88. Plasterers (*Kuwakata Keisai's Pictures of Tradesmen*)

90. Woodcarvers (*Kuwakata Keisai's Pictures of Tradesmen*)

ure 90 wood carvers (*horimonoshi*) produce delicately rendered floral-patterned fittings for a temple or shrine, while in figure 89 metalworkers (*kaji*) use hammers and tongs to shape the red-hot metal they have taken from the coals. Though metalworkers are primarily known for their work on swords and tools, they were vital to architectural projects as well, as they produced hinges and other metal fittings, not to mention nails, fashioned painstakingly one at a time. In figure 88 plasterers (*sakan*) knead clay into balls and toss them to others, who flatten them against the wall with trowels. In figure 87 *tatami* makers (*tatamiya*) put the finishing touches on the woven straw tatami mats and sew decorative strips along both sides. Though not illustrated, building projects also called for lacquerers (*nushi*), workers in fine metal ornamentation (*kazarishi*), and makers of interior and exterior partitions and other wooden fittings (*tategu daiku*).

91. Sawyers (*Hokusai's Thirty-Six Views of Mt. Fuji [Hokusai fugaku sanjūrokkei]*)

92. Stonemason (*Kuwakata Keisai's Pictures of Tradesmen*)

CONSTRUCTION TECHNIQUES
OF THE EDO PERIOD

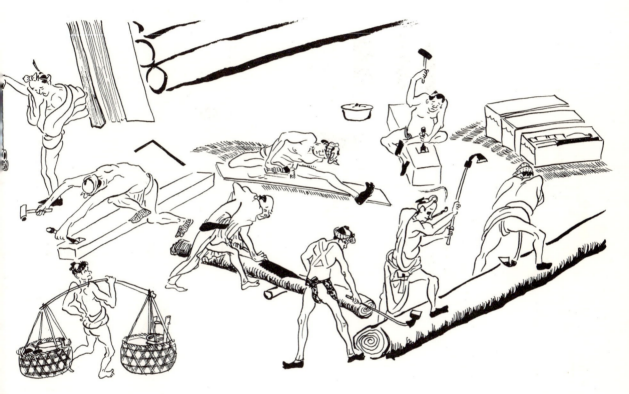

93. Carpenters (*Kuwakata Keisai's Pictures of Tradesmen*)

Workers and Tools Some of the most telling, yet humorous, of illustrations of workmen at their various crafts are those by Kuwakata Keisai (1764–1824), painted in 1804 (see figs. 85, 87–88, 90, 92, 93). These pictures, belonging to a genre called, appropriately enough, *Pictures of Tradesmen (Shokunin zukushi e)*, are accompanied by the topical remarks of three popular writers of the Edo period, Yomo no Akara (1749–1823), Tegara Okamochi (1735–1815), and Santō Kyōden (1761–1816). The workman in the foreground of figure 93, for example, is muttering "I'd like to cut it down a bit during the noon break." Clearly the time is just before lunch, as food boxes are being carried in at the lower left. The carpenter in the middle is using a bench plane, which was invented in the late middle ages and had come into wide use by the time the illustration was made.

The *Sino-Japanese Illustrated Encyclopedia* Very few of the actual tools used by carpenters remain from the Edo period and illustrations are consequently an important source of information on them. One of the best compilations is the *Sino-Japanese Illustrated Encyclopedia* (*Wakan sansai zu e*) from 1713, which gives pictures of contemporary carpenter's tools, together with explanations (fig. 94). For ''adze'' (*chōna*), for example, the caption in the *Encyclopedia* reads, ''A hand axe with either a single or a double blade.'' Most of the tools depicted have changed little in basic

shape during the intervening centuries and continue to be used with minor improvements by carpenters today.

A second source of illustrations depicting the tool of the era was made by the Nagasaki painter Kawahara Keiga (1786–?). It is now in the collection of the National Museum of Anthropology in Leiden, The Netherlands. Through pictures of this kind, we can more effectively understand the huge amounts of skill and labor contributed by craftsmen who worked on the monuments of the period.

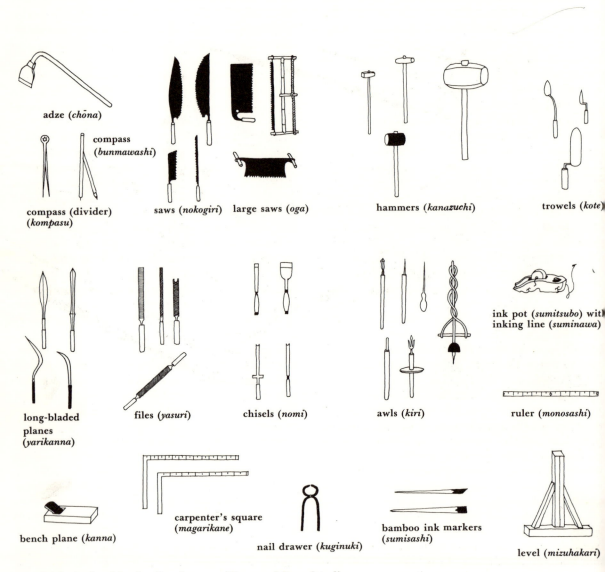

94. Tools depicted in the *Sino-Japanese Illustrated Encyclopedia*

DAILY LIFE

Residential and Urban Architecture

Homes should be built for summer. In the winter one can live anywhere, but dwellings unsuited to the hot months are unendurable.

Yoshida Kenkō (1283?–1350?) had left the world of the imperial court for the contemplative life of a Buddhist priest when he wrote the above remarks as part of his collection of short anecdotes and observations entitled *Essays in Idleness* (*Tsurezuregusa*, entry 55). The early fourteenth-century work is thought by many to be the quintessence of medieval Japanese literary expression. In it Kenkō makes pronouncements on a wide range of human experiences and concerns, from history and court usages to aesthetics and the qualities of an ideal man, always with an engaging idiosyncratic subjectivity. His remarks on the ideal house are a case in point—they are uncompromisingly presented, but suited only to homes near the Heian Capital in central Japan and certainly not to the snowy northern hinterlands. But his statement is nevertheless a forceful apology for the integration of house and natural environment, a central theme throughout the history of traditional Japanese architecture.

A century before Kenkō, another medieval courtier-turned-recluse, Kamo no Chōmei (1155?–1216), turned his attention to domestic architecture, in this case his own. The very title of his contemplative essay, *Tale of the Ten-Foot-Square Hut* (*Hōjō ki*), written in 1212, suggests the central role his thoughts on architecture play in his composition. The evanescence of all things is the theme of his work, and it is evoked in the first line, familiar to nearly every Japanese: "The river flows on without cease, yet its waters are never the same." It is perfect metaphor for the permanence of change. Chōmei then illustrates this supremely Buddhist truth by recalling the great mansions of the past and the calamities that swept them all away. Faced with the certitude of a similar fate, Chōmei recounts how he abandoned his own home in the capital for a tiny hut, "ten feet on either side and seven from floor to roof," deep in the mountains to the south. He called his hut *hōjō*, the name taken from the dwelling of the Indian Buddhist sage Vimalakīrti and later used to indicate the abbot's quarters in Zen monasteries. Vimalakīrti is said to have miraculously enlarged his modest dwelling when visited by a great host of divine beings, and the Zen sect reveres his example of virtue and wisdom.

The lavish manors of the aristocracy notwithstanding, the theme of simplicity and modesty has been another touchstone of traditional Japanese architecture. Even the masters of the great castles and palaces of the Momoyama and Edo periods would retire to tiny rustic tea houses when they wished to calm their hearts of the impurities of the outside world.

This chapter will look at traditional residential architecture from its beginnings, through the time of Chōmei and Kenkō, up to the end of the Tokugawa shogunate, as well as at the villages and cities of which these residences formed a part. The dwellings can be divided along two main lines—those of the aristocracy and those of the common folk.

The Heian-period nobles immortalized in Murasaki Shikibu's *The Tale of Genji* (*Genji monogatari*) or Sei Shōnagon's *The Pillow Book* (*Makura no sōshi*) lived in mansions built in the *Shinden* style, which usually consisted of a central hall facing a pond and bounded by hallways leading to subsidiary structures. Logically enough, it developed out of the mansions of the Nara-period aristocrats and was in turn the ancestor of the second main type of upper-class residential mode, the *Shoin* style, which continues to strongly influence Japanese domestic architecture today. Japanese houses therefore show a remarkable undercurrent of design consistency from early history to modern times.

The houses of the common people were understandably influenced by those of their superiors, though to varying degrees. When the first great palaces of the early Nara emperors were constructed, many of their subjects still lived in houses little changed from prehistoric "pit dwellings." But in the later Edo period, village headmen and rich urban merchants often lived on a scale envied by many of their nominal superiors, the samurai.

But what exactly did the houses of the early Japanese look like, and in what directions did they subsequently develop? What was the Shinden of Murasaki and Sei really like, or the urban spaces experienced by Chōmei and Kenkō? The truth of Chōmei's remarks on mutability are all too amply proven by the paucity of extant evidence. We will nevertheless suggest some answers to these and other questions in the following pages on the basis of remaining structures and, much more importantly, information gathered from contemporary literature and painting.

HOUSES OF THE JŌMON AND YAYOI PERIODS

95. Restored Yayoi dwelling

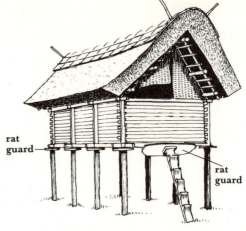

rat guard

rat guard

97. Restored Yayoi elevated storehouse

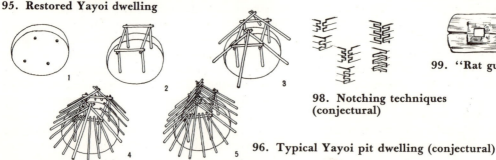

99. "Rat guard"

98. Notching techniques (conjectural)

100. Ladder

96. Typical Yayoi pit dwelling (conjectural)

Prehistoric Dwellings   Shelter ranks with food and clothing as one of the three basic necessities of life, but our knowledge of primitive dwellings is still quite limited. The distant ancestors of the modern Japanese appear to have sought protection from the wind and rain in natural shelters such as rocky overhangs or caves, or in simple huts built of the wood from nearby trees. Examples still exist of caverns or rocky outcroppings that were used in the earliest years of the neolithic Jōmon period, which dates from the end of the last ice age (9,000–10,000 years ago) to the start of the Yayoi era (200 B.C.–A.D. 250).

The earliest type of house about which we have much information is the pit dwelling (*tateana jūkyo*). It was built by digging a circular pit (or a rectangular one with rounded edges) fifty or sixty centimeters deep and five to seven meters in diameter, then covering it with a steep thatched roof.

The Toro Site   The Yayoi period brought with it wet-rice cultivation and the sophisticated use of iron tools, which in turn prompted advances in building techniques and the development of a second type of prehistoric building that was elevated on posts. The best example of a Yayoi community is Toro in Shizuoka Prefecture, where one can see the Yayoi pit dwelling (fig. 95) and elevated storehouse in conjectural reconstruction (fig. 97). The settlement probably contained about twenty structures originally.

The Toro pit dwellings (fig. 95) consisted of a six-by-eight meter oval living area. A double skirting wall thirty centimeters high was first built around it and the space in between the walls filled to the top with earth. Though it was therefore not a pit dwelling *per se*, since the floor was on the level of the ground outside, the basic idea of a sunken living area was the same. The dwelling was then constructed over this foundation with four posts sunk in the ground, beams connecting them at the top, and rafters radiating from those beams to the ground, forming the structure's periphery (fig. 96). The roof was thatched with miscanthus or some other grass, and a hearth was sunk in the earth floor inside.

Elevated storehouses were raised off the ground by posts to protect the contents from pests (fig. 97). Wooden discs or "rat guards" (*nezumigaeshi*; fig. 99) were placed at the top of the posts and the entrance ladder to provide additional security from rodents (fig. 97). The ladder was carved of a single piece of wood rather than assembled with individual rungs (fig. 100). Archaeological evidence suggests that these storehouses were built of planks that overlapped at the corners. Ingenious mortise and tenon joinery methods are believed to have been used, which suggests that the builders of the period already possessed marked technical expertise and sophisticated iron tools (fig. 98).

RECONSTRUCTING YAYOI AND TUMULUS-PERIOD DWELLINGS

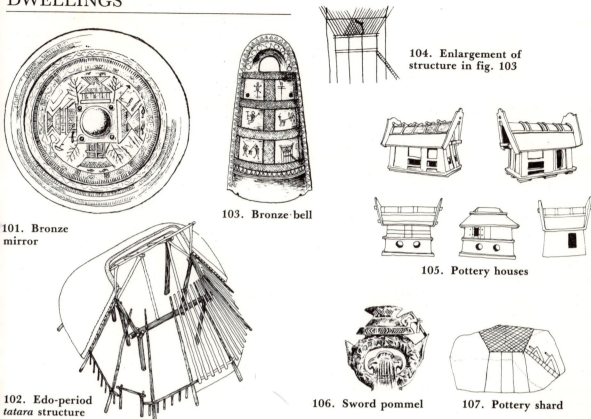

101. Bronze mirror

103. Bronze bell

104. Enlargement of structure in fig. 103

105. Pottery houses

102. Edo-period *tatara* structure

106. Sword pommel

107. Pottery shard

Archaeological Remains Excavations have clarified the plans of pit dwellings, but the positions of the post holes and the few surviving pieces of structural members have been insufficient to completely explain the roof configuration. Fortunately a number of other sources of information exist, many of them recovered from the great keyhole-shaped funerary tumuli in which members of the court were buried in pre-Buddhist Japan. These funeral mounds (see fig. 111, upper left) give their name to the Tumulus period (250–550 A.D.). One artifact is a bronze bell from Kagawa Prefecture, on which are shown pictures of people hunting and grinding grain in a large mortar, as well as of what appears to be an elevated building (figs. 103–4). The ridge of the roof is supported by two gable-end pillars (*munamochibashira*; see also figs. 70, 73), and there is a ladder leading up to the entrance. Similar evidence is found on a pottery shard from the Karako site in Nara Prefecture (fig. 107). The incised drawing shows two human figures climbing the ladder.

A bronze mirror discovered in the Samida tumulus in Nara shows on its back four early structures (fig. 101). Clockwise from the top they are a ground level hip-and-gable house, a pit dwelling, then two elevated buildings, the first with a gabled roof and the second with the hip-and-gable variety. The differences in style perhaps reflect different social strata of their occupants. Buildings elevated on posts, for example, were used not only for storehouses but also for shrines and chieftain's residences, due to the close connections between custodianship of food, divine sanction, and temporal power. Ise Shrine is representative of such a blend.

Eight pottery houses known as *haniwa* were also excavated from the Chausuyama tumulus in Gumma Prefecture, and these corroborate the designs on the bronze mirror (fig. 105). So too does a design atop a sword pommel uncovered at the Tōdaijiyama tumulus in Nara Prefecture (fig. 106).

The *Tatara* Illustration One last place to look for hints about early construction techniques is the *Tetsuzan hisho*, an Edo-period manual on iron making. The book contains an illustration of a temporary structure called a *tatara* (fig. 102) that seems to correspond quite well with what we know of pit dwelling plans from the Toro site. Sekino Masaru used the illustration in reconstructing the Toro structures.

THE ANCIENT CAPITALS

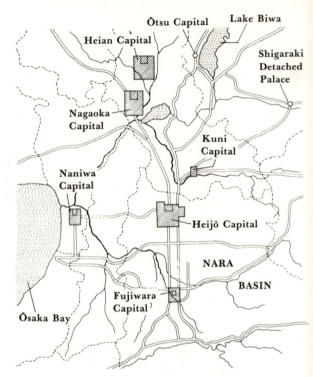

108. Relative sizes and locations of early capitals

Naniwa—The First Planned City   Japanese imperial palaces were traditionally rebuilt with the death of each sovereign for reasons of ritual purity, and the communities that grew up around each new palace tended to develop haphazardly. With the accession of Emperor Kōtoku in 645, however, a preconceived plan for his new imperial city was put into effect at Naniwa, located in present-day Ōsaka. The move to Naniwa had been occasioned by the Taika Reforms of that same year, wherein the court undertook revolutionary legal, economic, and social changes to modernize the country according to the Chinese Tang-dynasty model, the most advanced in the world at that time. As part of the effort to develop the nation, the capital was moved outside of the Nara Basin, the site of earlier centers of government, to a seaside location well suited to commerce (fig. 108). In 667, however, the capital was transferred to Ōtsu on Lake Biwa, and then soon thereafter the court returned to the Nara area.

The Fujiwara Capital   By the late seventh century, relations with the Asian continent had necessitated a fixed center of government. A splendid capital was accordingly built in 694 to the south of present-day Nara City, on a plain surrounded by the fabled Unebi, Kagu, and Miminashi hills. At this imperial city, called the Fujiwara Capital, the court presided over the burgeoning growth of the new, post-Taika Japan. Major temples such as Yakushiji were established, and great poets such as Kakinomoto Hitomaro composed verses that were later collected into Japan's oldest extant poem anthology, the *Man'yōshū*. The city was laid out on a rectangular grid about 3.8 km north to south and 2.1 km east to west. Entrance from the north was via three thoroughfares, the Upper (Kamitsumichi), Middle (Nakatsumichi), and Lower (Shimotsumichi) Roads.

The Heijō Capital   Though the Fujiwara Capital had been expected to be permanent, geographic considerations forced a move after less than two decades to what is now Nara City, twenty kilometers to the north. This first truly permanent capital was formally established in 710 and named Heijō-kyō, "Capital of the Peaceful Citadel" (see pp. 58–59). The Middle and Lower Roads that bounded the east and west sides of the Fujiwara Capital led to the east and center of Heijō, which was about twice as wide as its southern predecessor.

From Heijō to Heian   The court was to remain at the Heijō Capital for three quarters of a century, from 710 to 784. The Emperor Shōmu did leave Heijō for some years, though, first commanding the establishment of the Kuni Capital in 740, then electing to move it once more to Naniwa in 744, only to have a succession of earthquakes convince him to return to Heijō in 745. For much of those years he actually governed from yet another locale, the Shigaraki Detached Palace in present-day Shiga Prefecture (fig. 108).

Emperor Kammu made the final departure from Heijō in 784. He established his new capital, Nagaoka, some thirty-five kilometers to the north in order to distance the court from the growing influence of the Nara Buddhist temples. But it soon came to be feared that an evil influence had infested the site, and Kammu peremptorily quit the area in 794 to found a new imperial city even farther north, which he called Heian-kyō, "Capital of Peace and Tranquility." Heian was to remain the capital until Emperor Meiji (1852–1912) moved his court to Edo and renamed that city Tōkyō ("Eastern Capital") in 1868.

THE HEIJŌ AND HEIAN CAPITALS

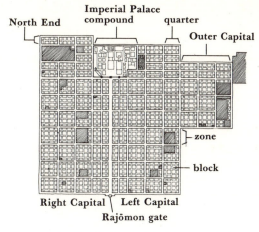

109. Heijō Capital in Nara period

The Heijō Capital The Heijō Capital was built at the height of a period of international commerce and exchange throughout Asia that centered on the Tang court and the Silk Road. Chinese prelates such as the blind master of the Lü (in Japanese, Ritsu) sect, Jian Zhen (Ganjin in Japanese; 689–763), came to Heijō to impart Buddhist teachings, and even an Indian monk attended the ceremony that marked the completion of the Great Buddha of Tōdaiji. It was not surprising then, that Heijō was designed as a copy on a smaller scale of the Tang-dynasty capital of Changan.

The city was composed of nine strips or ''zones'' (*jō*) running east and west, each one referred to by the number of the avenue at its southern border (fig. 109). Each zone was subdivided by north-south avenues into eight ''quarters'' (*bō*), numbered in terms of how far each was removed from the central Suzaku Avenue. That grand thoroughfare bisected the city into the ''Left Capital'' (Sakyō) and the ''Right Capital'' (Ukyō), the latter being to the west rather than the east for it was to the right of the Imperial Palace, which faced south. Thus the Ninth Zone, First Quarter, of the Left Capital was the southernmost quarter bordering Suzaku Avenue on the east. Each quarter was further subdivided into sixteen blocks (*chō*), which were 120 meters on a side, or a little narrower when bordered by a wide avenue, and these were further systematically broken down into even smaller subunits, with the result that any house lot in the capital could be pinpointed. The plan of the city was uniform save for a section of three half-quarters to the northwest, called the ''North End'' (Kitanobe), and the twelve wards to the east, known as the ''Outer Capital'' (Gekyō). The Imperial Palace compound was also slightly irregular in plan.

Living space in the Heijō Capital was apportioned according to rank and power: the more influential the resident, the larger the lot and the nearer to the Imperial Palace. It is recorded, for example, that the Tamura no Tei, mansion of the powerful mid-Nara-period figure Fujiwara no Nakamaro (706?–64), covered four blocks (one-fourth of a *bō*). Important temples also covered several blocks.

The Heian Capital The Heian Capital resembled that of Heijō in its basic grid layout, but it was com-

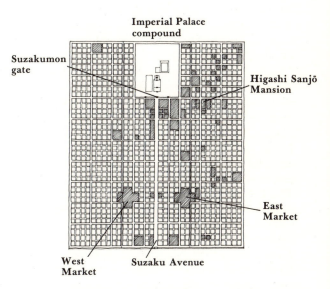

110. Heian Capital in Heian period

pletely regular in plan. The blocks too were a uniform 120 meters on a side and were not affected by varying street widths as they had been at Heijō. There, it had been the distance from the centers of two parallel streets that remained a constant 120 meters, but at Heian, it was the size of each block that stayed the same.

As at Heijō, the Heian Capital was bisected by a great avenue called Suzaku, as wide as a modern ten-lane highway, that ran to the Imperial Palace. Over the centuries, however, Heian, today the city of Kyōto, developed asymmetrically to the north and east, and the palace, which was frequently the victim of fires, was relocated in the early fourteenth century to the east of the Heian-period compound. The present palace complex contains only a fraction of the number of buildings it originally held.

HEIJŌ—FIRST OF THE GREAT CAPITALS

The Move from Fujiwara   The court of the Nara period (710–784) presided over a social and cultural efflorescence unprecedented in Japanese history. Its legal and governmental systems remained influential until the modern period, and its art and architecture became the classical norm against which later work was measured. Let us take a second look then at the birth and configuration of the Heijō Capital.

Preparation for the move north from the Fujiwara Capital officially began on the fifteenth day of the second month of 708, when Empress Gemmei (661–721) issued the proclamation of her intent. On the twentieth of the next month, she toured the Heijō site and then days later appointed two men to head the bureau in charge of the building project.

The move was effected on the tenth of the third month, 710. The empress is said to have composed this poem on the occasion, while viewing Mayumigaoka, the hill on which her deceased husband, Prince Kusakabe (662–89), was interred: "If I leave behind / The Asuka Capital / Of the coursing birds, / Will I ever see again / The place wherein rests my lord?" (*Man'yōshū*, no. 78). The "Asuka Capital" she left refers to Fujiwara. Work continued on the new capital well after the empress herself had arrived, and the strain on the treasury and labor force was immense. In the ninth month of 711, for example, a proclamation had to be issued forbidding corvée laborers from absconding.

Choosing the Site   The *Shoku Nihongi*, the second of Japan's national histories, records that the new capital was chosen on the basis of Chinese-style geomancy. This involved divination by interpreting cracks in tortoise shells (*plastromancy*), as well as satisfying the directional requirements of the "Four Birds and Beasts" (*shikin*), the Cyan Dragon, Vermilion Sparrow, White Tiger, and Dusky Warrior. These requirements stipulate a river to the east, low and damp area to the south, a long road to the west, and a rise to the north. The site satisfied all four. Moreover, its location in the north of the Nara Basin made it convenient for commerce and strategic for governing.

The Heijō Capital and Palace   As we have already seen, Heijō was designed on a Chinese-style grid plan (see fig. 109). Basically a rectangle, the capital measured 4.7 km north to south, and 4.2 km east to west, with additional sections extending beyond the rectangle to the northwest and east. At its height it is thought to have had a population of about two hundred thousand, including the immediate environs.

The main entrance to the city was through the Ra-

Uwanabe tumulus

Iwanohime-ryō tumulus

Konabe tumulus

jōmon (Rampart Gate) to the south, which opened on to the great Suzaku Avenue that bisected the city and ran for nearly four kilometers to the Suzakumon (Vermilion Sparrow Gate) at its northern end. The Suzakumon in turn was the main southern entrance to the Imperial Palace (Daidairi), a compound a kilometer north to south by a kilometer and a quarter east to west.

Within the Imperial Palace were located the East and West Imperial Assembly Halls (Chōshūden), then, to the north, the Court of Government (Chōdōin), with twelve buildings for the Eight Ministries and related functions symmetrically arranged along the central axis. North again was the Great Hall of State (Daigokuden), where the emperor supervised the governmental process. At the north of the com-

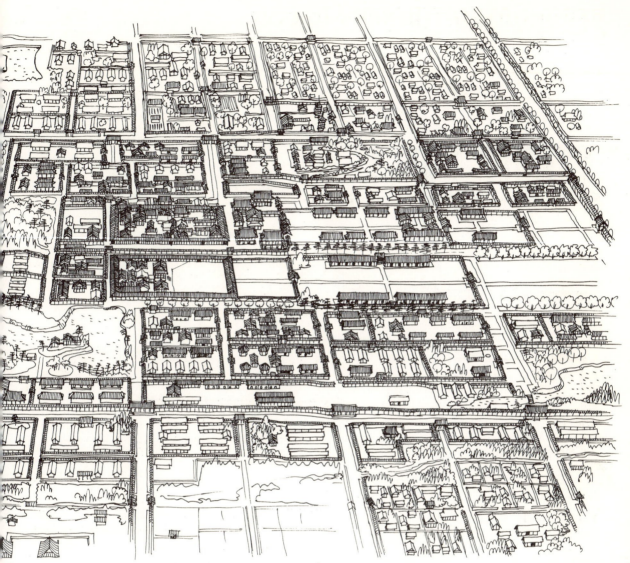

111. Imperial Palace and northern blocks of Heijō Capital, viewed from west

pound was the Inner Palace (Dairi), containing the Throne Hall (Shishinden) and the imperial residence halls. Dozens of other offices, stables, and storehouses surrounded the main subcompounds just mentioned.

The Court of Government and the Great Hall of State were dismantled when Emperor Shōmu temporarily established the above-mentioned Kuni Capital in 740, then built anew to the east of their original locations when he returned to Heijō in 745. The complexes are referred to as the First and Second Court of Government and Hall of State for this reason.

Figure 111 shows the northern part of the capital from the west. At right center are the Imperial Assembly Halls, followed to the left by the Court of Government with its twelve halls, the Great Hall of State, and the Inner Palace. The older compounds, nearly vacant, border them at the west. Yet another enclosure, the Palace of the Western Pond, is located at the northwest corner of the Imperial Palace compound. Beyond the compound to the northeast are the Iwanohime-ryō, Uwanabe, and Konabe tumuli.

Much of the old Heijō Capital returned to rice fields within four decades after Emperor Kammu departed. Since the small city of Nara today occupies only the eastern part of the site, archaeological investigation is much easier to carry out than at the site of the Heian Capital, which is still a large metropolis.

RESIDENCES OF THE NARA PERIOD

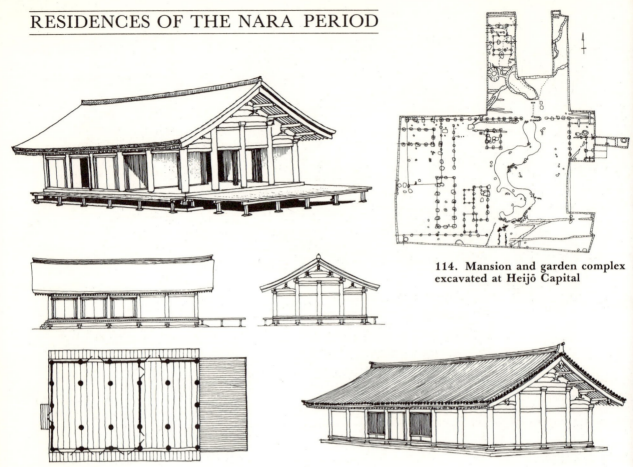

114. Mansion and garden complex excavated at Heijō Capital

112. Original Dempōdō as reconstructed by Asano Kiyoshi

113. Present Dempōdō

The Dempōdō ''Rich in blue-black earth, / The capital of Nara / Is now at its height, / Even as the crimson glow / Of petals in fullest bloom.'' As seen in this *Man'yōshū* poem (no. 328), the Heijō Capital in its efflorescence was a place of grandeur and beauty. But today only one of its residential structures remains, the Dempōdō (fig. 112) in the East Precinct of the Hōryūji temple. It was moved to the temple in 739 from the manor of a ''Lady Tachibana,'' thought to be Tachibana no Michiyo (?–733), mother of the Empress Kōmyō (701–60), consort of Emperor Shōmu.

The present Dempōdō, which means ''Hall for the Transmission of the Dharma,'' is seven bays long by four bays wide and, with its tiled roof, looks little like a residential building (fig. 113). It was, of course, given the name Dempōdō after it was moved to Hōryūji. The presence of a wood-plank floor, however, betrays its domestic origins, as temples of the period had floors of packed earth. Evidence obtained during a dismantling for repairs has allowed architectural historians to conjecture with relative certainty how the building originally looked.

When first built, the structure was five bays long by four wide and was roofed with cypress bark (fig. 112). In front stood a wide veranda. The rear three bays of the house were enclosed with walls or doors, and the front two were open, save on one side, thus effecting a gradual transition from the completely open veranda to the closed interior.

An Excavated Nara-Period Garden Complex The remains of a mansion and its garden and pond have been uncovered at Amagatsuji in Nara City, together with the well and remnants of the outer wall (fig. 114). This discovery has greatly contributed to our knowledge of Nara-period aristocratic residences. It was a spacious villa located in the east side of the capital (Sakyō) at the Third Zone (Sanjō), Second Quarter from Suzaku Avenue, close to the mansion of Fujiwara no Nakamaro. The garden is elegantly designed, with water-smoothed stones and boulders piled at the banks of the pond. One can easily imagine aristocrats at their ease by the pond banks drinking wine and composing poetry.

The Mansion of Fujiwara no Toyonari Though it no longer remains, another Nara-period residence,

116. Fujiwara no Toyonari's mansion (after Sawamura Hitoshi)

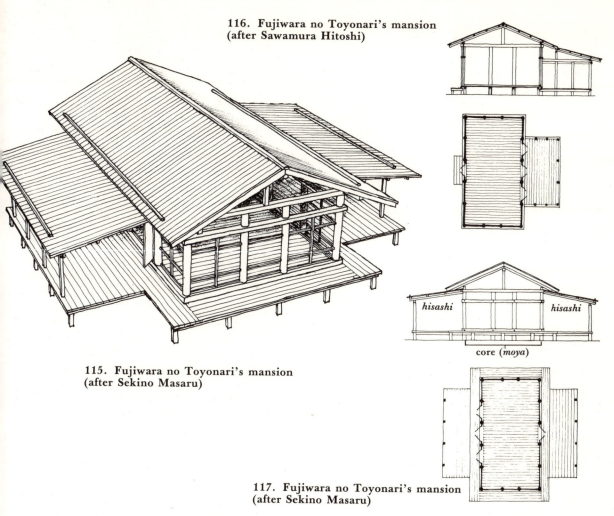

115. Fujiwara no Toyonari's mansion (after Sekino Masaru)

hisashi

core (moya)

hisashi

117. Fujiwara no Toyonari's mansion (after Sekino Masaru)

that of Fujiwara no Toyonari (704?–65), can be partially reconstructed thanks to a description in a collection of documents entitled *Shōsōin monjo* (figs. 115–17). The mansion is thought to have been five bays wide by three deep, with an elevated plank floor and no fixed interior partitions. The *Shōsōin monjo* also says there was one open veranda, and Sawamura Hitoshi has reconstructed it on this basis (fig. 116). But Sekino Masaru believes the *Shōsōin monjo* was miscopied and that there were actually two verandas, making the building symmetrical back to front (figs. 115, 117).

The brothers Toyonari and Nakamaro were two of the chief ministers of the mid Nara court. Toyonari rose to the rank of Minister of the Right in 749 and stood at the center of the government, but in 757 he fell out with his brother over a question of imperial succession. Nakamaro, who enjoyed the confidence of Empress Kōken (718–70), was the victor, and Toyonari was exiled to a governmental post in Kyūshū. Toyonari's mansion was built near the Shigaraki Palace in Ōmi Province (present-day Shiga Prefecture; see fig. 108) while he was in service there from 741 to 745, then moved to Ishiyamadera, a temple also in Ōmi Province, when he was exiled. But the fortunes of the brothers turned full circle late in their lives—Nakamaro opposed the rise of Dōkyō (?–772), a monk involved in a scandalous and self-aggrandizing liaison with Nakamaro's erstwhile benefactress Empress Kōken, and was killed for his trouble in 764. Toyonari, who had declined under the pretext of ill health to take up his Kyūshū post, was subsequently recalled from Naniwa and reappointed to the position of Minister of the Right.

The Forerunners of the Shinden Style   Though we cannot tell what function the original Dempōdō and Toyonari mansion performed in their respective residential complexes, they are still historically valuable as we know so little about any dwellings of that time. They clearly presage the development of the Shinden style of the Heian period (see pp. 64–67) in their use of both open and closed spaces, elevated plank floors, and unpartitioned central sections. The garden of the mansion in the eastern part of the Heijō Capital (fig. 114) is also a clear forerunner of those in later Shinden residences.

THE HEIAN CAPITAL

Heian—The Heart of Japan Through the centuries since the founding of the Heian Capital in 794, in which it saw the arrogation of monarchical prerogatives by the Fujiwara family, the establishment of three shogunates, and near-total destruction in the Ōnin War of 1467–77, the city continued to be thought of as the heart of Japan. Even today it bears the name Kyōto, "Capital City," though the emperor and the National Diet are located in Tōkyō, the "Eastern Capital." For most of Japan's history it was the center not only of government but of learning and the arts, and all other parts of the country bowed to its cultural ascendancy.

Heian was planned on an even larger scale than Heijō, being 4.5 km east to west and 5.2 km north to south. As at Heijō, the great Rajōmon gate, made famous in modern times as Rashōmon (a later pronunciation) by the author Akutagawa Ryūnosuke and then the film director Kurosawa Akira, was the main entrance to the south, opening on to the imposing Suzaku Avenue that bisected the city. The Left Capital later came to be also called Rakuyōjō or "Luoyang City" and the Right Capital, Chōanjō or "Changan City," both names borrowed from those of the Tang-dynasty capitals. Due, though, to the inhospitable dampness of much of Chōanjō, the population gravitated to Rakuyōjō at the east, and the term Rakuchū, "within Luoyang," came to be synonymous for the capital as a whole.

Suzaku Avenue was lined with willows celebrated in folk songs such as the following: "Into the distance / All along Grand Avenue, / The light-green willows! / The light-green willows! / See them all so laden low, / Now in fullest bloom! / Now in fullest bloom!" At its northern terminus was the Imperial Palace, 1.4 km north to south and 1.1 km east to west, that housed the governmental and residential buildings as it had at Heijō, though with many additional structures, such as the Court of Abundant Pleasures (Burakuin), a complex as large as the Court of Government and built as a banquet facility.

The present Kyōto Imperial Palace, now used only for accession ceremonies, is located two kilometers to the east of the original. The palace burned often throughout its history, and while rebuilding took place the emperor would live at the mansion of his regent or chancellor, who usually was his maternal relative. These temporary lodgings were called "town palaces" (*sato dairi*). By the early twelfth century, emperors were starting to reside permanently in these town palaces and return to the Imperial Palace only for state occasions.

The present Imperial Palace compound is also

118. Heian Capital in late Muromachi period

much smaller than the original, and its buildings are rebuilt versions of those of the domestic quarters, which had by the mid Heian period already taken over most of the functions of the government buildings to the south. But the style of the old Great Hall of State can be seen today at Heian Shrine (Kyōto City), which was built as a two-thirds scale replica of the original. But the original roof of the Great Hall was hipped and did not take on the hip-and-gable design of Heian Shrine until a rebuilding in 1072. The Heian Shrine replica was made from information assembled from such secondary sources as the "Picture Scroll of Annual Rites and Ceremonies" (*Nenchū gyōji emaki*), originally painted in sixty scrolls in about 1173 by Tokiwa Mitsunaga, at the behest of Emperor Goshirakawa, but now surviving only in a copy ordered by Emperor Gomizunoo (1596–1680) in 1626. Only a portion of the reproduction exists, and none of the original. Another valuable source was an Edo-period study of the Imperial Palace, the *Dai Dairi zukōshō*, completed in 1797 in fifty parts by the expert on ancient usages Uramatsu Mitsuyo (1736–1804).

Urban Culture There are a number of theories concerning the population of the Heian Capital at

various times in its history, but it seems reasonable to estimate that at the height of Fujiwara power in the tenth century the city held about 150,000 people. In the shops and residences lining the streets of that bustling metropolis a distinctive culture took shape that prized *miyabi* or courtly elegance, a taste for the refined that set the capital and its residents apart from the coarser world beyond. In a society that seldom had recourse to the death penalty for aristocratic transgressors, exile from this cultural center was the worst fate imaginable for members of the upper class. Estate owners too tended to stay in the city and left the on-site administration to deputies.

The Development of Commerce   As had been the case in the Fujiwara and Heijō Capitals, there were two areas officially set aside for markets in Heian, one in either half of the city. They were accordingly called the East and West Markets. With the decline in the southwestern part of the city, the West Market ceased to be used. Over time, the East Market too changed in character, developing from a place of commerce to a location for festivals. Buying and selling concurrently expanded into the city itself and centered at the intersections of various thoroughfares that became known for trade. Some of the most bustl-

ing of these commercial areas were located at the intersections of Machi Street (modern Shimmachi Street), which ran north and south near the middle of the Left Capital, and Second, Third, Fourth, and Seventh Avenues, and Rokkakunokōji and Nishinokōji Streets as well.

City Dwellers   The quality of life in medieval Heian can be gathered to some extent from a section of a pair of screens entitled "Scenes in and around the Capital" (*Rakuchū rakugai zu*; fig. 118). The screens are believed to have been presented to the warrior Uesugi Kenshin (1530–78) by the brilliant general Oda Nobunaga. There is more activity than usual in the streets in the illustration for it depicts a famous Kyōto annual event, the Gion Festival. Young men pull the various gaily decorated floats through the streets as the population looks on. Each float was built and maintained by a certain neighborhood, and competition was fierce (and still is today) to determine who could outfit the finest. It was, in fact, the neighborhood organizations and not the central government that arranged and financed the display, suggesting how strong independent commerce had become by the late Muromachi period.

THE SHINDEN STYLE

gate

inner
gate

corridor

pavilion

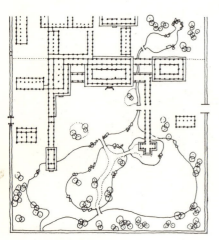

119. Hōjūji Mansion

120. Hōjūji Mansion (reconstructed)

Residences of the Heian Aristocracy The Shinden style (*shinden zukuri*) takes its name from the *shinden*, the central structure in such complexes. The word literally means "hall for sleeping." Though every known Shinden-style complex had its own unique aspects, most faced south over a courtyard where ceremonies and entertainments were performed. South of the courtyard a pond was dug with a central island reached by bridges. At the pond's periphery might be a hill, made from earth excavated to create the pond, with trees planted on it. Boating on the pond was a favorite form of relaxation for the fortunate residents of such mansions.

Shinden Buildings and Grounds The *shinden* hall was the residence of the master of the house and place where he met guests and officiated at rites and festivities. Projecting from one or more sides of the *shinden* hall were hallways (*watadono*) leading to subsidiary spaces called *tainoya* (literally meaning "opposed halls"), mostly allotted to family members

and their servants. Corridors (*rō*) led from these tainoya to the pond, where they ended in small "fishing pavilions" (*tsuridono*) or "fountain pavilions" (*izumidono*). Midway along these southern corridors were "inner gates" (*chūmon*) through which one entered the complex, and the corridors were accordingly called "inner gate corridors" (*chūmonrō*). These corridors were quite spacious and contained the offices of the household staff.

Shinden residences were usually built on one-block lots (120 square meters), though some, like the Higashi Sanjō mansion of the Fujiwara, was two blocks north to south. The lot was surrounded by thick earth walls (*tsujibei*), which were faced with planks on both sides and topped by tiled roofs. Gates were set into the eastern and western walls, one being the Main Gate (Seimon) and the other the Rear Gate (Uramon). Inside the gate was a place for ox carts, the elegantly lacquered vehicles that were the preferred conveyance of the Heian aristocracy, and

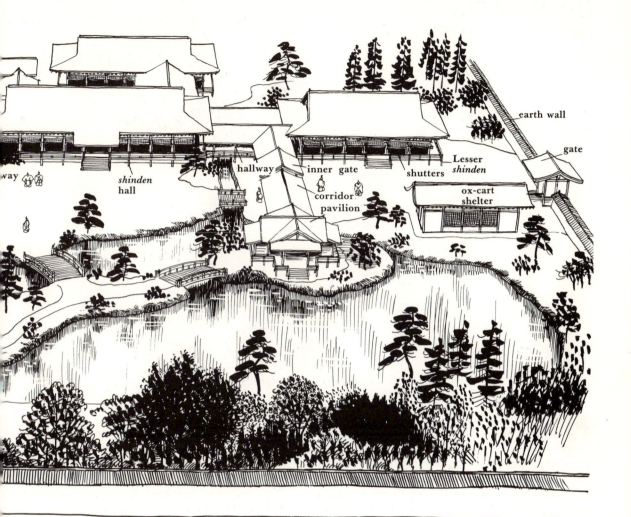

earth wall

gate

Lesser *shinden*

shutters

ox-cart shelter

inner gate

corridor pavilion

hallway

shinden hall

...way

also places to shelter the escorts and servants of guests. Most buildings were connected by hallways or corridors. The grounds were lower at the southwest, and the pond was accordingly fed by a stream that flowed in from the northeast. Water flowed by and large to the southwest in Heian, and this accounts for the dampness and consequent undesirability of that quarter of the city.

Bilateral symmetry is thought by some to have been the ideal for Shinden structures, but the actual examples we know of do not seem to have been so constructed. One possible reason for this is that the main hall faced south, but due to the garden and pond the main entrance was to one side, making the opposite side the rear. The arrangement of spaces thus progressed east to west though the buildings faced south, and irregularity was the result.

The Hōjūji Mansion The "Picture Scroll of Annual Rites and Ceremonies" and other sources have allowed historians to reconstruct on paper the Hō-

jūji Mansion, one fine example of the Shinden style (figs. 119–20). It was a huge complex, with western and northern tainoya, an eastern "lesser *shinden*" which corresponded to an eastern tainoya, and eastern and western fishing pavilions. The eastern of the two pavilions had a unique cross-shaped plan and was located not on the bank of the pond, as was usually the case, but actually on the island itself. It thus helped integrate the garden and the architecture of the site.

The mansion was built in what is now southeast Kyōto by Chancellor (Daijō Daijin) Fujiwara no Tamemitsu (942–92). He made it into a temple after the death of his daughter Kishi (d. 985), a favorite of Emperor Kazan (968–1008), who took holy orders after her death. The Emperor Goshirakawa later added other structures nearby, such as the Thirty-Three-Bay Hall (Sanjūsangendō or Rengeō-in), when he assumed ownership.

DAILY LIFE IN A SHINDEN MANSION

121. Hōjūji Mansion

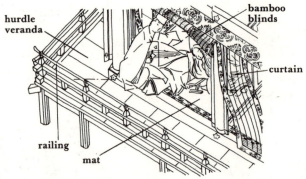

hurdle veranda

bamboo blinds

curtain

railing

mat

122. Hurdle veranda and peripheral chamber (*hisashi*)

The Shinden Style as Seen in Picture Scrolls Not a single Shinden complex survives today, and though excavations can suggest representative building plans and garden configurations, we must rely on secondary sources for information on elevations and interiors. Perhaps the best such sources are the narrative picture scrolls (*emakimono*), some interspersed with text, that provided entertainment and instruction to members of the Heian and medieval upper classes. Many of these scrolls, which could reach to ten or more meters in length, are illustrated versions of the literature of the day, such as *The Tale of Genji Picture Scroll* (*Genji monogatari emaki*) and *The Pillow Book Picture Scroll* (*Makura no sōshi emaki*). Others portray the lives of Buddhist saints, the history of holy places, or famous legends. Such accounts obviously required the depiction of interior and exterior architectural environments, and the scrolls are consequently invaluable tools for the historian of residential and religious buildings styles.

Figure 121, from the *Picture Scroll of Annual Rites and Ceremonies,* shows the formal visit made at the beginning of the year by the emperor to the residence of the retired emperor and empress. The event, called the *chōkin gyōkō*, involved entertainments and a banquet. The chōkin gyōkō depicted in the scroll is that of the Emperor Nijō (1143–65), which he made in 1163 to the Hōjūji Mansion of his father,

the Tonsured Retired Emperor Goshirakawa.

Aesthetic Rivalry In the section of the *Picture Scroll of Annual Rites and Ceremonies* shown in figure 121 dance is being performed in front of the Emperor Nijō and the Tonsured Retired Emperor Goshirakawa, both of whom, though not shown out of deference to their exalted status, sit on the decorated mats partially visible behind the front stairs of the central *shinden* hall. Normally, the two monarchs would be shielded by reticulated shutters (*shitomido*, described on pp. 30–31), but on this day the shutters have been removed to allow them to view the performance. To the left, on the veranda of the *shinden* and on the open hallway (*sukiwatadono*), members of the nobility sit and watch the dance. They wear court costumes called *sokutai*, with long trains (*kyo*), which they drape over the railings. The longer the train, the higher ranked the wearer. White was stipulated for winter and brown (*suō*) or double indigo (*futaai*) for summer, but at observances of this sort individual color preferences were countenanced. The color combinations chosen for the various underrobes reflected the taste and panache of each wearer, and such gatherings became fashion shows with no small element of competitiveness.

The women that watch the proceedings through the blinds to the right of the central staircase are also deeply concerned with the aesthetic effect of their

blinds

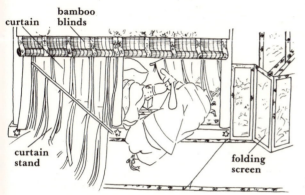

curtain · bamboo blinds

curtain stand

folding screen

123. Shinden interior

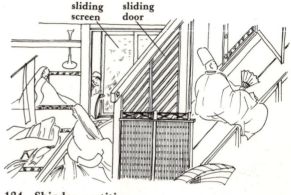

sliding screen · sliding door

124. Shinden partitions

clothing. They wear many layers of robes, with the various colors showing at the hems that are allowed to tastefully show beneath the blinds. In a society as aware of aesthetic subtleties as that of the Heian aristocracy, a solecism in choosing one's garments could brand the wearer as aesthetically insensitive and have major consequences in terms of social standing or even official preferment.

In the left foreground of the picture, a boat floats in the pond, and at the right, the roof of a temporary shelter for performances of court music (*gagaku*) is visible. The boat has a dragon-headed prow and is one of a pair customarily used; the other would bear the head of a *geki*, a mythical water bird said to resemble a cormorant but with white feathers.

Interior Decor of the Shinden Complex Picture scrolls about court life, such as the *Diary of Murasaki Shikibu Picture Scroll* (*Murasaki Shikibu nikki emaki*) and the above-mentioned *The Tale of Genji Picture Scroll* and *The Pillow Book Picture Scroll* are particularly good sources of information about Shinden-style interiors.

Evidence from these sources shows hurdle verandas (*sunoko en*), made of wooden planks laid down with slight gaps between each to prevent pooling of rain water (fig. 122). They were bordered by railings (*kōran*) elegantly curved at the ends. Floors were also of wooden planks, but thick, movable mats of woven straw with silk borders were used for sitting

or reclining. Swinging doors (*tsumado*) were often employed at the ends of buildings and sliding doors (*yarido*; fig. 124) on verandas. Exterior partitions consisted of the reticulated shutters noted earlier or simply of hanging bamboo (*sudare*), often with curtains (*kabeshiro*) behind. Interior partitions were occasionally built-in sliding screens, often with paintings (fig. 124). These screens were originally called *shōji* but later termed *fusuma*. The word *shōji* changed in subsequent years to denote the sliding translucent screens of white paper used on the exteriors of Shoin-style residences (see pp. 74–75). Far more frequently though, interior space was divided by means of movable screens or curtains. These included folding screens (*byōbu*; fig. 123), one-piece screens that did not fold (*tsuitate*), curtain stands (*kichō*; fig 123), and light, hanging tapestries with Chinese- or Japanese-style scenes (*zeshō* or *zejō*). But these movable partitions only shielded those behind from sight and not from sound. Nor did they protect against the cold, thus accounting for the many layers of clothing Heian aristocrats wore. But even with robes and such heating devices as "charcoal boxes" (*subitsu*) and hibachi, winters in Shinden houses were uncomfortable.

COMMONERS' DWELLINGS

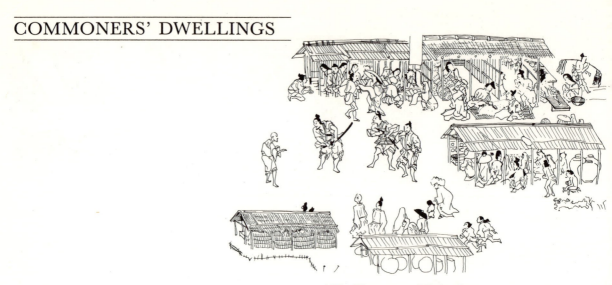

125. The town of Fukuoka

Urban Row-Houses If we know little of aristocratic residences in premodern Japan, we know less about the homes of the lower levels of society, and what information we do have is limited entirely to pictorial sources. The *Picture Scroll of Annual Rites and Ceremonies* is helpful not only for the aristocratic dwellings previously introduced but also for depictions of how the rest of society lived in the late Heian period, on the verge of Japan's middle ages.

The city dwellings illustrated in the scroll are of the row-house type, with the facade of each unit divided in half, the right side with a door and the left with a wall and a window above (fig. 126). Walls are made of woven strips of bamboo or thin wood, and partially planked. Short curtains (*noren*) hang over the entrance at the far right. Inside is an earth floor, though one section at the back not visible in the illustration was probably raised and floored with planks. The roofs are also of planks, reinforced by logs.

Provincial Towns Houses in towns further from

the Heian Capital were even simpler in construction. One example is the town of Fukuoka in present-day Okayama Prefecture, depicted in the *Picture Scroll of the Monk Ippen* (*Ippen Shōnin eden*), painted in 1299 (fig. 125). Ippen (1239–89) was a traveling priest who preached a new doctrine, that of the Ji sect, to the common folk. In the section illustrated, Ippen has arrived on market day and is being challenged by a burly samurai who is about to draw his sword. The houses of the residents are little more than huts, with posts sunk in the ground and simple plank roofs. Rooms are separated by plank walls. The people are selling cloth, rice, fish, ceramic pots, and other such basic commodities. In the fish stall (top, far right), the vendor has laid a fish on a cutting board and seems about to slice some sashimi for a customer. Behind, a man walks away carrying more fish suspended from the ends of a bamboo pole resting on his shoulder. The adjoining shop appears to be that of a rice vendor, who measures out his goods in a square wooden cup. The shops are so simple one

curtain

126. A street in the Heian Capital

127. A town in the suburbs of Nara

might take them for temporary huts set up just for market day, but many provincial towns were most likely built this way permanently. Another section of the *Picture Scroll of the Monk Ippen* depicts the outskirts of Kamakura, the city serving as the headquarters of Minamoto no Yoritomo's shogunate. It is a very quiet place despite its political importance, underscoring the fact that all cities were in no way the bustling commercial centers that the Heian Capital was.

The suburbs of Nara are portrayed in another famous work, the *Picture Scroll of the Legends of Mt. Shigi (Shigisan engi)*, believed to have been made in the twelfth century (fig. 127). In the section illustrated, we see at the far right the gable end of a row-house, with people issuing from the entrance on to the street. The back yard is reserved for trees and a garden. The side view of the house is convenient for showing its construction, which consists of a central two-bay section (*moya*) surmounted by a steep, plank roof and flanked by one-bay subsidiary spaces (*hisashi*) to the

front and rear, both with roofs of shallow pitch.

The house to the left, viewed from the front, shows an entry with *noren* curtains and an earth floor behind. In the rear, a cat sleeps on the step leading to the raised-floor section of the house. Beside the door, a man bends over a windowsill to drive off a pair of dogs. The windows are fit with small reticulated shutters propped up temporarily, and in the back of the room is a latticelike partition. As in the case of the houses in the other picture scrolls, the posts of these structures are sunk directly into the ground, the roof is of wooden planks, and the walls are wattle and daub.

The houses portrayed in these three city scenes are far removed from the luxurious Shinden-style residences of the aristocracy. It is important to remember too that many of the more outlying towns were even more crude, not to mention the houses of the poorer rural districts.

RESIDENCES OF THE SAMURAI

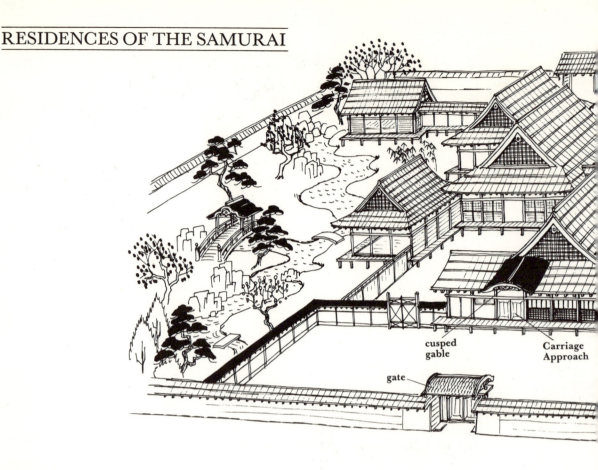

cusped
gable

Carriage
Approach

gate

Medieval and Early Modern Mansions of the Military in the Capital   The most powerful of the medieval warriors patterned their homes and many of their customs after those of the descendants of the Heian-period aristocrats, who had lost actual ruling power but still commanded enormous prestige because of their distinguished history and cultural attainments. These upper-level samurai adopted the Shinden style for their own mansions, including the added garden complex. But the Shinden style itself began to change in the medieval period. One major development was toward spacial division according to function, with more fixed partitions between public and private spaces in the main hall and more separate structures built for different purposes. One important new building that appeared particularly frequently in the homes of the nobility was the *kaisho*, literally ''meeting place,'' for audiences and entertainments with guests.

The pair of screens introduced earlier showing the Gion Festival (see fig. 118) depict in a different section the manor of the Hosokawa family, one of the powerful deputies of the Ashikaga shōgun (fig. 128). The constituent structures are arranged on a diagonal in the northeast of the compound, and a garden with a stream occupies the southwest. One approached the complex from the south through a gate, then entered the residence itself via the Carriage Approach (Kurumayose), here covered with a dark roof fit with a cusped gable (*karahafu*).

The Ninomaru Palace of Nijō Castle (fig. 129), also in the Heian Capital, has the same general placement of buildings as the Hosokawa Mansion (see pp. 72–73, 104, 122–23 for further discussion of Nijō Castle). The castle was built from 1601 to 1603, and the Ninomaru Palace is thought to have been added from 1624 to 1626 by the third Tokugawa shōgun, Iemitsu, in preparation for an imperial progress by Emperor Gomizunoo. Originally roofs of the Ninomaru Palace were not of tile but cedar bark, which would have made it resemble the Hosokawa Mansion even more strongly. Its various buildings are divided according to purpose, with, from the bottom right, the Carriage Approach for entering the complex, the Tōzamurai for samurai retainers, the Shikidai for initial reception of guests, the Ōhiroma for formal audiences, the Kuroshoin for more private interviews and daily business, and finally, just visible at the back, the Shiroshoin for the master's personal use. The kitchens, directly to the north behind the Tōzamurai, are extant as well, as is the pond to the southwest.

128. Mansion of the Hosokawa family in Kyōto

129. Ninomaru Palace of Nijō Castle in Kyōto

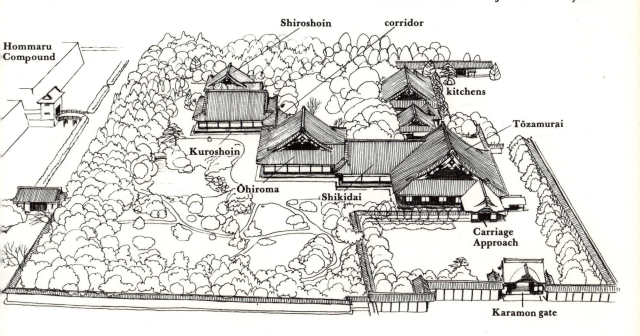

A FORMAL AUDIENCE IN A WARRIOR RESIDENCE

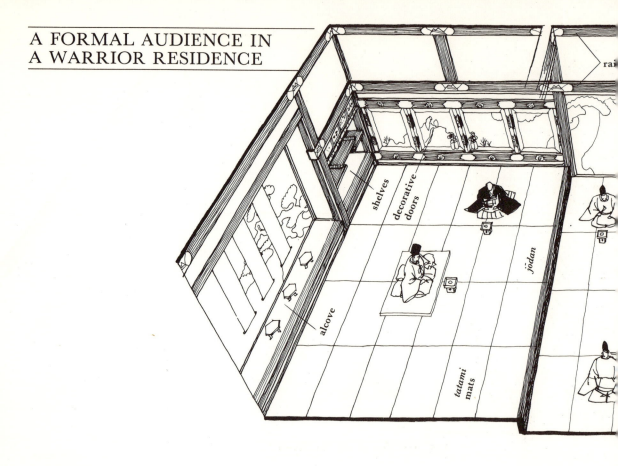

rai...

shelves

decorative doors

jōdan

alcove

tatami mats

A Meeting with Ieyasu On fourth day of the fourth month of 1603, Tokugawa Ieyasu, ruler of all Japan after his victory nearly three years earlier at the battle of Sekigahara, held an audience at Nijō Castle with members of the court and the military houses. The meeting with Ieyasu, who had been confirmed as shōgun by the emperor some weeks earlier, was held in the Ōhiroma, the most formal of the castle rooms (fig. 130). The space was designed on three levels, the *jōdan* ("upper step"), *chūdan* ("middle step"), and *gedan* ("lower step"), and the participants were assigned seats according to their exact position in the hierarchy of those in attendance.

On the uppermost level, the jōdan, were seated Ieyasu and, to his left, the prelate Gien (1558–1626), abbot of the Daigoji Sambōin and one of Ieyasu's advisors. The following seating arrangement was recorded in his diary as well as that of Yamashina Tokitsune, also present, which suggests how seriously such matters of precedence were taken by the company.

At Ieyasu's right, on the chūdan, sat the courtier and famous calligrapher Karasumaru Mitsunobu (1544–1606; Provisional Major Counsellor, Senior Second Rank, aged 59), Hirohashi Kanekatsu (1558–1623; Provisional Major Counsellor, Senior Second Rank, aged 45), also a main figure at court,

and Asukai Masatsune (1569–1615; Consultant, Junior Third Rank, aged 34), a courtier, poet, and scholar. Next to him sat the courtier Kajūji Mitsutoyo (1575–1612; Consultant, Junior Third Rank, aged 28), and then Kyōgoku Takatsugu (1563–1609; Consultant, Junior Third rank, aged 39), a warrior who had changed sides to support Ieyasu at Sekigahara. Across from them were Hino Terusuke (1555–1623; Provisional Major Counsellor, Senior Second Rank, aged 48), Yamashina Tokitsune (1543–1611; Former Provisional Major Counsellor, Senior Second Rank, aged 60), a courtier, diarist, and one-time stipendiary of Hideyoshi and Ieyasu, and then Maeda Toshinaga (1562–1614; Middle Counsellor, Junior Third Rank, aged 40), one of Hideyoshi's advisors who supported Ieyasu at Sekigahara and became a daimyō with vast holdings on the Japan seacoast. Next to him sat Matsudaira Tadayoshi (1580–1607; Gentleman-in-waiting, Junior Fourth Rank, Lower Grade, aged 22), and Mōri Terumoto (1553–1625; Middle Counsellor, Junior Third Rank, aged 49), another of Hideyoshi's advisors who had opposed Ieyasu at Sekigahara but did not personally take part in the fighting. Last on the left was Hosokawa Tadaoki (1563–1645; Consultant, Junior Third Rank, aged 39), who fought at Sekigahara with Ieyasu and also made a name for

72

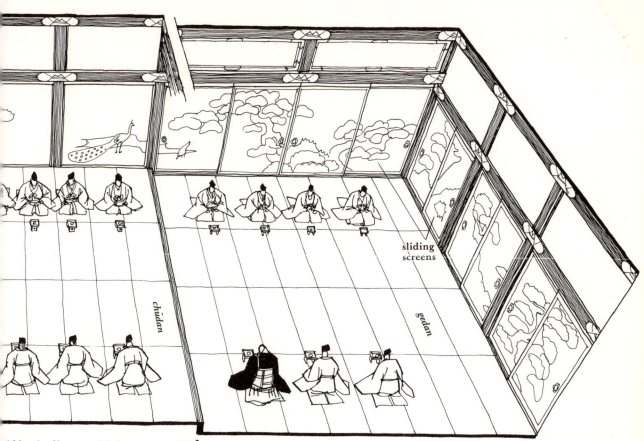

130. Audience with Ieyasu in old Ōhiroma of Nijō Castle (reconstruction with details after extant Ōhiroma)

himself as an artist, poet, and man of tea.

Below this group sat seven lower-ranked men on the gedan, also in strict order of precedence. The overall seating arrangement graphically demonstrates a hierarchy based by and large on office and rank, then age. The only major exception was Matsudaira Tadayoshi, who was accorded a higher position as he was Ieyasu's fourth son. The fact that not only the hereditary courtiers but also the military men bore court titles and ranks shows the continuing prestige of the traditional nobility, despite their lack of real power. The courtier Kajūji Mitsutoyo was even seated above the warrior Kyōgoku Takatsugu, though both had the same office and rank and Mitsutoyo was eleven years younger.

Other Manifestations of Social Hierarchy The titles, ranks, and ages of each man present determined not only seating arrangement but other various details at the meeting. One examples is the type of tray each was to use to hold refreshments and gifts. Ieyasu and Gien use four-sided trays, so called because they bear ornamented legs on all four sides. Those on the chūdan have three-sided trays, with no legs at the back, and those on the gedan have two-sided trays.

After the audience, Ieyasu proceeded to the far end of the gedan, where the company watched a perfor-

mance of Nō drama, danced on a specially built stage (see fig. 246). The Nō was a dramatic art form that had reached artistic maturity through the support of the military aristocracy, and its presentation that day was another indication of Ieyasu's regard for the eminence of his guests.

Nijō Castle Ieyasu constructed the original Nijō Castle between 1601 and 1603 on the location of the Ninomaru Palace of present Nijō Castle. When Iemitsu undertook his massive remodeling program to prepare for Emperor Gomizunoo's stay in 1626, he used many of the structural members of the original castle. The Ōhiroma of Iemitsu's Ninomaru Palace has only a jōdan and gedan, but marks on some of the posts show that Ieyasu's Ōhiroma had three levels, as shown in figure 130.

The present Ninomaru complex is a rare extant example of a palace appended to a castle compound, though only the walls of the original castle remain. It is also one of the most impressive representatives of the opulent formal Shoin style of architecture, and its gold and polychrome screen paintings, intricate transom carvings, and coved and coffered ceilings serve as awe-inspiring symbols of the power and magnificence of its builders.

THE SHOIN STYLE—EARLY MODERN RESIDENTIAL ARCHITECTURE

Shoin Origins The Shoin style of residential architecture gradually developed during the Muromachi period (1338–1573) out of the Shinden mode. Early Shoin-style features were found particularly frequently in the *kaisho* hall of Shinden complexes and the abbot's quarters (*hōjō*) of Zen monasteries. The word *shoin* literally means "writing hall," and abbot's quarters often had a corner room with that name used by the abbot for study or conversation. The earliest extant example of the style is the Dōjinsai room of the Hall of the Eastern Quest (Tōgūdō or Tōgudō) in Yoshimasa's Silver Pavilion complex. Another early example of the type is the Shoin of the Reiun'in, a subtemple in the great Zen complex Myōshinji in Kyōto.

Characteristics of the Shoin Style The most formal room in a Shoin structure typically contains a decorative alcove (*tokonoma*), staggered shelves (*chigaidana*), built-in desk (*tsukeshoin*), and decorative doors (*chōdaigamae*; fig. 133). Relatively few Shoin structures contain all four elements, however. The Shoin style is also characterized by *tatami* mats over the entire floor, square posts (though with slightly beveled corners), ceilings (often coved or coved and coffered), *fusuma* (plain or painted sliding screens) between interior spaces, and *shōji* (white translucent paper screens reinforced with a wooden lattice; fig. 133) on the exterior, protected by heavy sliding panels (*amado*) moved in front of them at night or in inclement weather.

Decorative Shoin Elements To follow the development of the four fixtures of the Shoin style—that is, the decorative alcove, staggered shelves, built-in desk, and decorative doors—we must once again consult picture scroll illustrations. One good resource is the *Pictures of Longing for Extinction* (*Bokie*), the biography of the monk Kakunyo (1270–1351). The work is particularly valuable because its ten scrolls were originally painted in 1351, but numbers one and seven were subsequently lost and then repainted in 1482, thus allowing us to compare interior fixtures over time. Figures 131, 134, and 137, taken from part of the work painted in 1351, show prototypes of the decorative alcove, composed of a hanging scroll with a thin, low foretable before it supporting various *objets d'art*. By 1482, however, the foretable was already built into the wall (fig. 135). These early-period decorative alcoves are wide and shallow, only about sixty centimeters in depth. Decorative alcoves in today's traditional-style homes are deeper—about the width of a tatami mat (a little less that one meter)—

131. Foretable (precursor of the *oshiita*) and decorative doors

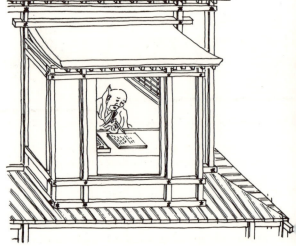

132. Built-in desk

and are known as *tokonoma*. While the earlier, narrow variety is also sometimes called a tokonoma, it is more accurately referred to as an *oshiita*. Originally the word tokonoma referred to an entire room containing a decorative alcove within it. Within the alcove are usually hung one or more scrolls, and before them are set out the "three *objets*" (*mitsugusoku*)—incense burner, flower vase, and candle holder (figs. 131, 134, 137; see also pp. 134–35).

The second of the four decorative Shoin fixtures is the staggered shelves (fig. 133). Originally the shelves could be moved about the room, but by the time of the illustration in the *Picture Scroll of the Kasuga Gongen Miracles* in the fourteenth century, they were already being built in (fig. 136).

The built-in desk alcove, the third of the Shoin features, usually protrudes into the veranda (fig

74

134. Foretable (precursor of the *oshiita*)

135. *Oshiita*

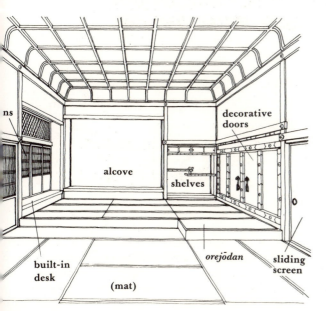

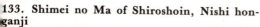

133. **Shimei no Ma of Shiroshoin, Nishi honganji**

136. **Staggered shelves**

137. **Strongroom and foretable (precursor of the *oshiita*)**

133). Also called *idashifuzukue* ("desk for taking out writings") in addition to the more common *tsukeshoin*, such desks were designed in that manner and fit with shōji screens so as to admit as much light as possible. The *Pictorial Biography of the Monk Hōnen* shows a good early example of the type (fig. 132).

The last of the four fixtures is the decorative doors (fig. 133). They originated as the single entrance to an otherwise totally enclosed and protected sleeping area (*chōdai*). Such spaces were relatively secure and thus doubled as strong rooms (*nando*), as in the example shown from the *Picture Scroll of Longing for Extinction*, where a sword stands against the wall (fig. 137). The doors are consequently sometimes called *nandogamae*, in addition to the more usual *chōdaigamae*. These doors, and for that matter the shelves and built-in desk as well, came to have purely decorative

uses, and together with the decorative alcove served to indicate the formal quality of the room in which they appeared.

The Shiroshoin The Shiroshoin of the True Pure Land (Jōdo Shinshū) temple Nishi Honganji ranks with the Ninomaru Palace as one of the quintessential examples of the formal Shoin style. The complex, which some date to 1632, is to the north of the Audience Hall (Taimenjo; see pp. 120–21) and southwest of the more relaxed and private Kuroshoin (see pp. 80–81). The main room, the Shimei no Ma (fig. 133), is gloriously opulent as befits the headquarters of a popular and worldly sect. A particularly interesting detail of the room is the ten-mat jōdan section, which includes one extra mat that projects into the gedan area. This design, known as an *orejōdan*, is of relatively old vintage.

THE DESIGN SYSTEM
OF THE SHOIN

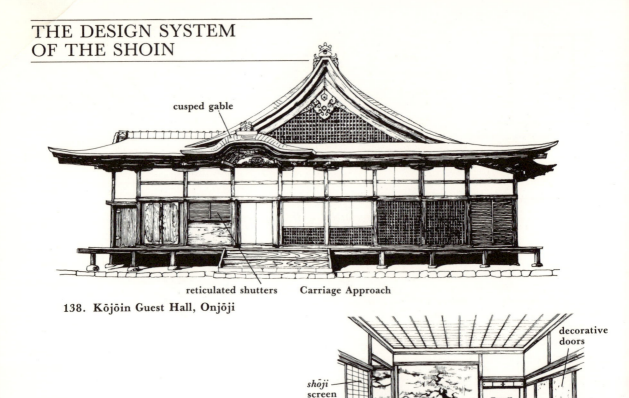

cusped gable

reticulated shutters   Carriage Approach

138. Kōjōin Guest Hall, Onjōji

shōji screen

decorative doors

shelves

built-in desk   alcove

139. Jōza no Ma of the Kōjōin Guest Hall, Onjōji

The Early Shoin Style: The Shuden Perhaps the two best-known early-period Shoin buildings are the Guests Halls (Kyakuden) of two subtemples of the great Tendai monastery Onjōji (also called Mii-dera)—the Kōjōin (fig. 138) and Kangakuin (not il-lustrated). The Kangakuin Guest Hall is the older of the two, dating to 1600; the Guest Hall of the Kōjōin was built the following year. Though the Kangakuin Guest Hall has only a decorative alcove in its main room, the equivalent room in the Kōjōin Guest Hall, the Jōza no Ma, has all four main Shoin fixtures—the alcove, staggered shelves, built-in desk, and decorative doors (fig. 139). The Kōjōin Guest Hall has two rows of rooms to the Kangakuin Guest Hall's three, but in general size and room layout they are quite similar (fig. 140). Their main facades re-semble each other even more closely. Both buildings are typical of the Shoin style in their use of ceilings, floors completely of tatami mats, square posts, wide verandas, and fusuma and shōji screens.

But a number of details mark the two guest halls as early examples of the style. These include the trun-cated vestige of the *chūmonrō* corridor (fig. 140) and reticulated hinged shutters (*shitomido*) on the facades (fig. 138), both reminiscent of Shinden designs (see pp. 64–65). They also incorporate a Carriage Ap-proach (Kurumayose) with steps below and cusped gable (*karahafu*) above, instead of the later entrance alcove (*genkan*). In addition, the decorative alcove is of the wide and shallow *oshiita* type. These early-stage Shoin buildings often bear the subclassification "Shuden," meaning "Main Hall."

The "Shuden Plan" and Its Modular Design System A plan for a building very like the Kōjōin Guest Hall is found in *Shōmei*, a collection of se-cret books of builder's illustrations belonging to the Heinouchi family, carpenters to the Tokugawa sho-gunate. The drawing is labeled "illustration of an old six-by-seven-bay Shuden." The word "old" sug-gests that the style was already well-established and perhaps even obsolescent by the time the drawing was executed in 1608.

Shōmei is the oldest complete manual on designing by means of set proportions (*kiwarijutsu*) that survive (figs. 141–42). It will be recalled (pp. 46–47) that the use of these proportions enabled the carpenter-builder to achieve overall architectural harmony by basing the major measurements in his design on a few set standards or modules, such as that of the width of the bays and posts. Books containing these sets of design proportions began to be written in the Muromachi period and were handed down from

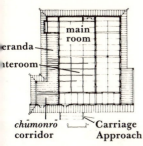

140. Kōjōin Guest Hall, Onjōji

Labels in figure 140: veranda, anteroom, main room, chūmonrō corridor, Carriage Approach

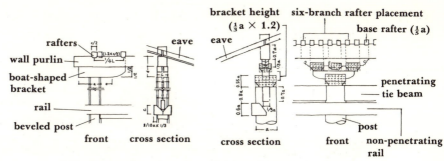

141. Proportions for eaves (left) and brackets (after *Shōmei*)

Labels: rafters, wall purlin, boat-shaped bracket, rail, beveled post, front, cross section, eave; bracket height ($\frac{1}{3}a \times 1.2$), six-branch rafter placement, base rafter ($\frac{1}{3}a$), eave, cross section, penetrating tie beam, post, front, non-penetrating rail

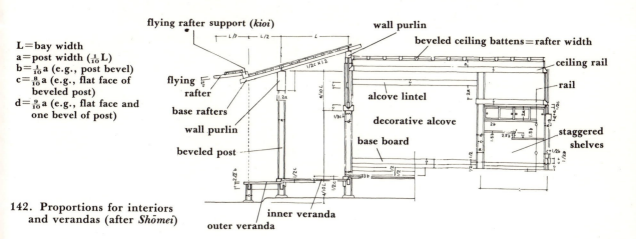

L = bay width
a = post width ($\frac{1}{10}L$)
b = $\frac{1}{10}a$ (e.g., post bevel)
c = $\frac{8}{10}a$ (e.g., flat face of beveled post)
d = $\frac{9}{10}a$ (e.g., flat face and one bevel of post)

Labels: flying rafter support (*kioi*), wall purlin, beveled ceiling battens = rafter width, ceiling rail, flying rafter, rail, base rafters, alcove lintel, wall purlin, decorative alcove, beveled post, base board, staggered shelves, outer veranda, inner veranda

142. Proportions for interiors and verandas (after *Shōmei*)

generation to generation as secret texts within carpenter families. But by the eighteenth century, printed books of design standards were widely circulating.

Shōmei was compiled by Heinouchi Yoshimasa and his son Masanobu, and bears the dates "autumn, 1608" and "spring, 1610" in the colophon. The extant version is a copy thought to have been made about a century later. The book consists of five chapters, covering gates, Shintō shrines, pagodas, Buddhist temples, and houses, with the "Shuden Plan" found in the last.

The Mathematics of Proportional Design The principle of design by means of interdependent modules works as follows. If we label as L the width of one bay (fig. 142), i.e., the distance from the center of one post to the center of the next (usually a little less than two meters), then the width of the staggered shelves may also be L, as may be that from the lower runner (*shikii*) to the upper runner (*kamoi*) into which are set the sliding screens. Likewise the decorative alcove may be set at 2 L and the width of the posts at 1/10 L. Carrying the system one step further, if we make 1/10 L equal to a, then the post may be beveled at the corners so that the bevels measure 1/7 a (called a "seven bevel"), or 1/10 a (a "ten bevel").

Another module that contributes to internal harmony is the tatami mats, rectangles about one by two meters in size that cover the floors in a Shoin residence. Room area is generally expressed in terms of the number of mats it contains. Though the dimensions of the mats vary somewhat in different parts of Japan, it is usually constant for all the rooms in a single structure, and it relates to the intercolumnar span as well, which effectively imparts a proportional unity to the whole.

These proportions were not indicated in *Shōmei* on the drawings themselves as we have done here, but were instead given in the text. It must also be remembered that no carpenter ever relied exclusively on these measurements. They were guidelines to be learned, then creatively applied. Moreover, they allowed for considerable leeway: the width of a decorative alcove might be fixed at 1 L, 1 1/2 L, 2 L, or even more, depending on the other design considerations of the space. In Heinouchi Yoshimasa's colophon, he wrote that the ideal carpenter was a master not only of designing on paper but also of visual estimation and "hands-on" building skills. He had to be a good carver and have the talents of a painter as well.

77

KATSURA DETACHED PALACE
AND THE SUKIYA STYLE

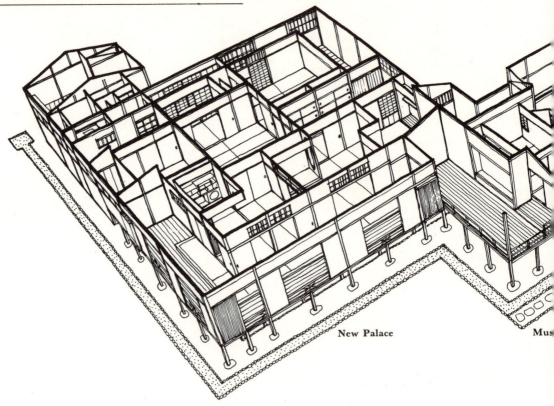

New Palace

Mus

A Relaxed Yet Elegant Shoin Variation The formal Shoin style of the type seen at the Ninomaru Palace of Nijō Castle was appropriate for grandiose ceremony, with its brilliantly painted walls, coved and coffered ceilings, square-cut posts, and heavy circumferential rails (*nageshi*; see fig. 130). But such spaces were far too imposing for the day-to-day activities of the members of the upper class. A different kind of Shoin style consequently developed in concert with the formal type, substituting posts with rough, unbeveled corners (*menkawabashira*), delicate structural members, and understated decoration for the more staid accoutrements of formal Shoin chambers. Intimacy and caprice were the hallmarks of this type of Shoin, which is frequently referred to as the Sukiya or Sukiya Shoin style (see also pp. 132–35). Much of the atmosphere of Sukiya structures was created by ideas borrowed from the architecture of the tea ceremony, the art of preparing and drinking tea with mental discipline, physical control, and aesthetic sensibility (see pp. 105–19). The humble tea cottage, with its coarsely finished walls, open ceilings, and surrounding garden, contributed

much to the formation of a canon of rustic simplicity that informs Sukiya dwellings. But tea ceremony architecture itself draws on even older traditions, such as the hermitages of medieval scholar-recluses and the simple yet refined homes of the Kyōto aristocrat of the early middle ages.

The Katsura Detached Palace Katsura, the country villa of the Katsuranomiya line of princes beginning with Hachijōnomiya Toshihito (1579–1629) and his son Toshitada (1619–62), has often been presented by Japanese and Western critics alike as the quintessence of Japanese taste. The complex is located in southwest Kyōto, near the Katsuragawa river, and is made up of the Old Shoin, Middle Shoin, Music Room, and New Palace (fig. 143). In the garden around it are five teahouses—the Tower of Moonlit Waves (Gepparō), Pavilion of the Lute in the Pines (Shōkintei), Hut of Smiling Thought (Shōiken), Pavilion of Admired Blossoms (Shōkatei), and Hall of the Garden Forest (Enrindō).

The Old Shoin and part of the garden were built by Toshihito and date to about 1616. Toshihito's son is responsible for the Middle Shoin, possibly built in

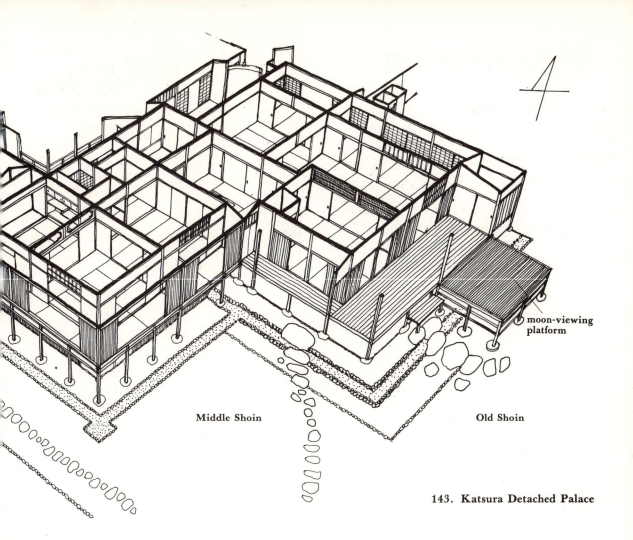

Middle Shoin

Old Shoin

moon-viewing platform

143. Katsura Detached Palace

1641. The Music Room and New Palace are thought to have been added by Yasuhito, third in the Katsuranomiya line, in preparation for an imperial progress by his father, the Tonsured Retired Emperor Gomizunoo. The date 1660 was found in the lining of one of the fusuma screens in this section of the residence, suggesting that it was completed or remodeled at about that time. The Katsura complex was thus built by degrees, but from the first was meant to be used for days or weeks at a time. In the beginning, what is now called the Old Shoin no doubt had a kitchen, bath, and toilet in the rear. Similar amenities probably were added to the Middle Shoin later as well. Bath and toilet areas still accompany the Music Room and the New Palace.

Integration of Palace and Garden The Katsura Detached Palace is a nobleman's private Xanadu and was built in the countryside to allow unimpeded relaxation in the midst of nature. Toshihito, Toshitada, and their guests would admire the cherry blossoms in spring and the crimson leaves in autumn at their elegant retreat while preparing tea and enjoying exquisite cuisine, or while floating in boats on the spacious garden pond. The grounds form an integrated whole with the buildings within it. The tastefully situated rocks and artfully maintained trees and bushes are not meant to be the occasional object of an admiring glance or quarter-hour's stroll, but to be the constant, active companions of the residents (see also pp. 132–33).

"The Katsura Teahouse" In the diary of the Hachijōnomiya family, the villa is called simply "The Katsura Teahouse." The family also had "teahouses" in Misasagimura, near Uji to the southeast, and Kaidemmura, close to the old Nagaoka Capital. The latter was a short distance from Nagaoka Temmangū shrine, once called Kaiden Temmangū, and was a convenient place from which to make shrine visits or to hunt the rare and delicious *matsutake* mushrooms. Nor did the Hachijōnomiya family have a monopoly on such retreats. Most nobles had residences for rest and relaxation to which they could repair to enjoy tea, quiet study, or the beauties of nature.

SUKIYA-STYLE DECOR

144. Manshuin Greater Shoin with Lesser Shoin in background

145. Twilight Room, Manshuin Lesser Shoin

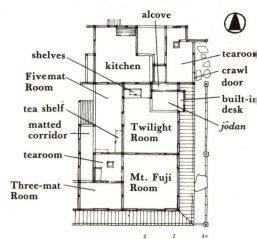

146. Manshuin Lesser Shoin

Distinguishing Sukiya Characteristics The word *sukiya* literally means "abode of refinement," and the most successful examples of the Sukiya style combine the elegance of the formal Shoin style with the relaxed atmosphere and artistic idiosyncrasies appropriate to a man of taste. Each Sukiya structure is accordingly unique, but all share certain general characteristics. Perhaps the most important of these is the understatement and irregularity, at times bordering on rusticity, borrowed from tea taste. As pointed out earlier, this accounts for the roughly hewn posts and simple ink paintings, where paintings exist at all. But the best Sukiya were created by social elites, and their understated atmosphere goes hand in hand with elegant details of the most expensive kind. Many Sukiya rooms have ogee-arched (cusped) windows (*katōmado*; figs. 147, 154; see also fig. 24) and tracerylike latticework in their transoms (figs. 145, 151), intricate openwork on shelves (figs. 152–53), and even figured metal nail covers (*kugikakushi*; fig. 149). Sukiya rooms also show eccentric reinterpretations of the typical Shoin plan. Formal Shoin rooms usually have the decorative alcove and shelves side by side at the back wall of the jōdan, with the writing desk to one side on the veranda wall and the decorative doors across from it (see fig. 133). Sukiya spaces, by contrast, almost never use the decorative doors, and they constantly rethink the traditional placement of the other formal Shoin fixtures (compare, for example, figs. 145, 147 with figs. 133, 139).

The Manshuin One of the most congenial representations of the Sukiya style is found in northeast Kyōto, where the land begins to rise toward Mt. Hiei. This is the Manshuin, a *monzeki* temple built for an abbot who was also a member of the imperial family. It was completed in 1656, after the temple was moved to its present location from the north of the Imperial Palace.

The Manshuin has two Shoin, the Greater (Daishoin) and the Lesser (Kojoin; fig. 144). The Lesser Shoin in particular is very well known (figs. 145, 46). The main room of the Lesser Shoin complex, called the Twilight Room (Tasogare no Ma; fig. 145), shows the creative reconsideration of traditional Shoin elements that is a touchstone of the Sukiya style. The decorative alcove and shelves are side by side on the back wall and the built-in desk, projecting into the veranda, sits at right angles to the alcove on a raised jōdan area. Thus far, the description sounds like a formal Shoin layout. But the designs of the constituent fixtures are quite original—the jōdan is only two mats in size and does not include the shelves. More remarkably, it is mirrored above by a canopylike ceiling irregularly coffered to suggest the pattern of the transom. The desk has an ogee-arched window, and the shelves show a unique three-tiered design with cupboards included as well.

The anteroom, called the Mt. Fuji Room (Fuji no Ma), is eight mats in size and is divided from the Twilight Room by a transom of most original design, including carvings in bas-relief and openwork chrysanthemums, which are the emblem of the imperial family (the transom is seen in fig. 145). Every detail

147. First Room, Kuroshoin, Nishi Honganji

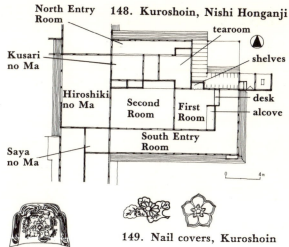

148. Kuroshoin, Nishi Honganji

149. Nail covers, Kuroshoin

150. Roof corner tile, Kuroshoin

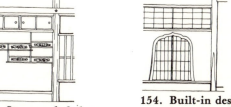

151. Transom, Kuroshoin

152. Openwork shelf backing, Kuroshoin

153. Staggered shelves, Kuroshoin

154. Built-in desk and ogee-arched window, Kuroshoin

of these two rooms has been planned—even the nail covers on the circumferential rails in the Mt. Fuji Room are made in the shape of that mountain. Appended to the Mt. Fuji Room is a tiny tea chamber with an area of only one mat plus another three-quarter-length mat (the latter mat called a *daime*).

The Kuroshoin of Nishi Honganji Behind the opulent Shiroshoin and the enormous Audience Hall of Nishi Honganji (see pp. 74–75, 120–21) is a series of rooms where the abbot of that great temple can carry out personal interviews or take his ease. Known as the Kuroshoin (figs. 147–48), the complex was built a year after the Manshuin in 1657. In the First Room (Ichi no Ma), there is a decorative alcove (one and a half bays in width) and a built-in desk side by side on the back wall, and shelves on the wall adjoining at the north—a definite departure from the formal Shoin arrangement. Nor is there a jōdan. The trademark rough-hewn posts are in evidence as is an ogee-arched window (figs. 147, 154), and the shelves, separated from the built-in desk by a one-bay expanse of wall with inset shōji screens, are fitted with superbly crafted openwork backings (figs. 152–53). Between the First Room and the Second Room (Ni no Ma) is a complex transom (fig. 151, right), and both rooms have nail covers of floral pattern (fig. 149). Even the corner tiles (*onigawara*) of the roof are molded with a design of wisteria, a flower used in the crest of the Nishi Honganji temple (fig. 150).

Family Relations and Design Influences Clearly the Sukiya designs of the Manshuin Lesser Shoin and the Nishi Honganji Kuroshoin are remarkably similar in spirit. The reason is not only that they were built at much the same time, but that there was a close personal bond on the part of the builders. The first resident of the Lesser Shoin was the Priestly Prince Ryōshō (1622–93), second son of the builder of the Old Shoin at Katsura, Prince Hachijōnomiya Toshihito, and that of the Kuroshoin was the abbot Ryōnyo (1612–62), whose wife (monks of the True Pure Land sect may marry) was Toshihito's daughter Umenomiya. It will be recalled that Toshihito's eldest

son, Toshitada, was also a builder and added much to his father's Katsura complex. Toshitada, Ryōshō, Ryōnyo, and Umenomiya all visited Katsura when it contained only the Old Shoin and Middle Shoin, and no doubt there was a good deal of discussion on matters of design, resulting in mutual influence.

Other Well-known Sukiya Buildings Four additional examples of superlative Sukiya styling are the Teahouse (Ochaya) of Fushimi Inari Shrine (Kyō-to; said to have been moved from the Imperial Palace in 1641), the Kokin Denju no Ma (Kumamoto City, Kumamoto Prefecture; originally a study area in the mansion of Prince Hachijōnomiya Toshihito, then moved to his teahouse at Kaidemmura in the Kan'ei era [1624–44], and then again to its present location in the Meiji period), the Tōshintei of Minase Shrine (Ōsaka City; built for an imperial progress by Tonsured Retired Emperor Gomizunoo in the Kan'ei era), and the Rinshunkaku of the Sankeien Park (Yokohama; originally built in 1649 as a villa of the Wakayama Tokugawa and moved to its present location in this century).

MINKA—DWELLINGS OF THE COMMON PEOPLE

Guest Room
anteroom
Saya no Ma
Entry Alcove
Sitting Room
storeroom
entry alcove
Ima
Oie no Ma
Dei
Hiroshiki
earth floor
oven area
store room

155. Yoshimura House

Varieties of Minka The term *minka*, literally meaning "houses of the people," covers a great variety of residential types, from the great houses of village headmen and rich merchants to the huts of the poorest farmers. It even applies to the houses of Shintō priests and the lower levels of the warrior and even courtly hierarchies; in short, to all houses not belonging to the members of the very highest social strata in premodern Japan.

The types of minka are as diverse as their owners, and most have been renovated or enlarged in accordance with the changing needs and incomes of successive generations of inhabitants. Most of the very old minka that still survive belonged to village headmen or other wealthy commoners, which makes it difficult to generalize about minka as a whole. Undoubtedly these large minka formed a relatively small percentage of the total. Those owned by village headmen began to incorporate Shoin-style elements as the Edo period wore on, particularly in the sitting rooms (*zashiki*) where representatives of the shōgun's government were received. But the use of these upper-class accoutrements was limited, in theory at least, by sumptuary laws designed to preserve rigid class distinctions.

The Yoshimura House The Yoshimura House, located in Habikino City, Ōsaka Prefecture, preserves the simple vitality and solidity of the best of the minka tradition, together with no small degree of sophistication and even elegance. The Yoshimura family, which still owns the house today, boasts a venerable and distinguished lineage. One if its patriarchs, Yoshimura Shichiemon, is listed as "overseer" (*mandokoro*) at the head of a document dated 1591, and he appears again as "headman (*shōya*) Shichiemon" in a cadastral record of 1594. The successive heads of the family retained the position as

headmen of Shimaizumi village until the fall of the Tokugawa government in 1868.

As with nearly all minka, the history of the Yoshimura House is incomplete, but it is said to have been burnt during Tokugawa Ieyasu's Ōsaka Summer Campaign of 1615 when he crushed the last pocket of resistance to the national hegemony he had won at the battle of Sekigahara fifteen years before. The Yoshimura House was rebuilt soon thereafter. The formal sitting room area appended to the west of the main house is believed to have been built somewhat after that, and the storage and oven sections to the east date to after 1798 (fig. 155).

The central section of the Yoshimura House is divided, like most minka, into earth-floored (*doma*) and elevated, tatami-matted areas. The transition between the two parts is made possible at the Yoshimura House by a raised interior veranda, called the Hiroshiki, that projects into the earth-floored portion (figs. 155–56). Above, huge rough-hewn beams

156. Hiroshiki in earth-floored area, Yoshimura House

crisscross below a bamboo ceiling (*sunoko tenjō*)—an unexpectedly refined conception. A family of standing such as the Yoshimura would be expected to have a number of servants and, in a novel touch, a small room thought to be for maids was accordingly hung over the Hiroshiki's south side. It is reached via a ladder of half-moon shaped rungs cut into the wall. The wooden screen with the elegant design that stands on the Hiroshiki was made of a transom that once divided the earth-floored section but was removed when the house was restored.

West of the Hiroshiki are six tatami-matted rooms for daily living and meeting with callers. A wooden-floored storeroom is located in the middle of the northern row. In feudal times, most visitors came and went via doors in the earth-floored section, while important personages made formal entries via the Entry Alcove Room (Genkan no Ma), which leads either back toward the earth-floored area or toward the sitting rooms at the far west.

The formal guest area is made up of two main rooms, the Guest Room and the anteroom, which are separated by an openwork transom. The Guest Room includes a Sukiya-style decorative alcove and, projecting into an interior corridor to the north, a built-in desk with an ogee-arched window. There are shōji screens with high wainscoting and cleverly designed latticework, ink monochrome mural paintings, and fine metal door pulls and nail covers. The posts are unplaned at the corners, save for those in the corners of the room, which are square-cut in the formal manner. Outside to the north is a garden with a spring and a man-made hill. The total effect was most appropriate for a family of prominence with important local responsibilities.

In its heyday in the Edo period, the Yoshimura House had a large number of subsidiary structures, and today a number still survive, such as the gatehouse (*nagayamon*), fireproof storage building, and bulletin-board area.

MINKA DIVERSITY

157. Former Emukai House (mid 18th cen.)

158. Kawauchi House (first half of 18th cen.)

159. Typical Kudo-style house in Taku, Saga Prefecture

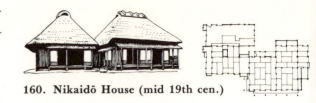

160. Nikaidō House (mid 19th cen.)

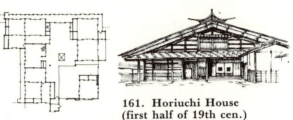

161. Horiuchi House (first half of 19th cen.)

162. Kuriyama House (1607)

Regional Variations Though relatively small in land area, the Japanese archipelago covers over twenty degrees of latitude, roughly from Maine to Miami in the United States. Differing climates have given rise over the years to a large number of regional minka types.

Northern Honshū (Tōhoku) One characteristic building style of northern Japan is the Chūmon style, so named for the *chūmon* ell that projects from the dwelling proper (*shuya*) in homes from Akita and Yamagata Prefectures south to Fukushima. The chūmon ell developed from the projecting corridor of the same name in Shoin structures (see p. 76) and earlier homes. The ell usually includes an entrance on the facade, earth-floored area, stable, and toilet, thus ensuring access to those areas in the snowy winter months.

A variant of the style is seen in the so-called Ell Houses of Nambu (*Nambu no magariya*) in the region of the old Nambu fief in present-day Iwate Prefecture. The former Kikuchi House in Tōno City is an example of this type (fig. 166). The ell houses in general include only a stable and earth-floored area in the ell, with an entrance not on the ell's facade but on the side.

Another exemplary minka of the northern area is the former Shibuya House, originally located in Tamugimata, Higashitagawa District, Yamagata Prefecture (fig. 164). It has large windows on its second and third floors due both to the heavy snows of the region and also to the growing of silkworms carried out in the upper stories. Silkworm production was a popular cottage industry in the area when the home was built in 1822. The roof is in the Kabutoyane style, so called for its resemblance to a samurai helmet (*kabuto*).

North-Central Japan (Kantō and Chūbu Regions) Many of the old minka of Ibaragi, Chiba, and Miyagi Prefectures have their earth-floored and tatami-matted areas under separate roofs. The former Sakuta House is a case in point (fig. 167). The Sakuta family were important fishermen of the Kujūkuri area on the coast of present-day Chibu Prefecture.

The former Kitamura House is another very old residence in the region (fig. 168). A farmhouse that once stood at the foot of Mt. Tanzawa outside Hadano City in Kanagawa Prefecture, it is noted for its Hiroma (literally "large room") set on the level of the elevated tatami rooms but three-quarters covered by bamboo flooring.

Moving toward the Sea of Japan, we find the Gasshō style used in many minka of Gifu and Toyama Prefectures. The name of the style is derived from the steep roofs of the houses, which resemble hands held in an attitude of prayer (*gasshō*). A representative example is the former Emukai House, originally located in the village of Kamitairamura, Toyama Prefecture, in the area drained by the Shōgawa river (fig. 157). As with the former Shibuya House, the

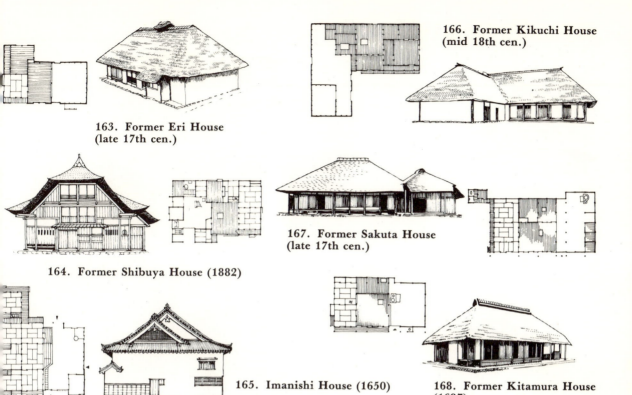

163. Former Eri House
(late 17th cen.)

166. Former Kikuchi House
(mid 18th cen.)

164. Former Shibuya House (1882)

167. Former Sakuta House
(late 17th cen.)

165. Imanishi House (1650)

168. Former Kitamura House
(1687)

three-story structure was used for silkworm cultivation.

Nagano Prefecture is known for its houses in the Hommune style. Our example here is the Horiuchi House in Shiojiri City, built by a prominent local family who served as overseers (*ōjōya*) for the area (fig. 161). The house is nearly square in plan, with a gently sloping pitched roof of planks. The facade is particularly noteworthy for its three-pronged roof ornament, called a "sparrow dance" (*suzume odori*) or "sparrow scare" (*suzume odoshi*), and for the impressive half-timbering of the gable beneath.

South-Central Japan (Kinki and Chūgoku Regions) According to the certification found on the roof ridgepole, the Kuriyama House, in the city of Gojō, Nara Prefecture, dates to 1607, making it the oldest minka to which a reliable date can be affixed (fig. 162). It is an imposing residence with thick plaster walls and a tiled hip-and-gable roof given added interest by a carefully designed smoke vent.

Another very old town house in the region was built for the Imanishi, headmen of Imaichō, a self-governing township built around a True Pure Land Temple (fig. 165). Walls and a moat were built to protect the town's autonomy. The date 1650 was discovered on the ridgepole certification. The house is famous for its huge tiled roof, and the complex system of gables gives it the name Eight-roofed style (*yatsumune zukuri*).

There are a number of other very old houses in the region, among them the Nakamura House in Gose City, Nara Prefecture, dated 1632. Other undated houses may be older than even the Kuriyama family residence. These include the Hakogi House in Kōbe City and the Furui House in Hyōgo Prefecture. Both are familiarly known as Thousand Year Houses (*sennen'ya*) and are thought to date to the late Muromachi period.

Shikoku and Kyūshū A number of homes in eastern Kagawa Prefecture have pitched roofs and particularly large earth-floored areas. One such residence is the former Eri House (fig. 163). Its massive walls give it a very inward-looking and protected appearance.

Saga and Nagasaki Prefectures are known for the Kudo style of minka, which has a roof with a U-shaped plan (fig. 159). The design may have been developed to withstand the frequent typhoons that strike southern Japan. The name is said to be derived from the style's resemblance to a *kudo* oven. Another example of the type is the house of the Kawauchi family, but it was remodeled in later years (fig. 158). The plan shows an earlier form of the house more representative of the Kudo style.

In the southern prefecture of Kagoshima, some minka are composed of two sections with separate roofs. At the Nikaidō House, the section under the roof with the east-west ridgepole is called the Omote and that with the north-south ridgepole, the Nakae (fig. 160).

PROVINCIAL TOWNS IN THE EDO PERIOD

Types of Towns Farming villages (*nōson*), port towns (*minatomachi*), temple or shrine towns (*monzenmachi*) that grew up around places of worship, post towns (*shukubamachi*) that catered to the traffic along the great roads, and castle towns (*jōkamachi*), all developed to serve different purposes, and all have unique features that are further particularized through adaptations to differing regional climates and topographies. The logic behind the organization of these varied communities is sometimes obvious, sometimes obscure. The Gasshō-style minka on the Tonami Plain in Toyama Prefecture, for example, seem at first glance to stand helter-skelter within their windbreak of trees, but on closer inspection prove to form a definite interrelated whole. Towns like this are called "dispersed communities" (*sankyo shūraku*).

Mitsuchō, in Ibo District, Hyōgo Prefecture, is a typical port town. It has a long history, reaching back to the days when it was called Murotsu and daimyō stayed at its sumptuous inns, and the town still re-flects its ancient appearance today.

A representative post town is the former Ōuch Station in Shimogōmachi, Minamiaizu District Fukushima Prefecture. Inns line both sides of the ol Aizu Nishikaidō road, and their gable-entry facade preserve much of their old flavor. The water tha flows in fosses to both sides of the street must hav refreshed many a weary traveler over the centuries Other old-fashioned post towns are Motoyama, Na rai, Midono, and, perhaps most notably, Tsumago all of which served travelers on the Kiso Road (als called the Nakasendō) that ran between Edo an Kyōto through the mountains of central Japan.

The Town of Tsumago Tsumago, in present-da Nagano Prefecture, was one of the dozens of pos towns on the Kiso Road. As it is located in a moun tainous region, harvests in Tsumago have alway been scant. In modern times many young people o the village have gone to the cities in hopes of bette employment. The town consequently has changed lit

169. The town of Tsumago

tle over the years, and recent restoration programs have been instituted to turn this old-fashioned quality to historical advantage. Even telephone poles have been moved behind the houses and out of sight. Today Tsumago presents a close approximation of its appearance over a century ago. The rows of simple houses that stand to either side of the three-to-four-meter-wide road still retain their old latticed fronts and their plank roofs, weighted down with rocks for reinforcement (fig. 169).

Urban Design The town of Tsumago does not ostentatiously advertise its historicity, and this understated integrity is one of its most charming and aesthetically effective qualities. The character of the town was not planned outright but rather evolved over years of unself-conscious trial and error. Civic pride expressed in terms of architectural display was in any case discouraged by the officials of a feudal government dedicated to the preservation of the status quo, and village carpenters were of limited

originality. The result of this de jure and de facto conservatism, however, was an extremely pleasing and successful uniformity of design, enlivened by occasional understated flourishes. It would be a mistake, though, to credit this effect entirely to good fortune. Instead, a clear design sense—conscious or otherwise—on the part of all those anonymous builders who contributed to the town's architecture helped make Tsumago what it is today.

In the same way that laws are necessary once people begin to live in groups, so are aesthetic rules required when houses are massed together to form cities. That we continue today to find pleasure in Edo-period urban design is a measure of the success of earlier generations in formulating such architectural rules. No doubt there is much we can continue to take from these early towns and apply to the urban problems of the present and the future.

JAPAN'S PREMODERN CITIES

Lake Biwa

Hikone Castle

lagoon

170. A castle town: Hikone

Castle Towns   Most of the main cities in present-day Japan developed in the early modern period as towns built around a central castle. Tōkyō, for example, grew up around Edo Castle, headquarters of the Tokugawa shōguns (see pp. 88–89). Ōsaka was centered on Ōsaka Castle, administered by Toyotomi Hideyoshi and later by Tokugawa Ieyasu, and so too was Nagoya built around the castle of a branch family of the Tokugawa, the Matsudaira of Owari Province, now Aichi Prefecture.

Hikone   Hikone, in present-day Shiga Prefecture, had its beginnings as a castle town when the warrior Ii Naokatsu established himself there in 1604. His castle remains today, overlooking Lake Biwa from atop a low hill (see fig. 206). At the height of its prosperity it was surrounded by the residences of the Ii family's highest retainers, and then, further out, by the houses of stipendiaries of the one hundred to one thousand *koku* class, a *koku* being equal to about five bushels of rice, the amount theoretically necessary to support one man for a year. The houses of the townsmen radiated outward from there (fig. 170). Temples were built around the castle's outer moat, as the castle residents were well aware of their usefulness from the point of view of defense.

Unlike towns such as Tsumago that took shape in an arbitrary and intuitive way, Hikone and most other castle towns were based initially on plans. The general apportionment of samurai, tradesmen, and artisan homes was established beforehand, and moats, roads, and water availability were given careful consideration. The exact layout of Hikone in the year 1736 is clear from an extant source entitled "Map of the Hikone Castle Town" (*Hikone jōka sō ezu*; fig. 170). Similar visual evidence exists for many other castle sites. One particularly valuable source is a group of city maps ordered made by the Tokugawa shogunate. Known as the *Maps of the Shōhō Era* (*Shōhō zu*) or *Maps of Shōhō Era Castles* (*Shōhōjō ezu*) by virtue of their date of compilation in the first year (1644) of the Shōhō era, the maps depict many of the cities of the day, with a high regard for fidelity and uniformity, making them a priceless legacy of the early days of the Tokugawa shogunate.

The Port City of Nagasaki   Nagasaki has a deep natural harbor, and its development as an urban center began in 1571. It flourished subsequently as a focus of foreign trade. In 1636 Dejima island was built to house the Portuguese traders who brought their wares to the city. Three years later, the shogunate decreed the country be closed off from most foreign intercourse, and the Portuguese were expelled. In 1641 the Dutch were moved to the tiny man-made island from their trade mission on Hirado Island to the north, and they remained the only Western traders allowed to deal with Japan until the

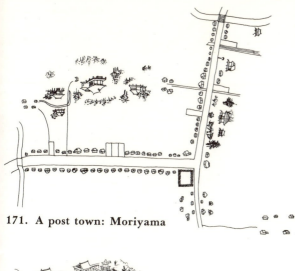

171. A post town: Moriyama

173. A post town: Moriyama

172. A port town: Nagasaki

174. A shrine town: Kotohira

reopening of the country in the middle of the nineteenth century. Nagasaki was thus Japan's only "window on the West," and free-thinking young men made the long trip to this bastion of comparative enlightenment to learn the secrets of European science and technology. Since its inception, the city has been known for its exotic flavor, lent by its European and Chinese influences.

The arrival of a European mission in 1672—an event notable for its rarity—was the catalyst for the painting entitled the *Nagasaki Screens of the Kambun Era* (*Kambun Nagasaki byōbu*). It gives a lively impression of the port, with ships moored in the harbor and people taking part in festival activities (fig. 172).

The Shrine Town Kotohira   Travel in the Tokugawa period was regulated by the government, and pilgrimages were one of the only excuses for leaving home during those centuries. One particularly famous pilgrimage center was the shrine to the god Kompira in Kotohira, located in present-day Kagawa Prefecture (see also pp. 126–27). Then as now, the main street of Kotohira was thronged by visitors buying souvenirs of their trip or hiring palanquins to ride up the hundreds of steps to the main place of worship. The *Illustrated Pilgrimage Guide to Kompira* (*Kompira sankei annai ezu*) survives from the Edo period to give a vivid impression of the town during those years (fig. 174).

The Post Town Moriyama   The *Map of Moriyama* (*Moriyama ezu*) shows the Edo-period plan of that post town on the Kiso Road near the east coast of Lake Biwa (fig. 171). Houses line the route, which turns ninety degrees near the center of town. The junction was chosen as the place for the bulletin board (*kōsatsu*) by which the town fathers conveyed laws and other civic information to the general populace. The map shows Moriyama to be delineated by bridges at its south and east ends. Thirty houses flank the north and west sides of the street and forty-one, the south and east. Several more are set back from the main road to the north and south. The town had a number of religious establishments as well. The map makes it clear that while castle towns tended to develop outward in all directions from a central fortress, post towns spread quite understandably along both sides of a highway.

The great woodblock artist of landscapes Andō Hiroshige (1797–1858) depicted Moriyama in his collection entitled *Hiroshige's Sixty-nine Stations of the Kiso Road* (*Hiroshige Kiso Kaidō rokujūkyū tsugi*; fig. 173). When compared to the map, Hiroshige's depiction of the town seems to include some artistic liberties, but it nevertheless evokes Moriyama's atmosphere quite well.

THE EDO METROPOLIS

176. Ōdemmachō Quarter

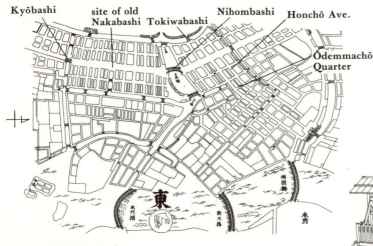

175. Nihombashi Quarter

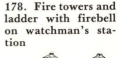

178. Fire towers and ladder with firebell on watchman's station

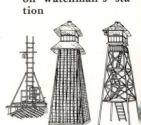

177. Bulletin board, Nihombashi Quarter

Ieyasu's City Planning On the first day of the eighth month of 1590, Tokugawa Ieyasu, still a subordinate of the great warlord Toyotomi Hideyoshi but master of most of north-central Japan, established himself in Edo Castle. Within a few decades the city that grew up around it, Edo, would become one of the largest on earth, a position it would continue to maintain after it was renamed Tōkyō and made the center of the Meiji government in 1868.

But when Ieyasu took up residence in Edo, the castle was so insignificant as to lack even stone parapets, and the bay was close enough to lap at the foundations of the central keep, which leaked in the rain. Ieyasu is said to have chosen the site at the suggestion of Hideyoshi. But the future founder of the Tokugawa shogunate no doubt saw for himself that the small town was ideally situated for land and sea trade and that it could control the entirety of the vast Kantō Plain.

Immediately Ieyasu began work on his new residence, not only expanding and strengthening the castle but planning the city that was to surround and supply it. He filled in the Hibiya Inlet that had bordered the castle, built a system of moats and canals, and reduced Mt. Kanda at present-day Surugadai.

Planning Edo's Great Roads The design of Edo is believed to have been heavily influenced by two distant mountains, Mt. Fuji and Mt. Tsukuba. Honchō Avenue, for example, one of the main arteries in the city, was laid out on the route connecting Mt. Fuji with the Tokiwabashi area. Similarly, the road from Kyōbashi to Nihombashi was laid out in the direction of Mt. Tsukuba (fig. 175). Standing on Honchō Avenue and looking southwest, one could see Mt. Fuji over eighty kilometers away, and travelers from Kyōbashi could glimpse Mt. Tsukuba over sixty kilometers to the northeast.

Mt. Fuji in particular became a point of reference and cultural pride for Edoites, and famous woodblock artists frequently incorporated it into their compositions. Torii Kiyonaga (1753–1815) used it, as did Katsushika Hokusai (1760–1849), who made it the subject of a whole series of prints, the famous *Thirty-six Views of Mt. Fuji* (*Hokusai Fugaku sanjūrokkei*; see fig. 91), some of which are depicted from vantage points within the city of Edo. The mountain was an inspiring centerpiece for some of Hiroshige's prints as well, such as *The Prosperous Ōdemmachō Quarter, the Eastern City* (*Tōto Ōdemmachō han'ei no zu*; fig. 176). The artist used the mountain as the focal point

179. Nakabashi Quarter

**180. Shop with second-floor residence
and earth-walled storehouse**

**181. Neighborhood watchman's
station and *kido* gate**

the entire composition, and he drew the eye to it through the use of the converging lines of the shops to both sides of the thronged avenue. Mt. Fuji had such charm for the artists of the period that some were no doubt inclined to include it in pictures of parts of the city from which it was not in fact visible. But in most cases it seems likely that artists were telling no more than the truth about the dominant role of the mountain in the consciousness of the citizens of Edo.

The Look of Edo As Edo was the site of the shōgun's government and the largest city in Japan, illustrations of it naturally proliferated. Many of these were in guidebooks such as the very detailed *Great Map of the Roads of Edo* (*Bundō Edo daiezu*) printed in 1716 from a painting by Ishikawa Tomonobu (fig. 175). Other artists chose to concentrate on city scenes such as the section around Nakabashi bridge, depicted, for example, in the *Folding Screens of Scenes in Edo* (*Edo zu byōbu*; fig 179). It gives a vivid and lively view of the area as it looked in the early years of the Edo period, before the bridge was dismantled and the canal beneath filled in. Nakabashi was clearly a thriving commercial center, with boats laden with goods and men on both sides of the river carrying

loads on poles over their shoulders. In front of the bridge, to the right, can be seen the gates called *kido* ("wooden doors") that demarcated the various city subsections and closed them off at night. Over them stand three-story towers that commanded a good view of the area. Kitagawa Morisada was another artist who focussed his talent on the city, particularly its architecture. His collection *Morisada's Random Sketches* (*Morisada mankō*; 1853) includes careful representations of a *kido* gate with a watchman's station (*jishimbansho*) to the left (fig. 181), a two-story house next to an even taller earth-walled storehouse (fig 180), and even examples of fire towers (*hinomiyagura*) together with the explanation "these are built about one per ten blocks" (fig. 178).

A final example of the illustrations devoted to Edo is the *Pictures of Famous Places in Edo* (*Edo meisho zue*) by Saitō Gesshin and others in 1836. The flourishing city is depicted therein section by section in very detailed representations. It also gives visual information on various everyday sights in the city such as the local bulletin boards on which ordinances and notices were regularly displayed (fig. 177).

SCHOOLS IN THE EDO PERIOD

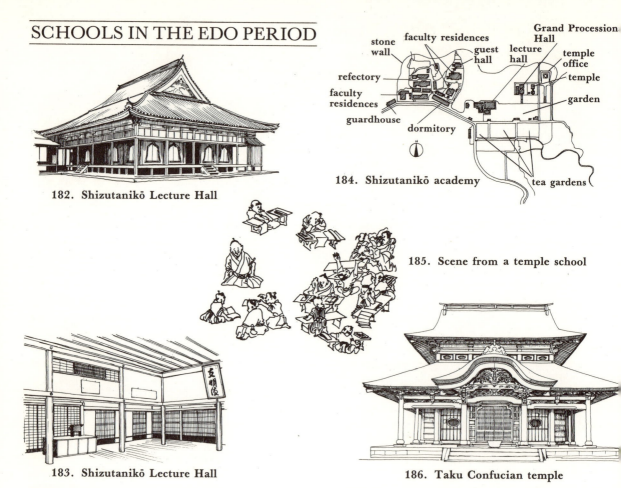

182. Shizutanikō Lecture Hall

184. Shizutanikō academy

stone wall · faculty residences · guest hall · lecture hall · Grand Procession Hall · temple office · temple · refectory · faculty residences · guardhouse · dormitory · garden · tea gardens

185. Scene from a temple school

183. Shizutanikō Lecture Hall

186. Taku Confucian temple

Fief Schools for Scions of the Samurai As members of the highest of the four basic social classes into which the population of Edo Japan was divided, the sons of samurai families were afforded special educational opportunities at academies (*hankō*) run by their fiefs (*han*). The Kōdōkan of the Mito fief and the Meirindō of the Owari are particularly well-known schools of this type. Another was the Shizutanikō of the Okayama fief, begun in 1670 when large numbers of trees were cleared to make a spacious site. Its Lecture Hall (Kōdō) was completed in 1673 and its temple to Confucius (Seidō) was built on a rise to the east in the following year (fig. 184). The present Lecture Hall, rebuilt in 1701, is a majestic structure with a spacious plank-floored interior to accommodate a large number of young scholars (figs. 182–83). The temple to Confucius was rebuilt in 1684.

These Confucian temples, where rites in honor of Confucius were performed, were a particular feature of fief academies. This is not surprising, as the curricula of these schools was overwhelmingly weighted toward the study of the Chinese classics, many of which are attributed to that master. It was also Confucian doctrine, as interpreted by later thinkers, that formed the philosophical underpinnings for the pre-

dominant social position of the samurai class.

Another good example of these temples belonged to the Taku School of the Saga fief (fig. 186). Finished in 1708, it is the only structure of the Taku School still standing. Appropriately enough, the temple is quite Chinese in atmosphere and perhaps was directly modeled on Chinese Confucian temples.

Temple Schools Children of the other three main classes in Edo society, the farmers, artisans, and merchants, attended "temple schools" (*terakoya*). There they learned the rudiments of reading, writing, and arithmetic, the last with the aid of the abacus (*soroban*). The teachers were usually samurai, monks, physicians, or Shintō priests. The term "temple school" developed in the medieval period when classes were held for the most part in Buddhist establishments, but by the Edo period it had come to mean any school for commoner children, and classes were held not only in temples but in shrines and the homes of samurai. The lively and somewhat undisciplined atmosphere of one such school was captured by the painter and philosopher Watanabe Kazan (1793–1841) in his notebook *Issō hyakutai ch* in 1818 (fig. 185).

BATTLE: Castles and Castle Towns

The sound of the bell of Jetavana Temple echoes the impermanence of all things. The hue of the blossoms of the double Sāla trees proclaims the truth that those who flourish must be brought low. The proud do not long endure, but are like the dream of a spring night. So are the mighty in the end destroyed, all as dust before the wind.

Like Kamo no Chōmei's *Tale of the Ten-Foot-Square Hut*, the first lines of the *Tales of the Heike* (*Heike monogatari*) announce the theme of mutability. Yet the subject of the *Tales* is not reclusion but war, war between two mighty military clans, the Minamoto and the Taira. The reader will recall that those two houses, also called the Genji and Heike, vied for national supremacy in the late twelfth century (see pp. 20–21). The *Tales of the Heike*, Japan's greatest military classic, is based on their struggle and recounts the rise of the Heike, the glory of its leader, Taira no Kiyomori, then the string of defeats and final extinction of his heirs at the hands of their enemies. The fall of the Heike in 1185 marked the birth of the medieval era, four hundred years of instability that ended in a protracted national conflict known as the Age of the Country at War (*sengoku jidai*). It was a time of devout popular Buddhism and the rise of Zen, of Sung-inspired ink monochrome paintings, the tea ceremony and the Nō drama. Most of all, it was a time of struggle to attain, then retain, power. As was characteristic of that violent age, the sons of Minamoto no Yoritomo, the first medieval shōgun, were both assassinated, and the Kamakura shogunate passed into the control of Yoritomo's maternal relatives, the Hōjō. The Hōjō overcame attempts to overthrow them by the imperial family and the Mongol army of Kublai Khan, only to collapse in a more successful imperial restoration attempt in 1333 by the army of the Emperor Godaigo (1288–1339). Three years later Godaigo himself was routed by an erstwhile retainer, Ashikaga no Takauji (1305–58), who established the second shogunate of the medieval period, the Muromachi, in Kyōto. Godaigo fled south carrying the emblems of imperial office, beginning a period of over a half century in which two courts, the Northern and the Southern, coexisted (1336–92). But Ashikaga control was never absolute, and its daimyō deputies perpetually thirsted for greater individual power. The fragile hold of the Muromachi shogunate over its subordinates collapsed in the Ōnin War (1467–77), which laid waste to the capital and led to the Age of the Country at War.

The man who finally rose supreme out of this anarchic century was Oda Nobunaga, a general of genius, audacity, and bloodthirsty cunning. After a number of great victories, Nobunaga finally marched into Kyōto and installed a new shōgun from the Ashikaga family in 1568, only to unseat him five years later,

thus ending the era of Ashikaga rule. Nobunaga went on expanding his holdings for nearly a decade thereafter, but in 1582 he died on the threshold of national hegemony, murdered by a subordinate.

Nobunaga's Azuchi Castle, built on the shore of Lake Biwa in 1576–77, was as epoch-making as the exploits of its master. Strongholds had, of course, been built throughout Japanese history and are mentioned in the earliest written records, but Azuchi represented a quantum leap over the large-scale but relatively crude construction of its predecessors. Its donjon rose six stories and seven floors in height (the interior configuration was not completely reflected on the exterior) and overlooked the surrounding countryside of Ōmi Province (present-day Shiga Prefecture) from atop a rise, announcing to the world the preeminence of its creator. The exterior was decorated with walls of scarlet, blue, and gold plaster, and the interior bore brilliant gold and polychrome mural paintings by the great painter Kanō Eitoku (1543–90). Virtually no interior surface was left unadorned, and this effort to dazzle the eye became one of the touchstones of the art of the period, referred to as the Azuchi-Momoyama, or simply Momoyama (1573–1600). Nobunaga held grand assemblies at the castle to display its opulence. Nor was he intent only on visual effect. The introduction of firearms by the Portuguese some decades earlier had revolutionized warfare and required much stronger fortifications, and this too was reflected in Nobunaga's edifice. He had already put his respect for firearms to good use in his monumental rout of the conventionally armed forces of Takeda Katsuyori at Nagashino in 1575. Azuchi Castle powerfully influenced all subsequent castle designs. But the prototype did not long survive its creator, and today all that is left is part of the foundation stonework. Despite the thick, plaster-coated walls used in the castles of the time, they were essentially built of wood, and most eventually fell pray to fire from either battle or other causes. Of the twelve donjons that survive today, only two, those of Maruoka and Matsumoto, antedate the battle of Sekigahara in 1600 (see pp. 72–73).

The height of castle building was to last less than half a century. After Tokugawa Ieyasu consolidated his hold over the country, he instituted measures in 1615 to limit the number of castles to one per domain in the interest of preserving peace and ensuring continued Tokugawa rule.

HIMEJI—THE GRANDEST OF THE SURVIVING CASTLES

cusped window

gu

187. Donjon complex of Himeji Castle, viewed from the Caltrop Gate (Hishi no Mon) to the south

"Egret Castle"   The donjon (*tenshu*) of Himeji Castle, built atop a forty-five-meter rise called Hime-yama, commands an expansive view of the surrounding Himeji City in Hyōgo Prefecture (figs. 187, 203). The thirty-one-meter donjon, the last stronghold and most heavily fortified castle structure, contains five stories and six floors, an additional floor being built into the fifteen-meter-tall stone foundation. This main donjon is surrounded by three smaller ones, the West Donjon (left of the main donjon in fig. 187), Northwest Donjon (left of the West Donjon), and the East Donjon (behind the main donjon and not visible in the illustration). The four donjons are connected by corridors (*watariyagura*). This central citadel is surrounded by a twisting maze of walls, gates, and corridors with turrets (*yagura*) at strategic points. The Ri Corridor is in the foreground of figure 187, with the Chi Turret at the far right.

But this complex formed only the Central Compound (Hommaru) of the castle—several subsidiary compounds stretched out before it to the south and west, all surrounded by walls and a great moat. The residences of high-level retainers were located outside this castle moat but were protected by another moat still further out. Then came another even larger residential area surrounded by yet another moat. An advancing enemy thus had to cross three moats before reaching the central citadel and to force several more heavily fortified gate areas before reaching the donjon complex, where fire could be concentrated on them from the four donjons and connecting corridors and turrets.

But the role of the castle was not only to defend but to impress, and ample attention was accordingly paid at Himeji to aesthetics. The dormers (*chido rihafu*), cusped gables (*karahafu*), gable ornaments (*gegyo*), and cusped windows on the minor donjons all attest to this concern for visual effect (fig. 187). As suggested by Himeji's nickname, "Egret Castle," its walls are finished with white plaster, creating a stark, yet immensely powerful, impression.

Himeji Castle's Strategic Location   Himeji Castle is located on a major route to the western provinces, and for that reason a number of fortresses had

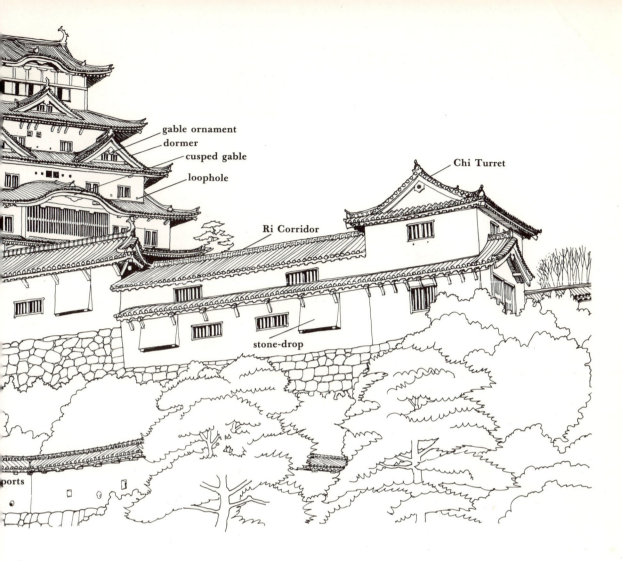

gable ornament
dormer
cusped gable
loophole

Chi Turret

Ri Corridor

stone-drop

ports

...een located on the site since at least the fourteenth century. Hideyoshi built a castle there with a three-story donjon in 1581. The present complex was be-gun when Tokugawa Ieyasu invested his son-in-law ...keda Terumasa (1564–1613) with the province of Harima (in present-day Hyōgo Prefecture) for his ex-ploits at the battle of Sekigahara. Construction was ...egun in 1601 and lasted until 1609, and materials ...rom Hideyoshi's old donjon were used in the new ...lesign. This was particularly ironic as the castle was ...neant to isolate Hideyoshi's son Hideyori in Ōsaka ...rom lords in the west, powerful leaders who had ...eceived favor from Hideyoshi in the past and were ...hus potential threats to Ieyasu. These included Katō Kiyomasa (1562–1611) of Kumamoto, Fukushima Masanori (1561–1624) of Hiroshima, and Mōri Te-...umoto of Hagi. Terumoto, it will be recalled, was ...resent at the audience with Ieyasu at Nijō Castle ...lescribed earlier (pp. 72–73). Masanori was in at-...endance at the same conference, as was Ikeda Te-...umasa. Another compound, the Nishinomaru, was ...dded to Himeji Castle in later years by the succes-

sors of the Ikeda, the Honda. Though the main don-jon seems quite close to that compound, the cleverly designed ground plan makes it extremely difficult to reach.

Construction and Design The six stories of Himeji Castle's main donjon are all tied to two huge central columns that run from the foundation to the roof. This configuration gives added stability to the mul-titiered structure. Viewed from outside the donjon, the basement story in the stone foundation is not visi-ble, but its inside walls that border the courtyard are fit with large windows to make for a more livable in-terior. The area contains a bathing room and a toilet, and a kitchen is located in the courtyard. The inner courtyard walls are not fit with loopholes for marks-men as are the outer walls. The residential part of the donjon was designed for sieges and not meant for long-term living, but it still has a more domestic quality that would be expected from the forbidding exterior.

THE HISTORICAL DEVELOP-
MENT OF CASTLES

**188. Ancient castle foundations on
Mt. Otsubo, Takeo City, Saga Prefecture**

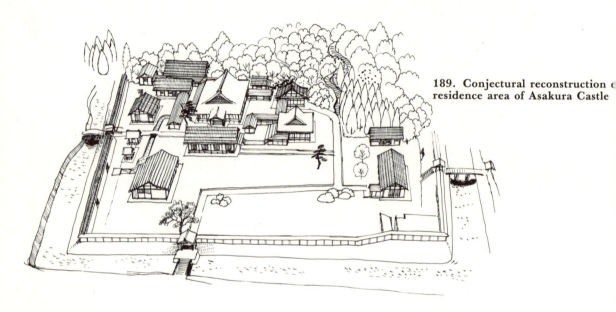

**189. Conjectural reconstruction of
residence area of Asakura Castle**

Ancient Fortresses At various sites from north
Kyūshū to the coast of the Inland Sea one can find
rock walls on the slopes of certain hills. The lines of
dressed stones stretch for several kilometers, and here
and there are found the remains of walls and sluice
gates. For years no one knew for certain what the
purpose of these ancient constructions was. Some
believed they had delineated holy areas, and they accordingly came to be called "sacred precinct stones"
(*kōgoishi*; fig. 188).

Much later, though, on the basis of scientific investigation, it became clear that these walls were the
remains of massive foundations, and that they had
been built not as sacred precincts but as early mountain castles. Possibly the technology for them was
brought to Japan by Korean immigrants. It is still
unknown, however, when and for what purpose these
castles were built.

Castles have a long history in Japan. The word

for castle appears in the oldest of Japan's official national histories, the *Nihon shoki* of 720, and we know
that structures built for warfare already existed in the
Asuka period (552–710). In the eighth century the
Nara court began pushing its borders further north
into the Tōhoku region, and its armies built strongholds as they progressed, such as Dewa Stockade
(709) and Taga Castle (724).

From Mountain Castle to Flatland Castle In the
medieval period, castles tended to be built atop
mountains or hills, where they could be easily defend-
ed. They often included a fosse around the compound
and a residential quarter as well, but tended by and
large to rely on the defensive properties of the terrain itself. What fortifications existed were thus quite
simple. Architectural historians have reconstructed
on paper one such establishment, the fortress of the
Asakura family in Ichijōdani, Echizen Province (in
present-day Fukui Prefecture). Built in 1471, the cas-

190. Remains of Takatenjin Castle

191. Donjon of Maruoka Castle

192. Jurakudai Castle and Palace

le itself stood at the summit of Mt. Ichijō, and a residential complex was built in the valley below with areas for retainers within it (fig 189). The mansion had a garden with elegant rock formations and a spring-fed pond.

This kind of "mountain castle" (*yamajiro*) was common even into the early modern period. And most early examples resembled the castle of the Asakura in locating the donjon on the mountain summit and the living area on lower ground. Another example of the type was Takatenjin Castle (Shizuoka Prefecture) where Takeda Katsuyori was defeated by Ieyasu in 1574 and again in 1579. But only the fosse of the castle remains today (fig. 190).

As the holdings of daimyō increased, however, mountain sites proved too rugged for use as centers of domainal government and commerce. Consequently "flatland-mountain castles" (*hirayamajiro*) came to be built on rises in the midst of surrounding

plains. Others, called "flatland castles" (*hirajiro*), were constructed on the plain itself. Himeji Castle is of the flatland-mountain type, as is Maruoka, the oldest extant donjon (fig. 191). Built in 1576, Maruoka Castle has a very early-type donjon, composed simply of a cupola set atop a manor-style roof.

The grandest of the Momoyama-period flatland castles was undoubtedly Hideyoshi's Jurakudai in Kyōto. The *Jurakudai Screen* (*Jurakudai byōbu*), a folding screen in the collection of the Mitsui family, shows a donjon with cusped windows and elegant railings on its cupola, surrounded by a maze of turrets, stone walls, and a multiroofed residential area. The whole complex is encircled by a moat. The complex was taken down in 1595, however, and though a number of temples over the succeeding years claimed to own parts of it, only the screen survives to show its immense grandeur in its entirety.

193. **Battle of Nagashin**

Firearms Revolutionize Castle Construction   On the twenty-first day of the fifth month, 1575, Takeda Katsuyori's army met the combined forces of Oda Nobunaga and Tokugawa Ieyasu on Shitaragahara Plain close to Nagashino Castle in what is now Aichi Prefecture. The battle was uneven in terms of numbers—Katsuyori's 15,000 against the 30,000 of Nobunaga and 8,000 of Ieyasu—and four hours later Katsuyori was in full retreat toward the province of Kai (present-day Yamanashi Prefecture). The battle was imaginatively dramatized by Kurosawa Akira in his film *Kagemusha*.

But it was not only numbers that won the day for Nobunaga: his forces were equipped with a large number of firearms. The arquebus had been introduced by the Portuguese a short three decades earlier in 1543 and had not been extensively used until Nobunaga, with his characteristic foresight, adopted it on a wide basis. More conservative leaders pre-

ferred their traditional bows, lances, and swords

As touched on in the introduction to this chapte the advent of firearms wrought great changes in cast design. Nagashino Castle, typical of late Muromac fortresses, is depicted at the far right of figure 19 (from the *Screen of the Battle of Nagashino* [*Nagashi kassenzu byōbu*]). It was of wood construction and di fered little from residential complexes. Atop one the structures is a small cupola that, if it is not sim ply a roof vent, may be a watchtower, and as suc constitute an embryonic donjon design with its even tual complement of loopholes for firearms and arrov as well as stone-drops.

Firearms, however, required builders to pay mo attention to fireproofing. Walls were coated wi plaster for this purpose, and made thicker as wel with a layer of sand and pebbles in the middle retard flame and projectiles. The result was the ty of construction seen at Himeji Castle.

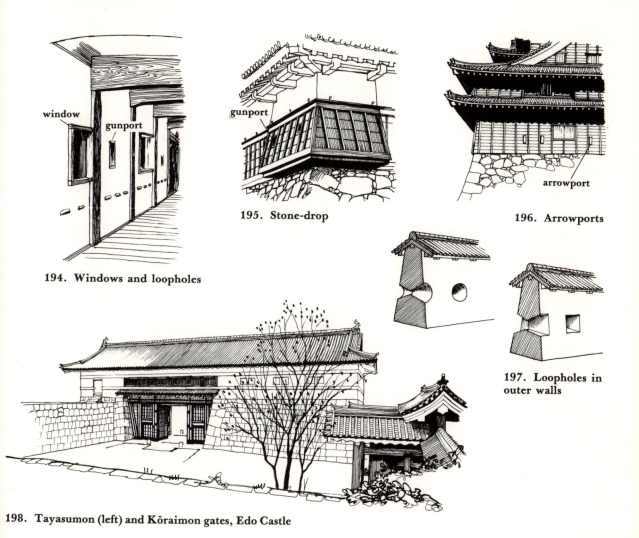

window
gunport

194. Windows and loopholes

gunport

195. Stone-drop

arrowport

196. Arrowports

197. Loopholes in outer walls

198. Tayasumon (left) and Kōraimon gates, Edo Castle

Loopholes and Stone-Drops An obvious necessity for any castle was openings in walls—loopholes—for soldiers to shoot through. Loopholes meant for the use of bows tend to be tall and narrow (*yazama*; fig. 196), while those for firearms are square or circular (*jūgan* or *teppōzama*; figs. 194–95, 197). Triangular loopholes were also used (see fig. 187). In cross section the loopholes are hourglass in shape, allowing for the greatest freedom of fire while providing the smallest target.

Another device for launching more primitive projectiles is the stone-drop (*ishiotoshi*), analogous in operation to the machicolations of European castles, which bulges out from a wall just enough to allow the defenders to rain rocks on attackers scaling the stone foundation wall (fig. 195). The stone-drop could also accommodate loopholes for shooting guns or arrows.

Double Gates and Enclosed Square Courtyards Care was also lavished on the castle layout (*nawabari*) in order to make it as difficult as possible for attackers to reach the donjon. Gates were a particular weak point, and builders consequently worked out a design to turn this inherent shortcoming to the advantage of the defenders within. On penetrating the first gate, attackers would find themselves in a square enclosed court (*masugata*) at right angles to a second, even stouter gate of two stories provided with loopholes for raking those trapped below.

One example of such double-gate designs is that at Edo Castle, built in 1636 (fig. 198). Once inside the Kōraimon gate at the right of the figure, any intruders would have been met by marksmen in the second floor of the Tayasumon gate behind it. Other gates at Edo Castle were likewise carefully outfitted for defense.

THE TWELVE SURVIVING DONJONS

201. Inuyama Castle (1601, 1620)

203. Himeji Castle (1609)

199. Maruoka Castle (1576)

secondary donjon

turret

pavilion

200. Matsumoto Castle (c. 1596)

202. Hikone Castle (1606)

204. Matsue Castle (1611)

A Chronological Survey When the Meiji Restoration took place in 1868, over forty donjons still survived. In the years that followed, though, as the country was engulfed in a wave of modernization and westernization, many donjons were dismantled as useless relics of a feudal past. Others met their end in the destruction of the Second World War—those at Ōgaki (Gifu Prefecture), Nagoya (Aichi Prefecture), Wakayama (Wakayama Prefecture), Okayama (Okayama Prefecture), Fukuyama (Hiroshima Prefecture), and Hiroshima (Hiroshima Prefecture) castles. When the donjon of a different Fukuyama Castle (Matsumaechō, Hokkaidō) burned in 1949, only twelve donjons from Japan's premodern period remained. A few donjons, at Kumamoto and Ōsaka castles, for instance, have been restored in modern times, but they are outside the scope of the present discussion.

The donjon of Maruoka Castle (Fukui Prefecture; 1576) was introduced earlier as the oldest extant (figs. 191, 199). The next oldest, that of Matsumoto (fig. 200; Nagano Prefecture, c. 1596), is strikingly situated on a plain against a backdrop of tall rugged mountains. Five stories and six floors in height, it is remarkable for its color scheme of white walls, black lacquered wainscoting, and red railings. Next to the main donjon is a secondary donjon of three stories and four floors to the northeast, a turret of two stories and three floors to the east, and a one-story moon-viewing pavilion at the far east end, surrounded by an elegant railing.

The first two floors of the Inuyama Castle donjon

(Aichi Prefecture) were begun in 1601, and the third and fourth were added in 1620 (fig. 201). The cusped gable was added still later. The watchtower that surmounts the roof is an old design, and for years the Inuyama donjon was incorrectly believed to be the oldest in Japan for that reason.

Hikone Castle (Shiga Prefecture; 1606) was introduced earlier (see fig. 170). It has a small but elegant donjon, with gleaming gold trim and cusped windows and gables (fig. 202). Three years after Hikone, Himeji Castle was completed (fig. 203), and it remains the grandest in the entire country.

Himeji is chronologically followed by the donjon of Matsue Castle (Shimane Prefecture; 1611), a structure quite large in size but of very simple and old-fashioned construction, being actually a three-story watchtower with a two-story main structure beneath it (fig. 204). The exterior is mostly black lacquered wood, giving it a grave exterior appearance and the nickname "Raven Castle." It is the last of the surviving castle donjons to antedate Ieyasu's 161? law limiting each domain to a single fortress.

Marugame Castle's donjon (Kagawa Prefecture) was completed in 1660 (fig. 205). It is a very simple three-story affair but commands a magnificent view for it stands on a three-tiered stone foundation atop a hill sixty-six meters high.

Uwajima Castle (Ehime Prefecture) was rebuilt in 1665 after an earlier version built at the end of the sixteenth century was taken down (fig. 206). The donjon incorporates no defensive structures such as stone-drops, which suggests that war was beginning

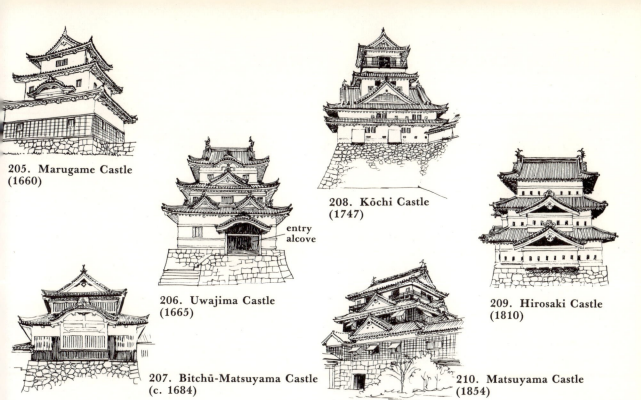

205. Marugame Castle (1660)

206. Uwajima Castle (1665)

entry alcove

207. Bitchū-Matsuyama Castle (c. 1684)

208. Kōchi Castle (1747)

209. Hirosaki Castle (1810)

210. Matsuyama Castle (1854)

to be perceived as a thing of the past by the time it was reconstructed. It also has a formal entry alcove (*genkan*) surmounted by a cusped gable.

The donjon of Bitchū-Matsuyama Castle (also called Takahashi Castle; Okayama Prefecture) was built around 1681–84 (fig. 207). It stands atop Mt. Gagyūzan and as such is the only mountain castle (*yamajiro*) in Japan to survive from the Edo period.

Kōchi Castle (Kōchi Prefecture) is likewise unique, as it is the only fortress in which both a donjon and a daimyō residential area remain intact (fig. 208). The donjon was rebuilt in 1747 after the original was burned twenty years before and was designed as a conscious reconstruction of the original, built from around 1601 to 1603. It represents a clear carry-over of the older watchtower type of donjon. The mansion, the Kaitokukan, is located at the southwest of the donjon and includes a main room elegantly outfitted in the formal Shoin style.

The Hirosaki donjon (Aomori Prefecture) is the northernmost surviving castle (fig. 209). Burned in 1627, it was not rebuilt until 1810, and even then in a very simple form at the southeast corner of the main compound. It looks as much like a corner turret as a donjon, and this impression is intensified by the fact that only the two faces overlooking the moat have projecting gables.

The last of the surviving twelve premodern fortresses to be built was Matsuyama Castle (Ehime Prefecture), sometimes called Iyo-Matsuyama to distinguish it from Bitchū-Matsuyama. It burned in 1784 and was rebuilt in 1854 (fig. 210). The com-

plex originally had three lesser donjons and various turrets, along the lines of Himeji Castle. Save for the main donjon, most of those buildings were burned in several fires in this century, but much of what was lost was restored in 1969.

The Various Donjon Types The word for donjon, *tenshu*, appears in writing toward the end of the Muromachi period at about the time the simple watchtower above a mansion roof was growing in size and solidity. The mature donjons fall into four main categories. Those that stand alone are called "independent donjons" (*dokuritsushiki tenshu*). Maruoka, Marugame, Uwajima, Bitchū-Matsuyama, Kōchi, and Hirosaki are of this type. Donjons with a subsidiary building such as a single lesser donjon or turret directly attached are known as "complex donjons" (*fukugōshiki tenshu*), exemplified by Inuyama, Hikone, and Matsue. When the main donjon and minor structures are linked by corridors, the design is termed a "connected donjon" (*renketsushiki tenshu*). Nagoya Castle, destroyed in World War Two, was of this type, but no example in its pure form now survives. The most highly evolved form is the "multiple donjon" type (*renritsushiki tenshu*), where two or more minor donjons are connected to the main one, as in the case of Himeji and Matsuyama. Combinations occur as well, as in the case of Matsumoto Castle, labeled a "complex-connected donjon" (*fukugō renketsushiki tenshu*).

CASTLE TOWNS

The Growth of Castle Towns As indicated in the preceding chapter, most of Japan's modern cities began as towns built around a daimyō's castle. The majority had their real start during the Age of the Country at War, when, in the absence of a cohesive central government, local daimyō established themselves in their own castles as independent rulers of as much territory as they could defend. These daimyō were the absolute masters of their domains, and they could establish their own laws, taxation rates, and even systems of weights and measures. The extreme decentralization of the period forced each domain to develop its commerce and trade in order to survive, which resulted in great economic expansion in areas previously dismissed as provincial backwaters.

The castle was the center of each domain's defense and government, and the towns that grew up around them became the focus of domainal commerce. They expanded culturally as well, as impoverished nobles were increasingly invited from the capital to tutor provincial potentates in poetry, the classics, and other courtly traditions.

The daimyō who survived the century of internecine fighting, and then the campaigns of Nobunaga, Hideyoshi, and Ieyasu, were allowed by the Tokugawa shogunate to continue as rulers of their domains, and this federal system survived until the end of the Edo period in 1868. At the end of the eighteenth century the daimyō numbered about 250, and more than half were of sufficient size to merit castles. The daimyō were obliged, however, to maintain second residences in the city of Edo and to spend alternate years or half-years in the city. Their families, moreover, were forced to live there permanently. This system of "alternate attendance" (*sankin kōtai*) was designed to discourage rebellion, and it kept most daimyō financially strapped as well. But it also resulted in flourishing post towns and huge growth in Edo.

The Castle Town of Kanazawa Kanazawa, in Ishikawa Prefecture on the Sea of Japan, is perhaps the best surviving example of an old castle town. It was the center of the Kaga fief, part of the domain of the Maeda family, the wealthiest daimyō in the land. The Maeda's castle was built on a rise between two rivers, the Saikawa and Asanogawa, and the town was laid out around it (fig. 218). Nearest the castle were set the residences of the highest retainers, with the size of the lot directly proportional to the stipend of the resident. The main thoroughfares were lined with merchants' shops, and back streets housed various artisans, with each trade assigned to a certain area. Even today one can find names such

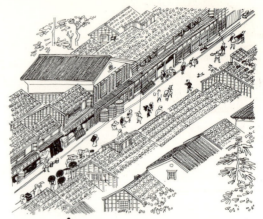

211. Road leading from Great Saikawa Bridge toward Kanazawa Castle [3]

212. Great Saikawa Bridge [4]

as Salt-Sellers' District, Metalworkers' District, Carpenters' District, and Lumbermen's District which remain from Kanazawa's premodern days. Buddhist temples, marked on the map by their traditional swastika symbol, also tended to concentrate in certain areas.

Kanazawa Castle Only two buildings remain in the castle compound of Kanazawa. These are the Ishikawamon gate and the thirty-bay Long House (Nagaya). The Ishikawamon (fig. 214), built in 1788, is actually a complex of eight structures around an enclosed square, including the Outer Gate (Omotemon), Kōraimon gate, Turret Gate (Yaguramon), Corner Turret (Sumiyagura), and so on. The gate is roofed with lead tiles. The Long House (fig. 213), built in 1858, is a two-story, two-floored construction that stretches for forty-eight meters atop the castle's outer wall. It was used for weapon storage. This type of structure was first used at the Yamato Tamon Castle and is consequently called a "tamon

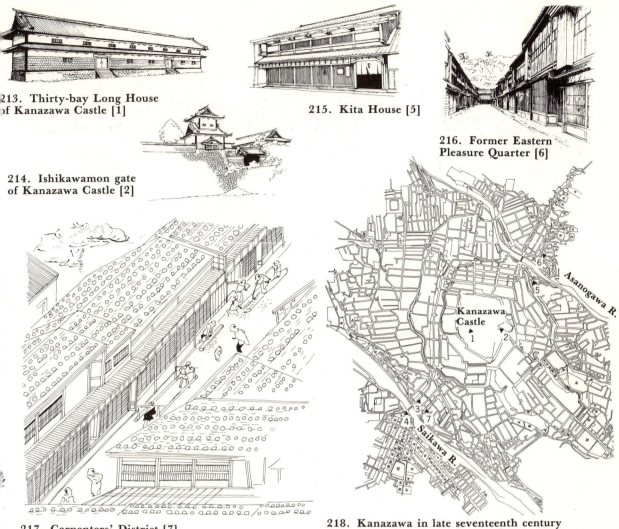

213. Thirty-bay Long House of Kanazawa Castle [1]

215. Kita House [5]

214. Ishikawamon gate of Kanazawa Castle [2]

216. Former Eastern Pleasure Quarter [6]

217. Carpenters' District [7]

218. Kanazawa in late seventeenth century (numbers correlated with other illustrations)

turret'' (*tamon'yagura*).

Near the castle was the daimyō's private park, now called the Kenrokuen. Within it is located a splendid Sukiya-style residence, built in 1863 for the mother of the last lord of Kaga, Maeda Nariyasu (1811–84). Ozaki Shrine, built close to the castle in 1643, used to be located within the castle compound and was named the Tōshōgū.

Beyond the Castle Walls　The Kanazawa area is rich in minka, such as the Kita House (fig. 215), now in Nonoichimachi but originally located in the Lumbermen's District (Zaimokuchō) of Kanazawa. Built at the end of the Edo period, the Kita House gives a good idea of what the city must have looked like on the eve of the Meiji Restoration. Its twenty-two-meter-long facade is especially grand. Rows of houses similar to that of the Kita family can be seen in a painting from the same period, the *Screen of Kanazawa* (*Kanazawazu byōbu*).

Figure 217, reproduced from this painting, shows the Carpenters' District with woodcutters finishing wood and carrying it in front of the town houses. Other sections of the painting depict the Great Saikawa Bridge (fig. 212) and the road leading from it to the castle (fig. 211). Both evoke the bustling activity appropriate to the central city of a daimyō's domain.

Kanazawa also had two licensed pleasure quarters, both outside the main city as defined by the Asanogawa and Saikawa rivers. One, popularly called Nishi (''West''), was just across the Great Saikawa Bridge. The other, known as Higashi (''East''), was across the Great Asanogawa Bridge northeast of the castle (fig. 216). The latter still resembles its appearance of the 1820s and was designated a Protected Area of Traditional Architecture in 1977. The streets are lined with the projecting lattice windows of the old houses, some of which have red walls in their sitting rooms, a clear Sukiya touch (see pp. 128–31).

CASTLE PALACES

219. Karamon gate, Ninomaru Palace, Nijō Castle

221. Ninomaru Palace and garden, Nijō Castle

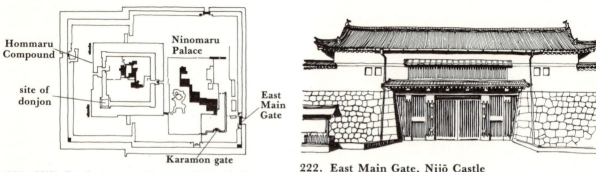

220. Nijō Castle (present-day configuration)

222. East Main Gate, Nijō Castle

Palaces of Tokugawa Castles To gain an idea of the vast size that a castle and palace could attain, we need only consider the Main Compound (Hommaru) of Edo Castle. The entire compound covered an astounding 357,000 square meters (slightly more than a third of a square kilometer), with 42,000 square meters of building space. Today, however, only a few minor structures and the stone foundation of the donjon remain. The same is true for the other great Tokugawa castles, including the once magnificent complex at Nagoya, which survived with its palace intact until 1945. Only the Ninomaru Palace of Nijō Castle remains to exemplify the splendor of the shōgun's castle complexes (figs. 220–21; see also pp. 70–73).

Ninomaru Palace of Nijō Castle As indicated earlier, the Ninomaru Palace consists of a main complex that recedes in a stepwise diagonal fashion from the Carriage Approach and Tōzamurai at the southeast to the private Shiroshoin at the northwest, flanked by separate kitchens to the northeast and a garden to the southwest (figs. 129, 220). A number of impressive gates survive as well. These include the East Main Gate (Higashi Ōtemon), the only entrance to the castle from the east, which was clearly built primarily for defense (fig. 222). By contrast, the cusped-gable gate, Karamon,

which opens into the Ninomaru compound inside the outer wall and moat, was intended chiefly for display and boasts splendid carvings and metalwork (fig. 219).

But these surviving structures are only a fraction of the original Ninomaru Compound. The kitchen and present palace complex were once surrounded by a maze of subsidiary spaces approximately equal in area to what now remains. Gone as well is the Palace of the Imperial Progress (Gyōkō Goten), built as Gomizunoo's temporary residence and located south of the pond. The stage for performances of Nō drama was lost as well (see fig. 246). And it must be kept in mind that the Ninomaru is only one of two compounds within the outer castle moat; the Main Compound, which once included the donjon and another huge building complex, is located within a second moat to the west of the Ninomaru structures. The palace of the retired shōgun, Tokugawa Hidetada, who was also present during Gomizunoo's visit, was built in this main compound at the same time as the Palace of Imperial Progress. The five-story donjon, which with its stone foundation rose forty meters in height, burned in 1750. The present structures in the Hommaru were built in 1847 and do not reflect the style of the originals.

ENTERTAINMENT: Architecture in the Sukiya Spirit

Prepare the tea so that in summer it is cooling and in winter warming, so that the charcoal brings the water to a boil and the tea is good to the taste—the secret is no more than this.

The great tea master Sen no Rikyū (1522–91) is reputed to have replied to that effect when asked about the essence of the tea ceremony. "But if you really think you can do it," Rikyū continued, "I will become your disciple." The account in which this exchange appears, the *Nambōroku*, was written after Rikyū's death, and it cannot be verified. It nevertheless gets at the heart of his attitude of approaching the ceremony naturally and without becoming obsessed by formality, remembering that it is a deceptive simplicity, one achieved only through long experience, dedication, and discipline.

The tea ceremony (*chanoyū*) was one of the most important upper-class entertainments in the late Muromachi, Momoyama, and Edo periods, and it continues to be practiced by millions today. It had its beginnings in the Nara period when tea was imported from China as part of Buddhist culture. Already by the Heian period the practice of tea drinking had been adopted from the monastery by the aristocracy, who became collectors of expensive Chinese tea utensils. The early Kamakura-period Zen masters Eisai and Dōgen were enthusiastic apologists for tea, and tea drinking thereafter became increasingly imbued with Zen philosophy. That set the stage for the development of the "Way of Tea" (*chadō* or *sadō*) in the Muromachi and Momoyama periods, when it became an artistic, philosophical, and religious system. Collecting and connoisseurship developed concurrently, and wealthy merchants, aristocrats, and warriors, including Hideyoshi himself, spent fortunes to obtain the finest tea bowls and build the most impressive teahouses. Tea taste, as we have already seen, subsequently exerted a powerful influence on the Shoin residence, resulting in the Sukiya style of architecture (see pp. 78–81).

But tea, of course, was not the only source of entertainment and artistic inspiration during and after the Muromachi period. Another was the Nō drama, which like tea, had risen out of humble traditions in the Nara and Heian periods to become a complex and esoteric art, again partly under the influence of Buddhist thought. This transformation was due primarily to the genius of two men, Kannami (flourished late fourteenth century) and his son Zeami (1363–1443), who as actors, playwrights, and theoreticians remade what had been a simple amalgam of playacting, song, and dance into a dramatic art of great richness and profundity. The Nō is performed by an elegantly robed and masked main actor who chants, mimes, and dances a text as poetic and religious as it is dramatic (fig. 243). He is accompanied by one or more subsidiary actors, a chorus, and a four-man orchestra. Like the tea ceremony, the Nō was performed throughout the Edo period and is today the oldest surviving professional theater in the world.

But not all the entertainments of the early modern period were as erudite as the Nō and tea ceremony. The Kabuki drama vied with the puppet theater (Bunraku) for the attention of the commoners of the Edo period, and the two theaters influenced each other to the artistic and dramaturgical improvement of both. Though Kabuki was to some extent also influenced by the Nō, it stresses bombast and display over suggestion and restraint, and it delights in swashbuckling heros and self-sacrificing heroines in byzantine plots full of bloodshed, coincidence, and amorous intrigue. Kabuki actors were the idols of the rising commoner class of the Edo centuries as well as one of the favorite subjects of woodblock artists and popular writers of the period.

No less central to the popular imagination were the courtesans of the pleasure quarters of the great cities. Those women held various ranks based on beauty and artistic accomplishment, and a *tayū* in the city of Edo required huge sums of money and extravagant gifts. Houses in the pleasure quarters, like the Sumiya in Kyōto's Shimabara, could be quite sumptuous and were appointed in a particularly innovative variety of the Sukiya style.

In this chapter we will discuss the architectural adjuncts of the pursuit of pleasure in the early modern period. We will begin with the rustic teahouse and the Sukiya philosophy of restraint, simplicity, and refinement that it embodies. Next we will describe the theater architecture of the Nō, then that of Kabuki, which developed out of the Nō stage but continued to grow in engineering sophistication as the Edo period progressed. The architecture of the pleasure quarter comes next, particularly that of the Sumiya house of assignation in Kyōto's Shimabara, which combines the taste and craftsmanship of the Sukiya style with the flair of the "floating world" of the courtesans. Concluding with a look at the courtly architecture of pleasure, we will show through excerpts from contemporary diaries how traditional court taste was blended with the Sukiya philosophy in gracious pastimes at the Katsura Villa and the Sentō Palace.

THE ARCHITECTURE OF THE TEA CEREMONY

The Maturation of Tea The tea ceremony began to reach maturity in the early Muromachi period when the shōgun and select members of his aesthetic circle met to admire choice Chinese tea wares and game at guessing the provenance of various types of tea. But its transformation into a true art form with spiritual dimensions is due to the influence of three men. The first was Murata Jukō (or Shukō; 1422–1502), a student of Zen and curator of Chinese art for shōgun Ashikaga Yoshimasa. He and Yoshimasa would meet at the latter's Silver Pavilion and drink tea in Chinese utensils in the Dōjinsai room of the Tōgūdō (see pp. 30–31).

Tea, and especially the collecting of utensils, was also popular among the wealthy merchants of Sakai City (near present-day Ōsaka). One of these merchants, Takeno Jōō (1502–55), took his interest in tea far beyond acquisition into the realm of philosophical appreciation and, under the influence of Jukō's thought, did much to develop the *wabi* ideal of refined rusticity that became one of the central elements of tea taste.

Wabi tea reached its mature expression under the third of these great tea masters, Sen no Rikyū. He continued the trend toward simplicity and naturalness, often incorporating folk objects into his tea ceremonies. Earlier warriors and aristocrats had made tea in one room, then served it in a large formal Shoin space, this practice being consequently referred to as Shoin Tea. The tiny tea area appended to the Mt. Fuji Room of the Manshuin Lesser Shoin, for example, may on occasion have been used in this way (see fig. 146). Rikyū, by contrast, often prepared and offered tea in the same room. He concurrently shrank the size of the tearoom from the four and half mats at the Dōjinsai (or even six mats or more in other teahouses) down to two mats in some of his designs. This type of extremely small and rustic teahouse is known as a *sōan*, literally "grass cottage." The larger tearooms continued to be used as well, though, for other tea ceremony styles. Despite the central role Rikyū played in the development of sōan tea, the design of only one of the extant sōan teahouses can be even tentatively ascribed to his hand. That is the Taian (figs. 223–25, 227).

The Taian Located in the town of Yamazaki, south of Kyōto, the Taian is part of the Myōkian temple. Though the provenance of the teahouse is unverified, it seems likely that Rikyū originally built it in his own house in Yamazaki and that it was later transferred to the Myōkian. He probably prepared tea for Hideyoshi there, which gave rise to the belief that Hi-

223. Taian Teahouse of Myōkian temple

deyoshi had ordered Rikyū to build it in 1582 while he was engaged in battle nearby with Akechi Mitsuhide (1526–82), Nobunaga's assassin.

The Taian consists of a two-mat tearoom (*chashitsu*) next to a one-mat anteroom bordered with wood-floor section (figs. 223). North of the anteroom is a one-mat space called the Katte, where preparations are made for the ceremony. The screens that normally separate the rooms have been removed in the figure for clarity. In the tearoom proper the west mat has a hearth (*ro*) cut into one corner, where the water for the tea is boiled. The other mat to the east is for the guests. This extremely small size is visually mitigated somewhat by the decorative alcove area and the anteroom can also be used when a larger number of guests are present.

The teahouse is entered via a low door called a *nu*

iriguchi (literally, "crawl door") only seventy-two centimeters tall. The design forces the participants to bend over to enter, which commensurately increases the apparent size of the tearoom inside and also reminds them of the attitude of humility appropriate to *wabi* tea.

Interior Decor   The design of the Taian sōan has been worked out in great detail. Even the ceiling is of a complex construction. The sections directly in front of the decorative alcove and over the server's mat are flat and consist of thin shingles reinforced beneath by light-colored bamboo. But the part above the guests' mat is inclined, and this again helps mitigate the feeling of constriction such a small space might otherwise generate. The decorative alcove is a so-called *murodoko*, as its rear posts have been plastered over. That is true also of the post in the

corner behind the hearth. The technique is yet another way of lending a more expansive feeling to the space and of making the design more arresting.

Every aspect of the Taian reflects rusticity and yet refinement, revealing a calculated use of natural materials for their inherent decorative qualities. The lattices of the shōji windows, for example, are made not of wood but of split bamboo. The delicate paper is protected on the exterior (fig. 224) either by vertical bamboo grills or by the wattle of the wall interior, left exposed for its rustic visual effect. Windows of the latter type are called *shitajimado*. The positions of the windows have been carefully calculated, as has the height of the transom of the decorative alcove and the alcove's ceiling. The baseboard of the decorative alcove was chosen for its three knots, which again enhances the rusticity of the space.

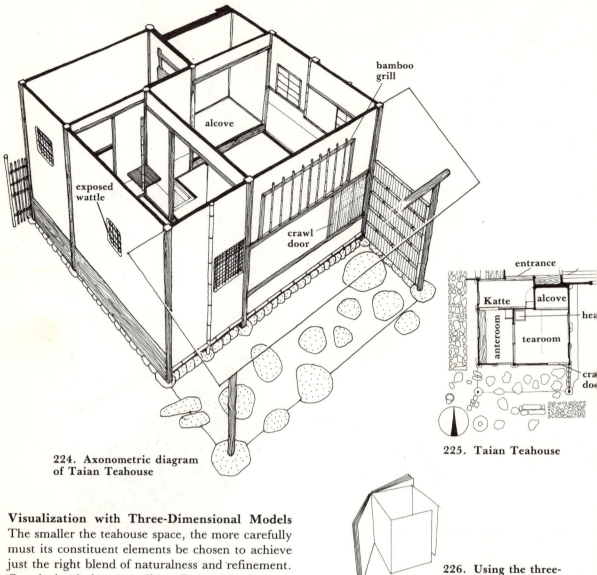

224. Axonometric diagram of Taian Teahouse

225. Taian Teahouse

226. Using the three-dimensional model

Visualization with Three-Dimensional Models

The smaller the teahouse space, the more carefully must its constituent elements be chosen to achieve just the right blend of naturalness and refinement. One device designers traditionally used for this purpose was a three-dimensional paper model called an *okoshiezu*. It was simple to make, and minute alterations in the placement of windows, doors, and interior partitions could be tested for potential effect. It could also be folded up and easily carried to the building site. In earlier religious and residential structures, the most critical aspect of the design had been the floor plan. A practiced builder could visualize in his own mind the basic elevation, as there were few variables in any one style. But as we have seen, in the teahouse every element of the design from the floor plan to the walls, ceiling, and roof could be freely manipulated, and a change in one element affected all the others. The three-dimensional paper model was a concrete way of visualizing such structures.

Three-dimensional models (*okoshiezu*) are assembled by gluing each wall to the floor section. It is impossible to provide a floor here, but folding the following pages as in figure 226 will give an idea of the effect. The gray section in figures 224–25 show the wall surfaces in question. Pages 110 and 115 are the south and east exterior walls; 109 is the anteroom side of the wall with sliding screens that divides the anteroom from the tearoom proper to the east; 112 is the tearoom side of that same wall; 111 and 114 are the inner sides of the exterior walls at the south and east; and 11 is the back wall with the decorative alcove. The alcove, of course, must be imagined as recessed. An even more realistic effect can be obtained by copying the floor in the plan and setting the walls on it, after cutting out the low entrance door.

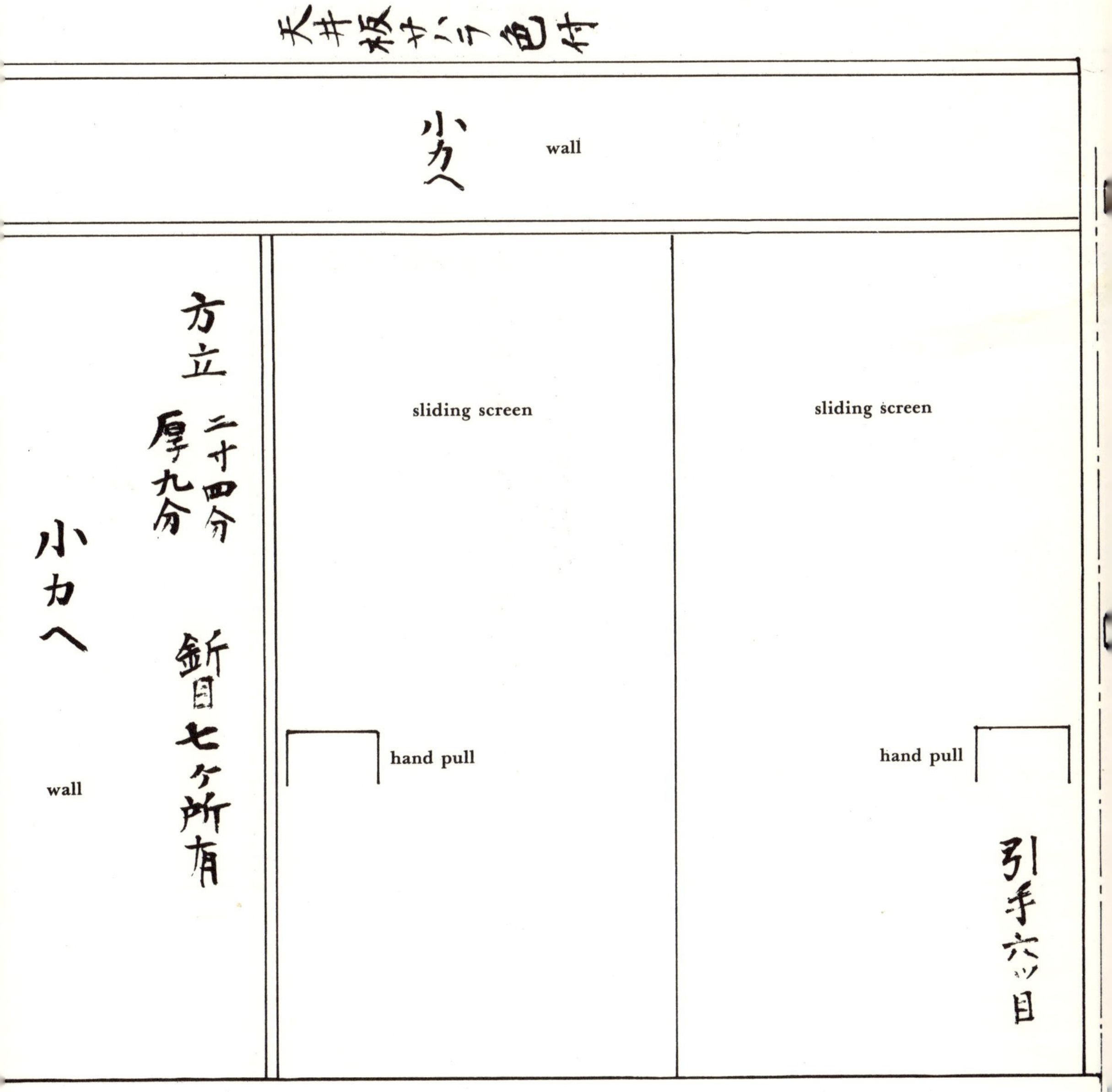

天井板サイフ色付

少ヘ　wall

方立　二寸四分
厚九分　釿目七ケ所有

小カヘ
wall

sliding screen

sliding screen

hand pull

hand pull

引手六ツ目

227. Three-dimensional model of
the tearoom of Taian Teahouse

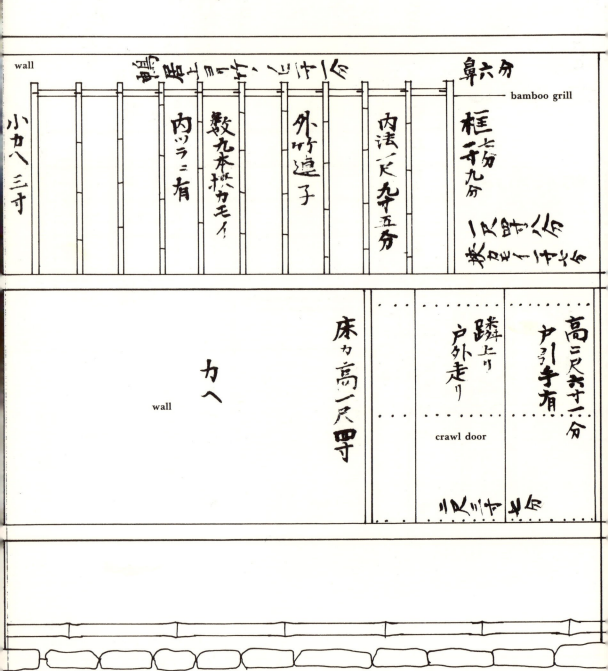

力へ

wall

wall

鼻六分

bamboo grill

框七分九分

内法一尺九寸五分

外竹連子

数九本扱カモイ

内ツラニ有

小力へ三寸

床ヵ高一尺四

力へ

wall

高二尺六寸一分

戸引手有

蹴上リ
戸外走リ

crawl door

110

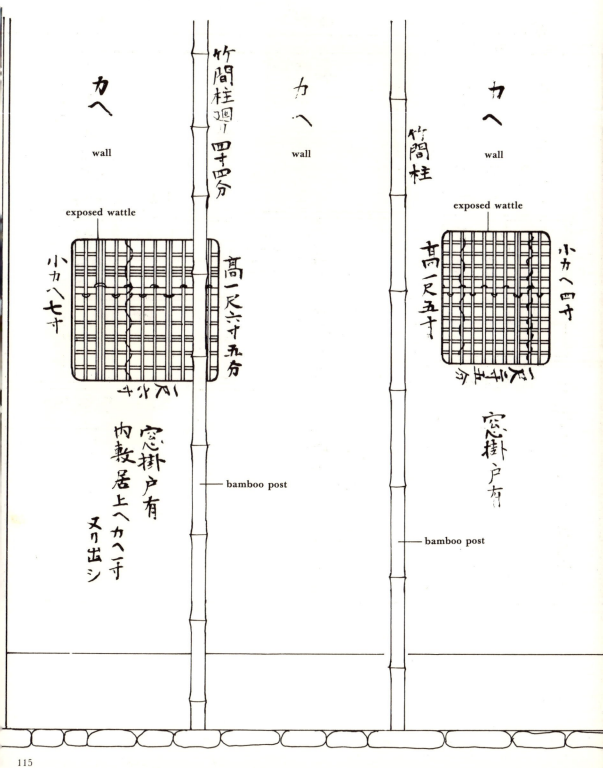

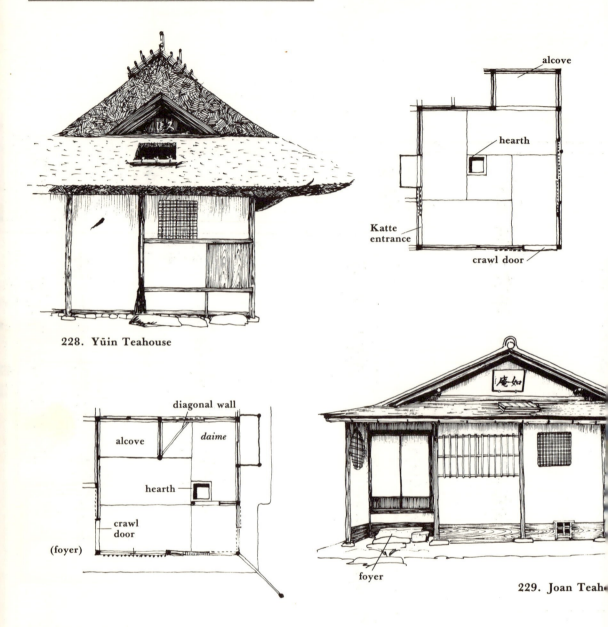

228. Yūin Teahouse

229. Joan Teah

Orchestration of Visual Effects Sōan teahouses are by definition small, between two and four and a half mats in size. Within this confined space, though, an unlimited number of visual effects can be attained. Window placement, for example, is calculated not only for ventilation and visual effect on the walls, but also to create just the right play of light and shade when the tea ceremony is performed. Some teahouses have windows that can be propped open at various angles to vary the quality of seasonal light that falls on the interior. The Yūin Teahouse (Kyōto City; fig. 228) and the Joan Teahouse (Inuyama City; fig. 229) also have

hatches on their eaves that can be opened to le light for the same purpose.

The Yūin Teahouse, four and a half mats in s has a particularly rustic quality thanks to its misc thus roof. The bamboo-handled broom hanging f the middle post next to the wattle *shitajimado* wine adds to that effect.

Connected to the Yūin is a second teahouse ca the Konnichian that contains only a three-quar length *daime* mat for the server and one full-len mat for guests (fig. 231, floor plan). Instead decorative alcove there is a wooden section set i the floor at tatami level and flanked by a thin

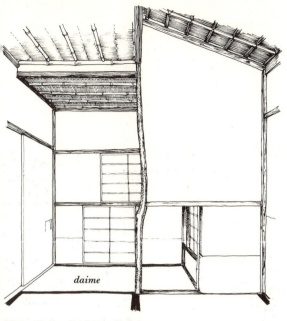

230. Teigyokuken, Shinjuan subtemple, Daitokuji

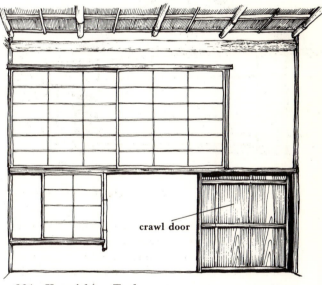

231. Konnichian Teahouse

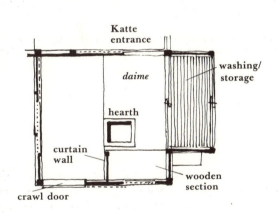

tain wall (*sodekabe*) supported by a center post. Such a design is perfect for such a small space, for it manages to suggest an alcove space while the curtain wall is thin enough to avoid altering the lines of the windows and low entry door behind. The elevation drawing in figure 231 shows this interior design with the curtain wall removed.

The Joan Teahouse contains a number of interesting touches. It is flanked on two sides by a packed-earth veranda protected by overhanging eaves. One enters the teahouse via a low door at the right of a foyer area that includes a high, flat stone on which to leave footwear before entering (fig. 229, elevation).

The sliding screens at the back of the foyer lead to the *mizuya*, a place for preparing the utensils for the tea ceremony, and to the Shoin proper. Inside the teahouse, the decorative alcove is flanked by a unique diagonally angled wall.

The Teigyokuken of the Daitokuji subtemple of Shinjuan (Kyōto City) is well known for the tiny inner garden court it has between the low entry door and the tearoom proper (fig. 230, floor plan). The interior, two mats plus a three-quarter-length daime mat, boasts a very intricate ceiling design as well as an artistically gnarled center post (*nakabashira*) made of Japanese red pine (fig. 230, elevation).

THE TEA GARDEN

232. Fushin'an Teahouse [1]

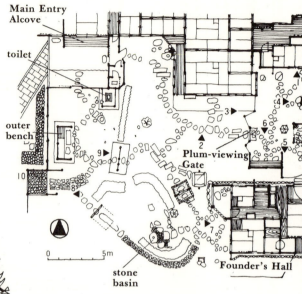

234. Garden of Zangetsutei and Fushin'an Teahouse
(bracketed numbers in other captions refer to this plan

233. Zangetsutei Teahouse [2]

A Space to Compose the Mind for Tea The tea-house is an isolated, spiritual space where the participants in the ceremony can cleanse their minds of mundane concerns. The transition from the world outside to the world of tea is aided by the tea garden, called a *roji*, literally "dewy ground," where guests await their host and then go with him or her to the teahouse itself. It is a world as carefully arranged as the teahouse and has its own conventions. But like teahouses, each garden is a unique experience. The trees that shield the teahouse from direct view, and likewise the steppingstones that lead along the paths, are chosen and arranged to give the impression of unassuming elegance. To generalize, the garden is divided by an inner gate (*chūmon*) or a low gate (*nakakuguri*) into two parts, a waiting area and the inner garden of the teahouse. Bending over to pass through this low gate makes tangible the transition into the world of tea. Inside is a bench where guests

pause before entering the teahouse, a low stone basin with water for cleansing the hands and mouth, and a stone lantern for lighting the path to the teahouse during evening gatherings.

A Tea Garden of the Omote Senke School After the retirement of Sen no Rikyū's grandson Sōtan (1578–1658), the family traditions were divided into three schools, each headed by one of Sōtan's sons. These were the Ura Senke, which now owns the Yūin and Konnichian Teahouses (figs. 228, 231), the Mushanokōji Senke, and the Omote Senke. The Zangetsutei and Fushin'an (Kyōto City) pictured above (figs. 232–33) belong to the Omote Senke branch, and their garden is a fine example of the genre (fig. 234; illustrations on this page are correlated by number to this plan).

The Zangetsutei is a Shoin-type building with large sitting-room–style tearooms, and the Fushin'an, connected to the east side of the Zangetsutei by a

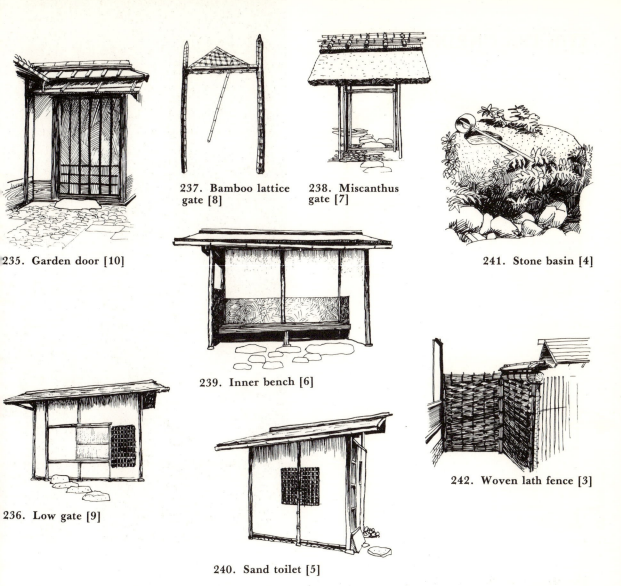

235. Garden door [10]

237. Bamboo lattice gate [8]

238. Miscanthus gate [7]

241. Stone basin [4]

239. Inner bench [6]

236. Low gate [9]

242. Woven lath fence [3]

240. Sand toilet [5]

wood-floored corridor, is a sōan teahouse three mats plus a daime mat in size. South of that complex is the Founder's Hall (Sodō; fig. 234).

Circulation into and through the garden is more complex than the general example just described because three structures are involved. Passage is orchestrated by means of gates, hedges, and stepping-stone pathways. One enters at the west via the "garden gate" (rojiguchi; fig. 235). Behind is a bench and toilet (fig. 234). Garden access to the Zangetsutei itself is obtained through the "low gate," fit with a small door in the middle flanked by a wattled window (fig. 236). One can also reach the Founder's Hall by this gate, or by the bamboo lattice gate (agesudo) to the south, the triangular lattice of which is propped open when guests are expected (fig. 237). A miscanthus gate (kayamon; fig. 238) stands in front of the entrance to the Founder's Hall.

The Plum-viewing Gate, flanked by a fence of woven laths (fig. 242), leads to the Fushin'an. Inside is a low basin (tsukubai) carved out of a boulder (fig. 241), an inner bench (fig. 239), and a "sand toilet" (sunazetchin; fig. 240), spread with river sand and naturalistic stones. Such toilets today serve only a decorative function. Before entering the low door of the Fushin'an itself, samurai guests would leave their swords on the rack hung from the eaves, for weapons had no place in the world of tea (fig. 232, left side).

Teahouse and garden complexes such as this were built on the grounds of the mansions of wealthy tea enthusiasts in Kyōto and the merchant city of Sakai. The Omote Senke example shows that the attention of the designers was focused as much on the garden setting for the teahouses as on the buildings themselves.

STAGING THE NŌ DRAMA

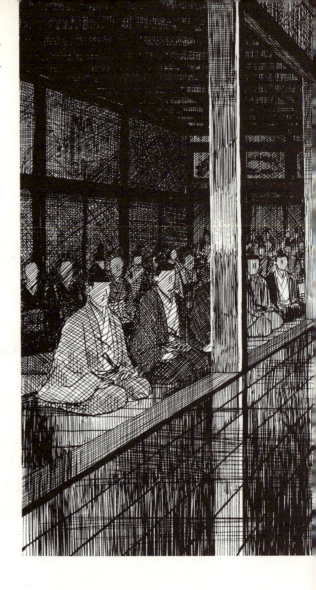

The History of Nō Kannami and his son Zeami transformed the Nō into the sophisticated form of dramatic art it is today from a number of simpler art forms. Two of these were *sarugaku* (literally, "monkey music"), which had grown out of Chinese-inspired variety shows in the eighth century and then become more religious in character, and *dengaku* ("field music"), derived from early agricultural religious rituals. By the fourteenth century these two forms had assumed a greater dramatic element and were very similar in nature. They were also immensely popular with all levels of the population. Kannami took these raw dramatic materials, added a *kusemai* (a popular rhythmic dance section), and evoked rich philosophical undertones.

In 1374 Kannami and his eleven-year-old son had become well enough known to perform for shōgun Ashikaga Yoshimitsu, builder of the Golden Pavilion (see p. 30). The shōgun was so impressed he gave them his personal support. Zeami later wrote down

and interpreted his father's dicta on the art in a book known as *Writings on the Transmission of the Flower* (*Kadensho*, 1400–1402, with later additions), the "flower" being a metaphor for the essence of Nō artistry. Zeami continued to write on the Nō for the rest of his life, building up a large body of theory that gave the art legitimacy in the eyes of educated audiences and still serves as the basic foundation of Nō study. His thought stresses mimesis tempered by stylization and grace, and it prizes the evocation of rich suggestion and mystery. Of the about 250 Nō plays currently performed, Zeami is credited with at least 25 and possibly twice that number. By the Momoyama period, the Nō drama was a highly respected art form, and warrior aristocrats in particular built Nō stages in their mansions for private viewing.

Early Nō Stages According to such contemporary sources as painted screens depicting scenes in the Heian Capital and its environs, late Muromachi Nō stages were open-air affairs that were roofed but not

243. Nō Stage in Audience Hall, Nishi Honganji Shoin

walled. This is also true for the North Nō Stage at the Shoin of Nishi Honganji (see fig. 245), which bears the date 1581 and is the oldest Nō stage extant. The Shoin also has an outside stage at the south, but of later date. Another such stage can be seen in the *Screen of the Jurakudai Castle and Palace*, just beneath the donjon (see fig. 192).

The Interior Nō Stages at Nishi Honganji By the Momoyama period, the Nō was also being performed on indoor stages. The Nishi Honganji temple has two such stages, one each in the Audience Hall (Taimenjo; fig. 243) and in the Shiroshoin.

The Audience Hall is a huge space in the most elegant Shoin style, measuring nine by nine bays with an added raised *jōdan* of nine bays by two and a half. On the back wall are set, from left to right, decorative doors, a huge decorative alcove, and, on a dais raised one step further (a *jōjōdan*), staggered shelves, behind the cusped window at the right in figure 243. A built-in desk is also on the jōjōdan at right angles

to the shelves, projecting into an inside corridor. The space is truly magnificent, with beautifully carved birds in the transoms and polychrome scenes from Chinese history on the walls. The room is believed to have been built in 1618 and moved to its present location in 1633, when the interior assumed its present appearance.

Normally the floor of the great space was completely covered with tatami mats, but when a Nō play was to be staged the central mats were removed, revealing a polished wood-planked floor beneath. At the south end of the room, opposite the jōdan, a diagonal entrance causeway, which could be fitted with railings, led back to the dressing room (*gakuya*; literally, "music room") where the actors prepared for the performance. In the dim illumination of the interior, the actors in their gold-embroidered robes must have presented a scene of ghostly mystery.

121

THE STRUCTURE OF
THE NŌ STAGE

244. Nō Stage of Itsukushima Shrine

Traditional Stage Design The main section of a Nō stage is traditionally a square, three by three bays in size. Behind is a "rear stage" (*atoza*) of one and a half bays for the orchestra and on the right side (stage left) is a half bay section for the chorus (figs. 244–46). Leading to the stage diagonally from the left is a covered causeway for entrances and exits. It is one and a half bays wide and from six to eleven bays long, with railings on both front and back. At the far end of the causeway is a curtain that covers the entrance to the "mirror room" (*kagami no ma*) where the actor establishes his mental and physical readiness before stepping into public view. Behind the mirror room is the dressing room.

The Nō drama is highly symbolic and few stage properties are used. The back wall, however, is tradi-

tionally painted with an aged pine, said to be a reminder of when a predecessor of the Nō was performed at shrines before a sacred tree.

Modern Nō stages are still constructed in the same fashion as that described above, save that the covered stage and causeway are enclosed in a much larger auditorium that houses the seated audience. But at premodern outdoor Nō stages such as those at the Nishi Honganji Shoin, the audience viewed the play from separate structures surrounding a central court covered with fine white gravel, into which the stage projected (figs. 245–46). Modern interior stages are surrounded by a periphery of fine gravel as a holdover from this tradition.

One particularly remarkable Nō stage is found at Itsukushima Shrine near Hiroshima (fig. 244). The

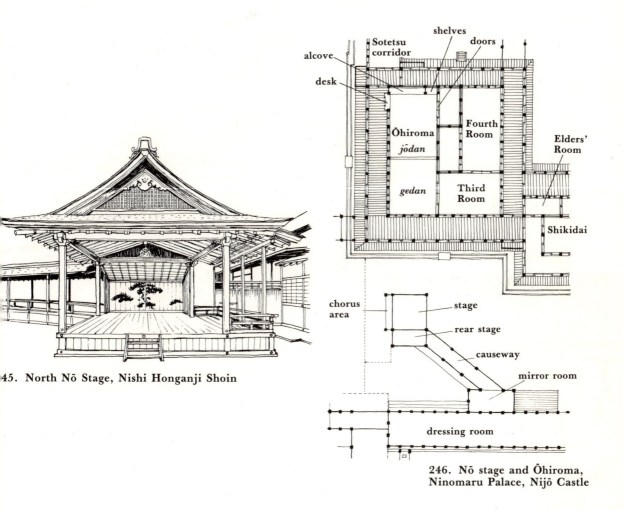

245. North Nō Stage, Nishi Honganji Shoin

Labels in plan (fig. 246, top): alcove, desk, Sotetsu corridor, shelves, doors, Ōhiroma, jōdan, gedan, Fourth Room, Third Room, Elders' Room, Shikidai

Labels in plan (fig. 246, bottom): chorus area, stage, rear stage, causeway, mirror room, dressing room

246. Nō stage and Ōhiroma,
Ninomaru Palace, Nijō Castle

tage projects from the shore and is surrounded by
vater at high tide, to brilliant and mystical effect.
The Nō Stage at the Ninomaru Palace of Nijō Cas-
le   When Iemitsu began his building project at Nijō
Castle in 1624 in preparation for the visit Emperor
Tomizunoo, he included a Nō stage directly south
f the Ōhiroma, the central building of the main
alace complex (see pp. 72–73). When the emperor
rrived in the ninth month of 1626, he watched a pro-
ram of Nō while seated in the Ōhiroma with Iemi-
u and Iemitsu's father, the retired shōgun Toku-
awa Hidetada (1579–1632).

Though the stage does not survive, an extant plan
hows one of the conventional dimensions set forth
arlier, together with a two-by-four-bay mirror room
nd a three-by-seventeen-bay dressing room (fig.

246). Modern Nō stages also have a low door (kirido)
at the right side of the rear stage for stage hands to
enter and exit unobtrusively during a performance
to straighten the robes of the main actor or help with
an onstage costume change. But there appears to be
no such door in this sketch.

Records show that the program of Nō shown to
the emperor began at ten o'clock in the morning with
the traditional Okina and Sambasō pieces, followed by
nine more plays, including the god play Naniwa and
the warrior play Tamura, then ending at about six
o'clock in the evening with a performance of Shōjō,
a standard finale piece, danced by the head of the
Kanze school of actors, the school descended from
Kannami and Zeami.

123

THE ARCHITECTURE OF THE KABUKI THEATER

The Birth of Kabuki By the mid eighteenth century, the Kabuki drama was the most popular form of entertainment among the commoner class, and thousands flocked to the huge Kabuki theaters in the great cities. This was a remarkable rise for an art form that had had its beginnings in bawdy skits and suggestive dances performed on the banks of Kyōto's Kamogawa river. Kabuki is traditionally said to have been begun in about 1600 by Okuni, an itinerant female performer who may have once been a priestess at Izumo Shrine. To curb immorality the government soon banned women from Kabuki, but the theater remained closely tied to the pleasure quarters. As opposed to the Nō drama, which by this time had a written repertoire of plays with high literary value, Kabuki for most of its early existence was improvised by its players on the basis of a general plot line laid out beforehand. Even after scripts came to be written down, the final emphasis was on the actors, some of whom had immense personal followings. By contrast, the puppet theater (Bunraku), also very popular in the seventeenth and early eighteenth centuries, required high-quality scripts since all the parts had to be narrated by a single chanter. Under the influence of puppet plays the quality of Kabuki plot and dialogue gradually improved, with the result that Bunraku found it increasingly difficult to compete for popularity.

Kabuki and the Shogunate Though considered a plebeian art by the upper classes, Kabuki nevertheless appealed to many members of the warrior stratum, who often risked official censure to attend the plays. In 1714 one such escapade caused a great scandal and had serious repercussions for the Kabuki theater. On the twelfth day of the first month, Lady Ejima (1681–1714), who was in the service of the shōgun's mother, made a visit to the Yamamura Theater in Edo's Kobikichō after having made a pilgrimage to Zōjōji, a temple closely tied to the Tokugawa. At the theater she was joined by her lover, Ikushima Shingorō (1671–1743), an immensely popular actor of romantic roles. The meeting was discovered by the shogunate, which declared that the lady had compromised the sanctity of the pilgrimage and had acted in a manner unbecoming to her station. She was taken into custody, Shingorō was banished to a distant island, and the theater was permanently closed, leaving Edo with only three others, the Nakamura, Ichimura, and Morita.

The shogunate had always pursued an ambivalent policy toward Kabuki and the pleasure quarters. On the one hand, it viewed them as offensive to Confu-

cian morality, but on the other recognized them as necessary evils that kept the public mollified and attracted provincial commerce. Furthermore, they could be confined to certain outlying sections of the city and effectively policed. But the Ejima-Ikushima affair was impossible for the Tokugawa regime to tolerate, and it imposed strict countermeasures. The managers of the three surviving theaters and the owners of the surrounding teahouses were summoned and presented with such directives as "in recent years two and three tiers of boxes have been used in theaters, but you will confine yourselves to one, as in the past," and "you will make no private passageways from the seats to backstage or to the theater manager's residence," and "bamboo blinds will not be permitted on boxes." These regulations show, for one thing, that already in the early eighteenth century the great theaters were being built on quite a majestic scale.

Building the Great Theater Ceilings Another 1714 regulation is even more illuminating regarding theater construction: "In recent years roofs on theaters have allowed performances to be held even on rainy days. You will hereafter limit yourselves to lightly constructed roofs, as in former times." Rec

247. Composite re-creation of a late Edo-period Kabuki theater

ords show that the ceiling beams of one Edo-period Kabuki theater were more than eighteen meters in length and that they were set at a height of over seven meters—a grand space by the standards of the day.

Evidence from contemporary woodblock prints shows how theater architects gradually mastered the art of spanning these large interiors. A print from 1739 depicting the Ichimura Theater indicates that at that time ceiling beams still had to be supported in the middle by vertical posts rising from the audience boxes. This was clearly an unsatisfactory solution, for it obstructed the view of the stage for some spectators.

These center pillars do not appear in a Torii Kiyotada print of 1743 showing the Nakamura Theater, but the beams are still supported by intermediate posts set along the front of the second-floor tier of audience boxes at both sides of the hall. They are further reinforced by diagonal trusses projecting from the side wall up to the intermediate posts and thence to the ceiling beams. The beams are still supported by intermediate posts at the front of the second- and third-floor tiers of boxes in an Utagawa Toyohisa print of 1806.

But a print of about 1830 by Utagawa Toyokuni of the Nakamura Theater shows that by this time the intermediate posts have disappeared in front of the side tiers of boxes. The same is true for a print by Toyokuni of the 1850s. All three Kabuki theaters were destroyed in the great Ansei-era fire of 1855, and a further improvement in ceiling design was developed for the rebuilding by Hasegawa Kambei (d. 1861), twelfth-generation head of a family of Kabuki carpenters bearing that name. His invention, ''tortoise-shell beaming'' (*kikkōbari*), called for parallel ceiling beams considerably shorter than the width of the hall to be assembled into a huge rectangular frame whose corners rested on four horizontal beams set diagonally into the corners of the hall. The design, first used at the Ichimura Theater, allowed large spaces to be spanned much more efficiently.

In figure 247 an actor addresses the audience while standing on a causeway (*hanamichi*) used for dramatic entrances and exits. Vendors of tea and food walk along narrow raised walkways purveying their goods to the audience. Kabuki performances could last an entire day, and spectators might eat and chat with each other, listening with half an ear for particularly affecting scenes.

IMPROVEMENTS IN KABUKI THEATER DESIGN

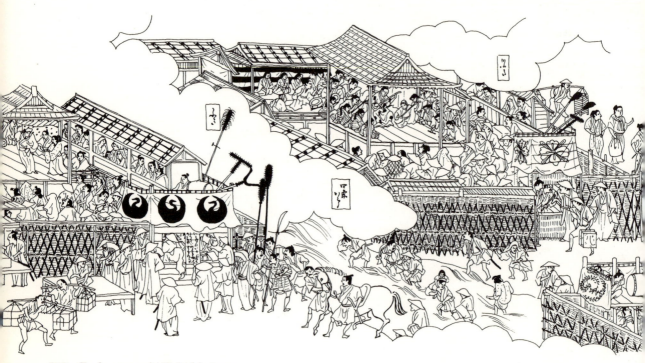

248. Early open-air Kabuki stages

The Early Kabuki Theaters   The genre of paintings entitled "scenes in and around the capital" comes to our aid once again in describing the earliest Kabuki theaters. One such screen, the former Funaki version now in the collection of the National Diet Library, shows the early open-air stages that were built on both banks of the Kamogawa river, near Shijō Avenue (fig. 248) in Kyōto, when Kabuki was still performed by women. The Kabuki stage is much like that used in the Nō theater, save that the stage roof is of wood shingle and the seats are of much simpler construction. The entrance to the theater at the left is beneath the banners emblazoned with a crane crest. Musicians are located at the back of both stages, again as in the Nō, and the three-stringed *shamisen*, newly arrived from the Ryūkyū Islands and not used in the Nō orchestra, is being played as well. Another such screen, the Yamaoka version, shows women's Kabuki at Kitano Shrine. Since Okuni

herself, the supposed founder of Kabuki, is said to have performed there in 1603, it may be she who is depicted.

The Nakamura Theater   The appearance of the Nakamura Theater in Sakaichō, an old theater quarter in Edo, has been reconstructed through the use of woodblock prints such as those by Okumura Masanobu (1686–1764) in 1740 and Torii Kiyotada in 1743 (fig. 249). By that time the entire audience section was roofed. The facade had entrances at both sides and a tower atop the middle. Along the facade were hung advertisements introducing the current plays and actors.

The stages of theaters of the time still contained the old pitched-roof center section over the stage, like that of the Nō stage. In the front was a smaller stage area (*tsukebutai*) that projected into the audience, and the causeway ran into the main stage from a point on the side wall near the theater entrance. Placards

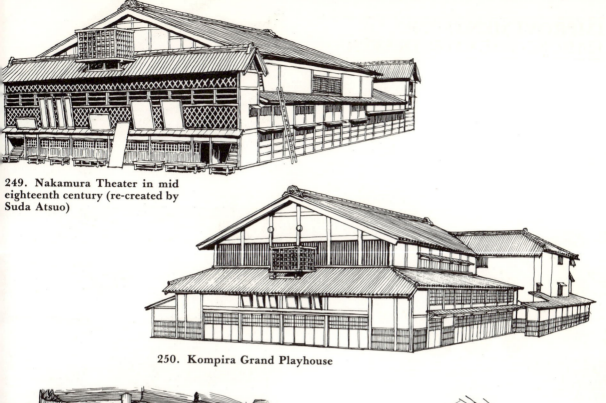

249. Nakamura Theater in mid eighteenth century (re-created by Suda Atsuo)

250. Kompira Grand Playhouse

251. Revolving stage

252. Trap-lift

bearing the name of the play currently being performed and the act and scene number were hung on the front posts of the stage roof. But the posts hindered the actors on stage and the view from the audience, and illustrations from the early nineteenth century no longer show the roof and posts. This, plus the design of the ceiling beams discussed earlier, suggests that by the late eighteenth and early nineteenth centuries the Kabuki theater had reached its mature configuration. Many pictures continue to show various buildings on stage, of course, but these are stage properties and are not built-in.

The Sole Surviving Edo-period Kabuki Theater
The Kompira Great Playhouse (Kompira Ōshibai) is the only extant example of Edo-period Kabuki architecture. Built in 1835 in Kotohira, Kagawa Prefecture (see fig. 174), it was moved to the less-crowded outskirts of the city in 1975 and restored at that time (fig. 250). It is an exceptionally large Kabuki theater,

measuring nearly twenty-four meters in width, just under thirty-seven meters in depth, and about eleven meters in height.

The Kompira Great Playhouse contains three stage devices common to the Edo period. One is a revolving stage (*mawaributai*) for quick scene changes (fig. 251). With a diameter of 7.72 meters, it turns on a central post sunk into the ground beneath the stage floor. The post is fit with a metal axle that projects into the large horizontal beam that supports the floorboards of the revolving stage. Within the revolving stage is a trap-lift (*seridashi*; fig. 252). Measuring about one by two meters, it is used for a variety of special effects or changes of scene. Another smaller trap-lift about sixty by seventy-five centimeters in size is located on the causeway. Used mainly for lifting actors to floor level, it is called a *suppon*. During performances stage hands labor for hours beneath the floorboards raising and lowering these devices.

127

THE ARCHITECTURE OF THE PLEASURE QUARTERS

The World of the Courtesan   One of the many names for the pleasure quarters was *keiseimachi*, denoting "courtesan district" but literally meaning "district of destroyers of cities." The allusion is to a phrase in the *Han shu*, the history of the Former Han Dynasty in China (202 B.C.–A.D. 8) that reads, "The hue and fragrance of a beautiful woman destroys cities and countries." The name suggests at once the condemnation and the fascination such women and the districts they inhabited have excited over the centuries.

Other common names for such areas include "the quarter" (*kuruwa*), "pleasure enclosure" (*yūkaku*), "pleasure quarter" (*yūri*), "blossom and willow district" (*karyūkai*), and simply "place of evil" (*akusho*). The women of the quarter lived in residences called *okiya*, meaning "storehouse," and went out to entertain customers at houses of assignation (*ageya*). The latter were decorated with exquisite decor called "the style of the place of evil," which, despite the name, was vastly and quite justly admired. The women of the finer houses of assignation were not only beautiful but superbly accomplished in the arts of poetry and music, and the best of them acquired great reputations among men of taste and learning. One such courtesan, Yoshino, became the paramour of Haiya Jōeki (1610–91), an admired essayist and disciple of the brilliant calligrapher and potter Hon'ami Kōetsu (1558–1637). For Jōeki and other men of taste, a visit to the pleasure quarter meant cultivated conversation in talented company as much as the more common bibulous revelry and sensual gratification.

Though the pleasure quarter was often frequented by men of the military class, its style reflected not their tastes and outlook but those of the townsmen (*chōnin*), who, despite their ignominious position at the bottom of the official Confucian hierarchy, continued to grow in wealth and influence as the Edo period progressed. Both Jōeki and Kōetsu, for example, were members of the wealthy upper reaches of the townsman class.

The pleasure quarters of Edo-period Kyōto was initially Rokujō-Misujimachi, located in the south central part of the city, about one kilometer north

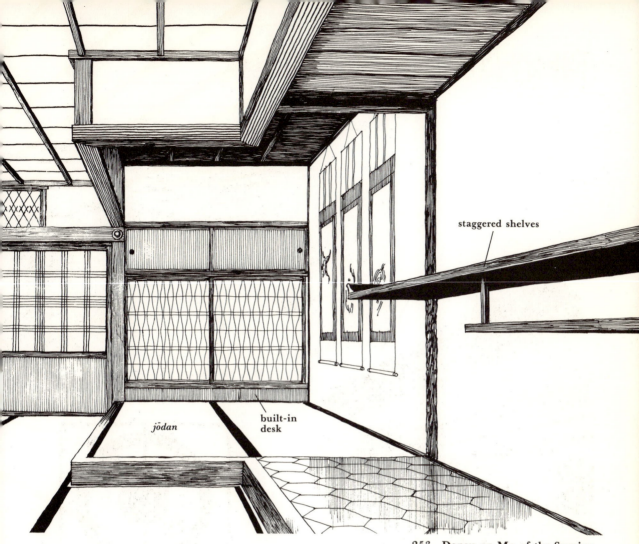

jōdan

built-in desk

staggered shelves

253. Donsu no Ma of the Sumiya

of the present Kyōto Station. The shogunate eventually became alarmed at Rokujō-Misujimachi's growing popularity and ordered it moved to a more remote area just west of Nishi Honganji temple, where it became known as Shimabara.

Yoshiwara, the Edo quarter, was first situated at Nihombashi Fukiyachō, northeast of the present Tōkyō Station. As suggested by the name Yoshiwara, ''Reed Field,'' it was at first an underdeveloped area specially chosen by the shogunate for its distance from the center of the city. After the devastating Meireki-era fire of 1657, it was moved north of the Asakusa area of Edo and renamed New Yoshiwara (Shin Yoshiwara).

The Sumiya—Last of the Premodern Pleasure Houses   Despite the efforts of the shogunate to limit the activities of the pleasure quarters, they grew and prospered. Elegant houses of assignation proliferated in such pleasure quarters as Shimabara and Yoshiwara, but today only one remains in more or less complete form, the Sumiya in Kyōto. The oldest section of the house dates to 1640, just after the quarter

was ordered moved from Rokujō-Misujimachi to Shimabara. Most of the Sumiya was built somewhat later, in the 1670s, and the entrance and south section were added in 1787.

The Sumiya is finished in a rich and unusually imaginative version of the Sukiya style. The Ajiro no Ma on the first floor has a ceiling of woven wooden strips (*ajirogumi*), an expensive design. The room also includes a built-in desk and cusped window. The wooden lattices of the *shōji* screens are applied in artistically patterned groups rather than in the more usual regular grid.

On the second floor, the Donsu no Ma has a large, stylized decorative alcove on a two-mat raised *jōdan* (fig. 253). To the left is a built-in desk and shōji with a wave lattice pattern. At the right of the jōdan are staggered shelves with a raised floor beneath, incised in a tortoise-shell pattern (figs. 253, 257).

The second floor also contains the Aoyagi no Ma, the walls and built-in fixtures of which are inlaid with mother-of-pearl.

DESIGN IN THE PLEASURE QUARTERS

254. Shimabara Pleasure Quarter

255. Facade of the Sumiya

256. Screen design
in the Wachigaiya

The Atmosphere of Shimabara and the Sumiya
The pleasure quarter of Shimabara was surrounded
by a moat and wall with a great gate at the east, making it look from the outside as much like a fortress
as an entertainment area. The quarter was divided
by one road going east and west and three north and
south, initially arranged in such a way as to form six
blocks. Each block had its own name, and that which
contained the Sumiya was known as Ageyamachi.
A collection entitled *Pictures of Famous Places in the
Capital* (*Miyako meisho zue*) provides a good idea of
Shimabara's atmosphere (fig. 254). Particularly poig-
nant is the silhouette of the customer listening to a
courtesan plying a shamisen in the second floor of
the house to the right.

The denizens of this "floating world" prized men
and women with *iki* (chic) and *tsū* (savior-faire) who
lived for the moment but who knew the pathos of

worldly evanescence. And the pleasure quarter offered an escape from the regimentation and hierarchy outside. The impoverished samurai might defer
to the moneyed merchant within its walls, whereas
he was likely to despise him beyond its gate.
The Sumiya and the Wachigaiya Passing through
the front gate of the Sumiya, one first enters a pleasant courtyard. Directly ahead is the entrance to the
kitchens, and the formal entry alcove is to the right.
From the street, one can see the outside of three
rooms on the second floor, the Ōgi no Ma, Suiren
no Ma, and Donsu no Ma (fig. 255). The shōji-
screened outer walls of both the first and second floor
are recessed half a bay and fronted by wooden grills,
which gives visual unity to the facade. In the rear
of the Sumiya is a gracious garden and a teahouse.

Another house in the quarter, the Wachigaiya, is
noted together with the Sumiya in the *Detailed Map*

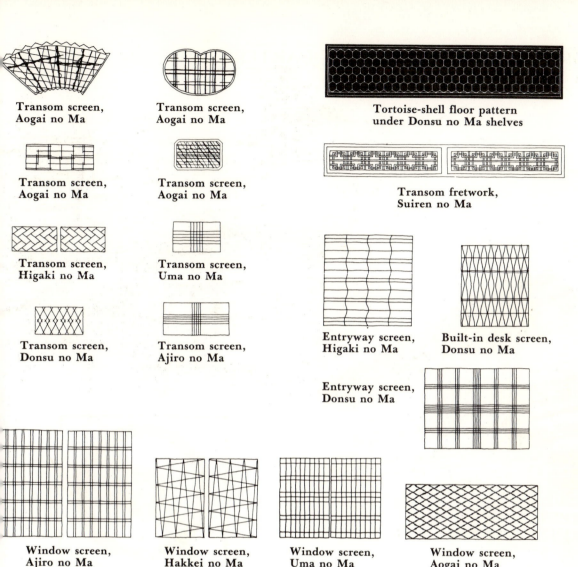

Transom screen,
Aogai no Ma

Transom screen,
Aogai no Ma

Tortoise-shell floor pattern
under Donsu no Ma shelves

Transom screen,
Aogai no Ma

Transom screen,
Aogai no Ma

Transom fretwork,
Suiren no Ma

Transom screen,
Higaki no Ma

Transom screen,
Uma no Ma

Transom screen,
Donsu no Ma

Transom screen,
Ajiro no Ma

Entryway screen,
Higaki no Ma

Built-in desk screen,
Donsu no Ma

Entryway screen,
Donsu no Ma

Window screen,
Ajiro no Ma

Window screen,
Hakkei no Ma

Window screen,
Uma no Ma

Window screen,
Aogai no Ma

257. Design in the Sumiya

Shimabara (*Shimabara saiken zu*), dated 1716. It is located in Nakanomachi, another of Shimabara's six blocks. Unlike the Sumiya, which survives in more or less its original form, the Wachigaiya was heavily remodeled in succeeding generations. But the bold, stylized umbrella design on its fusuma gives evidence of the elegance it once possessed (fig. 256). The imaginatively painted character "Sumi" on the lamp in front of the Sumiya shows the same spirited taste (fig. 255).

Shōji Screen Designs in the Sumiya The decor of each of the rooms of the Sumiya is elegant and unique. The tracerylike curved lattices on the shōji in the Higaki no Ma and Donsu no Ma are especially interesting in construction—they were not bent into position, but rather carved from larger planks in curvilinear patterns to assure that they would not spring out of shape years later. The transoms are cut

with intriguing fan or heart shapes and are backed with white screen paper. Other unbacked transoms have fretwork of an almost Chinese cast. Such details suggest the care with which all aspects of the decor were planned and executed.

Though partially obscured by soot from oil lamps, the paintings on the sliding screens are also worthy of note. The Suiren no Ma on the second floor takes its name from the trompe-l'oeil green bamboo blinds (*suiren*) painted on the walls. The blinds appear to hang from the upper screen runner and are rolled up to mid-wall height. The Ōgi no Ma has groups of fans (*ōgi*) painted on the ceiling. They show a blend of delicacy and eccentricity that must have pleased the most discriminating of guests.

GRACIOUS PASTIMES AT A SUKIYA COMPLEX

Emperor Gomizunoo's Visit to Katsura   On the sixth day of the third month, 1663, the Tonsured Retired Emperor Gomizunoo made an imperial progress to Katsura Detached Palace. As had been the case for the ex-emperor's stay at the Ninomaru Palace of Nijō Castle thirty-seven years before, the Katsura complex, to our best knowledge, was expanded in preparation for his arrival, and great pains were taken to put the existing buildings and gardens in perfect order.

One day's events during the imperial sojourn are recorded in the diary of the monk Hōrin Jōshō (?–1668) of Kinkakuji (the Golden Pavilion). The day began with a tour of the main Shoin complex and then a walk through the garden and around the various teahouses. One particular focus of attention was the New Palace (Shin Goten) and Music Room (Gakki no Ma), thought to have been newly added for the ex-emperor (see pp. 78–79). Particularly impressive was the Imperial Dais in the New Palace's Ichi no Ma, a three-mat raised *jōdan* space with a marvelously intricate confection of shelves and cup-

boards flanking a built-in desk and stylized cusped window. These so-called Katsura shelves are made of variety of exotic woods such as zelkova, chinese quince, red sandalwood, ebony, and bombay black wood—they are justly famous.

Outside, the cherry trees were in full bloom around the pond. Jōshō exclaimed in his diary that the splendor of the scene left him "bereft of speech," and that the delicacies provided in the teahouses were "amazing to mortal eyes." Returning to the Shoin complex, the party dined on *kirimugi*, a noodle dish appropriate to the season.

Boating, Dining, and Poetizing   After the kirimugi the party went boating on the nearby Katsuragawa river. On board were candies and other dainties. But the river was swollen due to rain the day before, and the group elected to return and boat on the gentler waters of the garden pond, at which time Jōshō composed a poem in Chinese and presented it to the monarch. Disembarking sometime later, the entourage moved indoors for the midday meal and two rounds of tea.

258. Katsura Detached Palace, viewed from the garden

The afternoon was given over to poetry. The tonsured retired emperor composed a poem in Japanese that was recorded by the host, his eleventh son Hachijōmiya Yasuhito, third-generation owner of the villa. Later the poets indulged in humorous verses in both Japanese and Chinese.

Toward evening Jōshō departed. He had left Kinkakuji early that morning and would not arrive back until late that night. Katsura seems relatively close to downtown Kyōto today, but in the seventeenth century it was part of the surrounding countryside. He had spent the day partaking of elegant pleasures—viewing the graceful architecture and gardens, eating delicious cuisine and drinking excellent tea, composing both serious and humorous verse, boating on the river and pond, and appreciating the breathtaking natural surroundings. These were all cultivated pursuits, fully enjoyed only by those of learning and culture, who were deeply imbued with the way of tea, the Nō drama, the great poetry anthologies, and the intricacies of ritual and court usage. It was to engage the intellect and sensibilities of connoisseurs

such as these that the Sukiya style was developed.

The Sukiya World The Katsura Villa is perhaps the most perfect example in Japan of the integration of architecture and its natural surroundings. The rustic teahouses sequestered in garden corners, the stones leading from the pond up to the Shoin complex, the open verandas and removable exterior screens, all contribute to that interrelation. But the present form of Katsura's Sukiya world is no doubt somewhat different from that enjoyed by Gomizunoo, Yasuhito, and Jōshō. A later owner of the Katsura Villa in the middle of the Edo period, Prince Yakahito (seventh head of the Katsuranomiya line), was particularly fond of the villa and probably altered it to some extent to suit his personal tastes. The Katsuragawa river, too, has a continual tendency to overflow its banks, and this has perhaps affected the configuration of the garden and pond. But the spirit of the old Katsura continues to survive for visitors enjoy today.

ENTERTAINMENTS FIT FOR AN EMPEROR

Sukiya Taste at the Sentō Palace of Gomizunoo
Besides leaving a record of the Tonsured Retired Emperor Gomizunoo's visit to Katsura, the monk Jōshō also noted in his diary the pastimes and entertainments he enjoyed on various occasions at the ex-emperor's own residence, the Sentō Palace. There, as at Katsura, Sukiya taste flourished. In 1636, for example, Jōshō attended a moon-viewing party on the fifteenth of the eighth month. By the lunar calendar, the moon is at its fullest on the fifteenth day of each rotation, and the full moon of the eighth month was, and still is, a traditional occasion for drinking *sake* and composing poetry. A similar gathering was held on the thirteenth of the next month in anticipation of the full moon, during which guests in boats made verses on the theme "the moon over the pond." Five days later the ex-emperor sponsored a *kuchikiri* gathering to open the jars of new tea sealed since the summer. Jōshō sampled three types of tea at the tasting. Calligraphy appropriate to the season had been hung for the occasion in the decorative alcove, and the shelves beside it were graced with finely wrought incense burners and small boxes. A banquet followed, and guests seated on the island in the pond watched the moon rise over the Eastern Hills. Others on board boats chanted poems. In the garden the dance *Otome* was performed on a temporary stage five bays square that had been set up earlier.

Perhaps the grandest occasion observed by Jōshō at the Sentō Palace was a party in the following year that lasted three days and nights, from the twenty-second to the twenty-fifth of the third month. A total of eighteen different events were enjoyed, including poetry composition in Japanese and Chinese, archery with miniature bows and arrows, *go*, incense judging, and *kemari*, a decorous and traditional form of kickball. Courtiers engaged in kemari can be seen by the bridge at the left in figure 258. The guests also drew lots for presents so lavish that Jōshō could only write that his brush failed to do them justice.

Delighting in Nature   Jōshō's entries reflect only a part of the annual round of activities at the Sentō Palace of the retired emperor. All the pastimes, though, were directly related to the current season and accompanying natural phenomena. When the camelias bloomed, for example, the ex-emperor's court went out to view them and bring home a few ~~rays~~ for the artful arrangements to be described ~~low~~. And when the time came for matsutake ~~mushrooms~~, the ex-emperor and his minions began ~~looking~~ forward to going out and picking them. In

259. Six of the dishes presented to Gomizunoo at Ninomaru Palace, Nijō Castle

260. Dishes for a formal visit (*Secrets of Ikuma-style Cuisine* [*Ikemaryū ryōri densho*])

261. Rikka flower arrangements (*Pictures of Ikenobō Senkō's Rikka* [*Ikenobō Senkō rikka zu*])

the autumn, they went north to Takao to view the changing leaves and enjoy rich food and drink (fig. 264). And no one ignored nights with a full moon; Katsura, in fact, has a special moon-viewing stage projecting from the pond side of the Old Shoin (fig. 262). Many of these activities had become staples of the court year, sanctioned by centuries of tradition, and were observed by the regnant emperor as well as by his retired predecessor. The principle of regulating and enjoying life through the changing seasons was accordingly the mark of a person of taste and cultivation. In his *Essays in Idleness* (entry 31) Yoshida Kenkō tells a humorous anecdote about a minor lapse in such sensitivity on his part:

> One morning after a pleasant snowfall, I had a matter to convey to someone and sent off a letter, but without mentioning the snow. The person replied "How can I have anything to do with one so perverse as to fail to inquire how I am enjoying the snow? Most regrettable of you." I found it quite amusing. . . .

The Art of Entertainment   Flower arranging was another way to bring the natural environment into the living space. The art developed as an adjunct to Buddhist ritual, and flowers arranged in a vase were one of the "three *objets*" (*mitsugusoku*; see pp. 74–75) placed in front of Buddhist icons. Out of this tradition developed the more complex and sophisticated

262. View of garden and moon-viewing platform from Old Shoin, Katsura Detached Palace

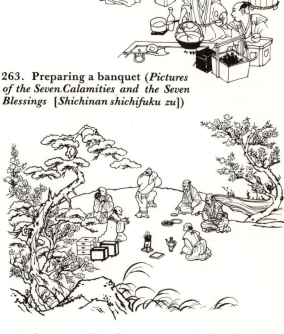

263. Preparing a banquet (*Pictures of the Seven Calamities and the Seven Blessings* [*Shichinan shichifuku zu*])

264. Merrymaking amid fall foliage (*Pictures of Maple Viewing at Takao* [*Takao kampū zu*])

art of *rikka* (literally, "flower placement") in the fifteenth century. The rikka technique, said to have been invented by the Ikenobō family, thrived in the sixteenth and seventeenth centuries, not only in aristocratic mansions but in teahouses and even castles. The art continues to flourish today under the name *ikebana*. Illustrations survive of some of the arrangements created by the famous early seventeenth-century master Ikenobō Senkō II (d. 1658?), who did much of his work in Gomizunoo's palace (fig. 261). Often flower arranging was pursued as an erudite game, with contestants vying to create the finest works of floral artistry.

The art of fine cuisine constituted another link between the people of the time and the outside environment. Their choice and preparation of various natural ingredients was sophisticated in the extreme, so much so that moderns have yet to duplicate some of their effects. Illustrations exist of some of the exquisite dishes served to Gomizunoo during his visit to the Ninomaru Palace in 1626 (fig. 259). Like so many Japanese arts, cooking techniques were eventually codified into schools. Some of the more exotic creations made in the Ikuma style for aristocratic visits also survive in early illustrations (fig. 260). And like flower arranging or poetry, it could be approached as a pleasant game or as an art worthy of serious and prolonged application.

The same can be said of the tea ceremony. We have already seen the way in which early practitioners

gamed at guessing the provenance of various teas while enjoying pleasant surroundings and good companionship. Others, like Rikyū, treated tea as a high art and a life's work. And just as tea could be either lighthearted or serious, so could it be either opulent or humble. One compromise between the various approaches is reflected in the tea ceremony of Kobori Enshū (1579–1647). Known as *kirei sabi*, Enshū's style of tea suggests a cross between rich beauty (*kirei*) and refined simplicity (*sabi*). His tea ceremonies were held in more spacious rooms than Rikyū's *sōan* and used a wide variety of Chinese, Japanese, and Korean vessels. An exemplar of the Sukiya spirit, Enshū was also a brilliant architect and garden designer, and his garden style is reflected at both Katsura and Gomizunoo's palace.

Another tea master, Kanamori Sōwa (1584–1656) practiced a related kind of tea ceremony whose elegance particularly appealed to members of the nobility as well as to Tokugawa Ieyasu, who summoned him to Edo. The Teigyokuken Teahouse (see fig. 230) is said to be one of his designs.

For most practitioners, the tea ceremony, like the other forms of artistic entertainment, was something to be respected, yet enjoyed in a relaxed way amid the changing panorama of the seasons. Even the teahouse itself could be dispensed with on occasion if the mood so warranted. Any natural setting was appropriate if approached with the Sukiya attitude.

SITES MENTIONED IN THE TEXT

Including Addresses and Hints on How to Get There

Asukadera
Asuka, Asuka-mura, Takaichi-gun, Nara Pref. Take bus or taxi from Kashihara Jingū station on Kintetsu Yoshino line.

Bitchū-Matsuyama Castle (Takahashi Castle)
Uchiyamashita, Takahashi City, Okayama Pref. Take bus or taxi from Bitchū-Takahashi station on Hakubi line.

Byōdōin
Ujirenge, Uji City, Kyōto Pref. Walk from Uji station on Keihan Uji line or J.N.R. Nara line.

Chōjuji
Higashidera, Ōaza, Ishibe-machi, Kōka-gun, Shiga Pref. Take bus or taxi from Ishibe station on Kusatsu line.

Chōkyūji
Kamimachi, Ikoma City, Nara Pref. Take bus or taxi from Tomio station on Kintetsu Nara line.

Chūsonji
Hiraizumi, Hiraizumi-chō, Nishi Iwai-gun, Iwate Pref. Walk from Hiraizumi station on Tōhoku line.

Daigoji
Daigo Garan-chō, Fushimi-ku, Kyōto City. Take bus or taxi from Yamashina station on Tōkaidō line.

Daisen'in *See* Daigoji

Daitokuji
Daitokuji-chō, Murasakino, Kita-ku, Kyōto City. Take bus or taxi from Kyōto station.

Daizenji
Kashio, Katsunuma-machi, Higashi Yamanashi-gun, Yamanashi Pref. Take bus or taxi from Katsunuma station on Chūō line.

Eiheiji
Eiheiji-chō, Yoshida-gun, Fukui Pref. Walk from Eiheiji station on Keifuku line.

Emukai House *See* Former Emukai House

Engakuji
Yamanouchi, Kamakura City, Kanagawa Pref. Walk from Kita Kamakura station on Yokosuka line.

Enjōji
Ninnikusen-chō, Nara City. Take bus or taxi from Nara station.

Enryakuji (Hieizan)
Sakamoto Honchō, Ōtsu City, Shiga Pref. Take bus or taxi from Hieizan station on Kosei line, or take cable car from Sakamoto station on Keihan Ishiyama Sakamoto line, or bus from Kyōto station.

Eri House *See* Former Eri House

Former Emukai House
Originally at Kamitaira-mura, Higashitonami-gun, Toyama Pref. Now in Nihon Minkaen (Japanese Open-Air Museum), 7-1-1 Masugata, Tama-ku, Kawasaki City, Kanagawa Pref. Walk from Mukōgaoka-yūen station on Odakyū Odawara line.

Former Eri House

2948-7 Tazura, Ōkawa-machi, Ōkawa-gun, Kagawa Pref. Take taxi from Zōta station on Kōtoku line.

Former Kikuchi House
13-46 Otomo-chō, Tōno City, Iwate Pref. Take taxi from Masuzawa station on Kamaishi line.

Former Kitamura House
Originally at Horiyamashita, Hadano City, Kanagawa Pref. Now in Nihon Minkaen (Japanese Open-Air Museum), 7-1-1 Masugata, Tama-ku, Kawasaki City, Kanagawa Pref. Walk from Mukōgaoka-yūen station on Odakyū Odawara line.

Former Sakuta House
Originally at Kujūkuri-machi, Sambu-gun, Chiba Pref. Now in Nihon Minkaen (Japanese Open-Air Museum), 7-1-1 Masugata, Tama-ku, Kawasaki City, Kanagawa Pref. Walk from Mukōgaoka-yūen station on Odakyū Odawara line.

Former Shibuya House
Originally at Tamugimata, Higashitagawa-gun, Yamagata Pref. Now at Chidō Hakubutsukan (Chidō Museum), 10-18, Kachū-shimmachi, Tsuruoka City, Yamagata Pref. Take bus or taxi from Tsuruoka station on Uetsu line.

Furui House
Yasutomi-chō, Shisō-gun, Hyōgo Pref. Take taxi from Himeji station on Tōkaidō line.

Fushian and Zangetsutei Teahouses
597 Hompōjimae-chō, Ogawa Dōri, Teranouchi Agaru, Kamigyō-ku, Kyōto City. Take bus or taxi from Kyōto station.

Fushimi Inari Shrine
Yabunouchi-chō, Fukakusa, Fushimi-ku, Kyōto City. Take bus from Kyōto station, or walk from Inari station on J.N.R. Nara line.

Futarasan Shrine
Yamauchi, Nikkō City, Tochigi Pref. Take bus from Nikkō station on Nikkō line or from Tōbu Nikkō station on Tōbu Nikkō line.

Ganjōji
Shiramizu-machi, Uchigō, Iwaki City, Fukushima Pref. Take bus or taxi from Taira station on Jōban line.

Ginkakuji (Jishōji)
Ginkakuji-chō, Sakyō-ku, Kyoto. Take bus or taxi from Kyōto station.

Golden Pavilion *See* Kinkakuji

Hakogi House
Yamada-machi, Hyōgo-ku, Kobe City, Hyōgo Pref. Take taxi from Kōbe station.

Heian Shrine
Okazaki-chō, Sakyō-ku, Kyoto City. Take bus from Kyoto station.

Hieizan *See* Enryakuji

Hie Shrine
Sakamoto-honchō, Ōtsu City, Shiga Pref. Take bus or taxi from Ōtsu station on Tōkaidō line, or walk from Sakamoto station on Keihan Ishiyama Sakamoto line.

Hikone Castle
Konki-chō, Hikone City, Shiga Pref. Walk from Hikone station on Tōkaidō line.

Himeji Castle
Hommachi, Himeji City, Hyōgo Pref. Take train (either the Bullet Train [Shinkan-sen] or Sanyō line) to Himeji

station and from there a bus or taxi.

Hirosaki Castle
3 Shirogane-chō, Hirosaki City, Aomori Pref. Take bus or taxi from Hirosaki station on Ōu line.

Horiuchi House
117 Horinouchi, Ōaza, Shiojiri City, Nagano Pref. Take taxi from Shiojiri station on Chūō line.

Hōryūji
878 Hōryūji, Ikaruga-chō, Ikoma-gun, Nara Pref. Take bus or taxi from Hōryūji station on Kansai line, or bus from Nara station.

Imanishi House
3-9-25 Imai-chō, Kashihara City, Nara Pref. Walk from Yamato Yagi station on Kintetsu Ōsaka line.

Inuyama Castle
Inuyama, Inuyama City, Aichi Pref. Walk from Inuyama-yūen station on the Meitetsu Inuyama line.

Ise Shrine
Isuzugawakami, Ise City, Mie Pref. For Outer Shrine (Toyouke Daijingū), walk from Ise-shi station on Sangū or Kintetsu Yamada line. For Inner Shrine (Kōtai Jingū), take bus or taxi from Uji-yamada station on Kintetsu Yamada line.

Itsukushima Shrine
1-1 Miyajima-chō, Saeki-gun, Hiroshima Pref. From Miyajimaguchi station on Sanyō line, take ferry for Miyajima.

Izumo Shrine
Kizuki Higashi, Ōaza, Taisha-chō, Hikawa-gun, Shimane Pref. Take bus or walk from Taisha station on Taisha line.

Jishōji *See* Ginkakuji

Joan Teahouse
Urakuen, 6 Gomonsaki, Inuyama City, Aichi Pref. Walk from Inuyama-yūen station on Meitetsu Inuyama line.

Jōdoji
Kiyotani-chō, Ono City, Hyōgo Pref. Take bus or taxi from Sannomiya station on Sanyō line.

Jōrakuji
Nishidera, Ōaza, Ishibe-machi, Kōka-gun, Shiga Pref. Take bus or taxi from Ishibe station on Kusatsu line.

Kaijūsenji
Reihei, Ōaza, Kamo-chō, Sōraku-gun, Kyōto Pref. Walk from Kamo-chō station on Kansai line.

Kakurinji
Kakogawa-chō, Kakogawa City, Hyōgo Pref. Walk from Kakurinji station on Kakogawa line.

Kamigamo Shrine *See* Kamowakeikazuchi Shrine

Kamo Mioya Shrine (Shimokamo Shrine)
Izumigawa-chō, Shimogamo, Sakyō-ku, Kyōto City. Take bus from Kyōto station.

Kamowakeikazuchi Shrine (Kamigamo Shrine)
Motoyama-chō, Kamigamo, Kita-ku, Kyōto City. Take bus or taxi from Kyōto station.

Kanasana Shrine
Ninomiya, Ōaza, Kamikawa-mura, Kodama-gun, Saitama Pref. Take bus or taxi from Kodama station on Hachikō line.

Kanazawa
Kanazawa City, Ishikawa Pref. Take Hokuriku line to Kanazawa station.

Karako Site

Karako, Tawaramoto-chō, Shiki-gun, Nara Pref. Take bus from Sakurai station on Kintetsu Ōsaka line.

Kasuga Shrine
Kasugano-chō, Nara City. Walk or take bus from Nara station.

Katsura Detached Palace
Kiyomizu-chō, Sakyō-ku, Kyōto City. Take bus or taxi from Kyōto station. Visiting by appointment only. Call 075-211-1215 up to three months in advance, or apply in writing (with self-addressed return envelope) to Kunaichō Kyōto Jimusho, Kyōto Gyoen, Kamigyō-ku, Kyōto City.

Kawaradera
Kawahara, Asuka-mura, Takaichi-gun, Nara Pref. Walk from Okadera station on Kintetsu Yoshino line.

Kawauchi House
6300 Itaya, Ōaza, Taku-chō, Taku City, Saga Pref. Take taxi from Taku station on Karatsu line.

Kenchōji
Yamanouchi, Kamakura City, Kanagawa Pref. Walk or take bus from Kamakura station.

Kenninji
Komatsu-chō, 4-chōme Shijō Kudaru, Yamato Ōji Dōri, Higashiyama-ku, Kyōto City. Walk or take bus from Kyōto station.

Kikuchi House *See* Former Kikuchi House

Kinkakuji (Rokuonji)
Kinkakuji-chō, Kita-ku, Kyōto City. Take bus or taxi from Kyōto station.

Kita House
Originally located in Lumbermen's District (Zaimoku-chō), Kanazawa City. Now at 3-8-11, Hommachi, Nonoichi-machi, Ishikawa Pref. Take bus or taxi from Kanazawa station on Hokuriku line.

Kitamura House *See* Former Kitamura House

Kiyomizudera
Kiyomizu 1-chōme, Higashiyama-ku, Kyōto City. Take bus or taxi from Kyōto station.

Kōchi Castle
Marunouchi, Kōchi City, Kōchi Pref. Walk for take bus from Kōchi station on Dosan line.

Kōdōkan School
119 Kita Sannomaru, Mito City, Ibaraki Pref. Walk from Mito station on Jōban line.

Kōfukuji
48 Noborioji-chō, Nara City. Walk from Nara station.

Kokedera *See* Saihōji

Kokin Denju no Ma
Suizenji, Izumi-chō, Kumamoto City, Kumamoto Pref. Walk or take streetcar from Kumamoto station on Kagoshima line.

Kongōbuji
Kōyasan, Kōya-chō, Ito-gun, Wakayama Pref. Take bus or taxi from Kōyasan station on Nankai Kōya line.

Konjikidō *See* Chūsonji

Konnichian Teahouse
613 Hompōjimae-chō, Ogawa Dōri, Teranouchi Agaru, Ogawa Dōri, Kamigyō-ku, Kyōto City. Take bus or taxi from Kyōto station.

Kuriyama House
2-8 1-chōme Gojō, Gojō City, Nara Pref. Take taxi from Gojō station on Wakayama line.

Mampukuji
3 Gokanoshō, Uji City, Kyōto Pref. Walk from Ōbaku station on J.N.R. Nara line or Keihan Uji line.
Manshuin
Takenouchi-chō, Ichijōji, Sakyō-ku, Kyōto City. Take bus or taxi from from Kyōto station.
Marugame Castle
Ichiban-chō, Marugame City, Kagawa Pref. Take bus or taxi from Marugame station on Yosan line.
Maruoka Castle
Kasumi, Maruoka-chō, Sakai-gun, Fukui Pref. Take taxi or bus from Maruoka station on Hokuriku line.
Matsue Castle
1-5 Tonomachi, Tonomachi, Matsue City, Shimane Pref. Take bus from Matsue station on the San'in line.
Matsumoto Castle
Marunouchi, Matsumoto City, Nagano Pref. Walk or take bus from Matsumoto station on Chūō line.
Matsuyama Castle
Marunouchi, Matsuyama City, Ehime Pref. Take bus and then cablecar from Matsuyama station on Yosan line.
Meirindō School
Originally in Higashikado, Katabata, Nagashima-chō, Gifu Pref. Now in Hashima City, Gifu Pref., where it is the Main Hall of Eishōji temple. Take taxi from Gifu station on Tōkaidō line.
Miidera See Onjōji
Minase Shrine
Hirose 3-chōme, Shimamoto-chō, Mishima-gun, Ōsaka Pref. Walk or take bus from Yamazaki station on Tōkaidō line.
Miwa Shrine (Ōmiwa Shrine)
Miwa, Ōaza, Sakurai City, Nara Pref. Take bus or taxi from Sakurai station on Kintetsu Ōsaka line.
Myōkian
Ōyamazaki, Ōyamazaki-chō, Otokuni-gun, Kyōto Pref. Walk from Yamazaki station on Tōkaidō line or from Ōyamazaki station on Hankyū Kyōto line.
Myōōin
Kusado-chō, Fukuyama City, Hiroshima Pref. Take bus or taxi from Fukuyama station on Sanyō line.
Nakamura House
Nagara, Gose City, Nara Pref. Take bus or taxi from Gose station on Wakayama line.
Nijō Castle
Nijōjō-chō, Horikawa Nishi Iru, Nijō Dōri, Nakagyō-ku, Kyōto City. Walk or take bus from Kyōto station.
Nikaidō House
5595 Kaminoichi, Niitomi Aza, Koyama Ōaza, Kimotsuki-gun, Kagoshima Pref. Take taxi from Ōsumi Koyama station on Ōsumi line.
Nikkō Tōshōgū
Yamauchi, Nikkō City, Tochigi Pref. Take bus from Nikkō station on Nikkō line or from Tōbu Nikkō station on Tōbu Nikkō line.
Ninomaru Palace See Nijō Castle
Nishi Honganji
Honganjimonzen-chō, Hanaya-chō Kudaru, Horikawa Dōri, Shimogyō-ku, Kyōto City. Take bus or walk from Kyōto station.
Omote Senke Tea Garden See Fushian and Zangetsutei

Teahouses
Onjōji (Miidera)
Onjōji-chō, Ōtsu City, Shiga Pref. Walk from Miidera station on Keihan Ishiyama Sakamoto line. (At the Metropolitan Museum of Art, New York, there is an exact reproduction of the Ichi no Ma, or First Room, of Onjōji's Kangakuin.)
Rengeōin (Sanjūsangendō)
Myōhōin Maegawa-machi, Shibuya Kudaru, Higashi Ōji Kudaru, Higashiyama-ku, Kyōto City. Walk from Kyōto station.
Rinnōji
Yamauchi, Nikkō City, Toshigi Pref. Take bus from Nikkō station on Nikkō line or from Tōbu Nikkō station on Tōbu Nikkō line.
Rinshunkaku See Sankeien Park
Rokuonji See Kinkakuji
Ryōanji
1 Tamazushiba-chō, Ryōanji, Sakyō-ku, Kyōto City. Take bus or taxi from Kyōto station.
Saihōji (Kokedera)
56 Matsuo Kamigaya, Nishinokyō-ku, Kyōto City. Take bus or taxi from Kyōto station, or walk from Kamikatsura station on Hankyū Arashiyama line. Visits arranged by written application (accompanied by self-addressed return envelope) to Saihōji Sampai-gakari, Matsuo Nishigyō-ku, Kyōto City, with notation of applicant's nationality (tel. 075-391-3631).
Sakuta House See Former Sakuta House
Sanjūsangendō See Rengeōin
Sankeien Park
293 Hommoku Sannotani, Naka-ku, Yokoyama City. Take bus or taxi from Sakuragichō station on Tōyoko or Keihin Tōhoku line.
Sentō Gosho See Sentō Palace
Sentō Palace
Kōkyonai, Kamigyō-ku, Kyōto City. Walk from Imadegawa subway station. Visiting by appointment only. Call 075-211-1215 up to three months in advance, or apply in writing (with self-addressed return envelope) to Kunaichō Kyōto Jimusho, Kyōto Gyoen, Kamigyō-ku, Kyōto City.
Shibuya House See Kamo Mioya Shrine
Shimokamo Shrine See Kamo Mioya Shrine
Shinjuan See Daitokuji
Shinra Zenshindō See Onjōji
Shin Yakushiji
Fukui-chō, Takabatake-chō, Nara City. Take bus or taxi from Nara station.
Shizutanikō Academy
Shizutani, Bizen City, Okayama Pref. Walk from Bizen Katakami station on Akoo line.
Shitennōji
Motomachi, Tennōji-ku, Osaka City. Walk from Tennōji station on J.N.R. line or Shitennōji station on Tanimachi subway line.
Shōfukuji
4-chōme Noguchi-chō, Higashi Murayama City, Tōkyō. Walk from Higashi Murayama station on Seibu Shinjuku line.
Silver Pavilion See Ginkakuji
Sōfukuji

7-5 Kamiya-machi, Nagasaki City. Take bus or streetcar from Nagasaki station on Nagasaki line.

Sumiya
32 Ageya-machi, Nishi Shinyashiki, Shimogyō-ku, Kyōto City. Take bus or taxi from Kyōto station.

Sumiyoshi Shrine
Sumiyoshi-chō, Sumiyoshi-ku, Ōsaka City. Walk from Sumiyoshi Taisha station on Nankai line.

Taian Teahouse See Myōkian

Taimadera
Taima, Ōaza, Taima-chō, Kita Katsuragi-gun, Nara Pref. Walk from Taimadera station on Kintetsu Minami Ōsaka line.

Takahashi Castle See Bitchū-Matsuyama Castle

Taku School
Taku-chō, Taku City, Saga Pref. Take taxi from Taku station on Karatsu line.

Tayasumon Gate
Kitanomaru Kōen, Chiyoda-ku, Tōkyō. Walk from Kudanshita station on Tōzai subway line.

Teigyokuken See Daitokuji

Tenryūji
Susukinobaba-chō, Saga Tenryūji, Ukyō-ku, Kyōto City. Take bus or taxi from Kyōto station.

Tōdaiji
406 Zōshi-chō, Nara City. Take bus from Nara station.

Torinokosanjō Shrine
1948 Yamata, Ōaza, Batō-chō, Nasu-gun, Tochigi Pref. Take taxi from Ujiie station on Tōhoku line.

Toro Site
Takamatsu, Shizuoka City, Shizuoka Pref. Take bus or taxi from Shizuoka station.

Tōshōgū See Nikkō Tōshōgū

Tsumago
Tsumago, Minami Kiso-chō, Kiso-gun, Nagano Pref. Take bus or taxi from Minami Kiso station on Chūō line.

Udamikumari Shrine
Furuichiba, Ōaza, Udano-chō, Uda-gun, Nara Pref. Take bus or taxi from Nara station.

Ujigami Shrine
Uji Yamada, Uji City, Kyōto Pref. Walk from Uji station on Uji line.

Umpōji
Kamihagiwara, Enzan City, Yamanashi Pref. Walk or take taxi from Enzan station on Chūō line.

Usa Hachiman Shrine See Usa Shrine

Usa Shrine
2859 Minami Usa, Ōaza, Usa City, Oita Pref. Walk from Usa station on Nippō line.

Uwajima Castle
Marunouchi, Uwajima City, Ehime Pref. Take bus or taxi from Uwajima station on Yosan line.

Wachigaiya
Ageya-machi, Nishi Shinyashiki, Shimogyō-ku, Kyōto City. Take bus or taxi from Kyōto station.

Yakushiji
Nishinokyō-machi, Nara City. Walk from Nishinokyō station on Kintetsu Kashihara line.

Yoshimura House
3-5 5-chōme Shimaizumi, Habikino City, Ōsaka Pref. Walk from Fujiidera station on Kintetsu Minami Ōsaka line.

Yūin Teahouse
613 Hompōjimae-machi, Teranouchi Agaru, Ogawa Dōri, Kamigyō-ku, Kyōto City. Take bus or taxi from Kyōto station.

Zangetsutei Tea House See Fushian and Zangetsutei Teahouses

Zenkōji
Ōaza Nagano Motoyoshi-chō, Nagano City, Nagano Pref. Take bus or taxi from Nagano station on Shin'etsu line.

MUSEUMS AND OTHER FACILITIES OF ARCHITECTURAL INTEREST

Hida Minzoku Mura (Hida Folklore Village)
2680 Kamiokamoto-chō, Takayama City, Gifu Pref. Tel. 0577-34-5888. Take bus or taxi from Takayama station on Takayama line. A collection of over sixty minka and storehouses as well as approximately five thousand traditional tools and utensils from the Hida region.

Hyakumangoku Bunkaen Edo Mura (Edo Village)
25 He, Yuwaku-machi, Kanazawa City, Ishikawa Pref. Tel. 0762-35-1111. Take bus from Kanazawa station on Hokuriku line to Yuwaku Onsen. A collection of tools, utensils, clothing, and buildings—an inn designated for use by daimyō, a merchant's house, farmhouses, gates, the house of a lower-ranking samurai, and others—preserved from the Kaga fief of the Edo period, giving a good idea of class differences in architecture.

Nihon Minkaen (Japanese Open-Air Museum)
7-1-1 Masugata, Tama-ku, Kawasaki City, Kanagawa Pref. Tel. 044-922-2181. Walk from Mukōgaoka-yūen station on Odakyū Odawara line. A collection of minka relocated from various regions of Japan, including the former Emukai, Kitamura, and Sakuta houses described in this book.

Nihon Minka Shūraku Hakubutsukan (Japanese Village Farmhouse Museum)
1-2 Hattori Ryokuchi, Toyonaka City, Ōsaka Pref. Tel. 06-862-3137. Walk from Ryokuchi-kōen station on Midōsuji subway line. A collection of over ten minka relocated from various regions, including the gate from a overseer's residence, an Ell House from Nambu, a rice storehouse, an elevated storehouse, and many traditional tools and utensils.

Sankeien (Sankei Park)
293 Sannotani, Hommoku, Naka-ku, Yokohama City. Tel. 045-621-0635. Take bus to Sankeienmae from Yokohama station. A traditional Japanese garden in which buildings from throughout Japan were collected by Hara Sankei, including sukiya-style structures, minka, and Buddhist pagodas and halls. The Rinshunkaku found here is described in the text.

Shikoku Minzoku Hakubutsukan (Shikoku Minka Museum)
91 Yashima Nakamachi, Takamatsu City, Kagawa Pref. Walk from Yashima-tozanguchi station on Kotohira line. A collection of over twenty minka, a rural Kabuki stage relocated from Shōdoshima island, and traditonal tools

and utensils from the Shikoku area.

Shitamachi Fūzoku Shiryōkan (Shitamachi Museum)
2-1 Ueno Park, Taitō-ku, Tōkyō. Tel. 03-823-7451. Walk from Ueno station on J.N.R. or Keisei line. A collection of articles and exhibits from the old merchant and craftsmen quarter (*shitamachi*) of Tōkyō. While most date from the twentieth century and are not within the scope of this book, they do give a feeling for life in that quarter in the Edo period.

Takenaka Daiku Dōgu-kan (Takenaka Carpentry Tools Museum)
4-18 Nakayamate Dōri, Chūō-ku, Kōbe City, Hyōgo Pref. Tel. 078-242-0216. Walk from Motomachi or Sannomiya stations. Exhibits give an overview of the development of traditional carpenters' tools as well as the types of lumber used, construction methods, and tools used in daily life.

BIBLIOGRAPHY

(Compiled and annotated by the translator from English-language sources)

GENERAL

Drexler, Arthur. *The Architecture of Japan*. N.Y.: Museum of Modern Art, 1966.
A readable introduction to basic concepts in Japanese architecture.

Ōta Hirotarō, ed. *Japanese Architecture and Gardens*. Tokyo: Kokusai Bunka Shinkōkai, 1966.
Excellent introduction to the field, with separate chapters on historical overview, technology, gardens, Shintō and Buddhist architecture, and houses and castles, each by one of the foremost Japanese experts. Includes a good bibliography of Japanese sources and a glossary.

Paine, Robert Treat and Soper, Alexander. *The Art and Architecture of Japan*. 3rd. ed., with Part One brought up to date by D. B. Waterhouse and Part Two brought up to date by Bunji Kobayashi. Pelican History of Art series. Middlesex, England and New York: Penguin Books, 1981.
A standard reference work in the field. Includes glossary and extensive bibliography.

Sadler, A. L. *A Short History of Japanese Architecture*. 1941. Reprint. Tokyo and Rutland, Vermont: Tuttle, 1963.
A classic introduction still useful in many respects.

Sansom, George. *A Short Cultural History of Japan*. Rev. ed. Stanford: Stanford University Press, 1952.
Remains one of the most frequently consulted Western works on Japanese cultural history.

Tazawa Yutaka, ed. *Biographical Dictionary of Japanese Art*. Trans. Burton Watson, H. Mack Horton, Eugene Langston. Tokyo: International Society for Educational Information, with Kodansha International, 1981.
See "Architecture," pp. 495–521, and "Gardens," pp. 521–35.

Varley, H. Paul. *Japanese Culture*. 3rd. ed. Honolulu: The University of Hawaii Press, 1984.
An excellent summary that puts architecture and the other Japanese arts into their historical perspective.

———. *The Japan Architect*.
The English version of the Japanese architectural magazine *Shinkenchiku*. Often contains valuable articles on Japanese architectural history.

WORSHIP

Akamatsu Toshihide and Yampolsky, Philip. "Muromachi Zen and the Gozan System." In Hall, J. W. and Toyoda Takeshi, eds., *Japan in the Muromachi Age*. Berkeley, Los Angeles, and London: University of California Press, 1977, pp. 313–30.
Good introduction to the origin and historical developments of the Zen establishment, with minor sections on monastic succession, administration, and fiscal management.

Colcutt, Martin. "The Zen Monastery in Kamakura Society." In Jeffrey Mass, ed., *Court and Bakufu in Japan*. New Haven: Yale University Press, 1982.
Very clear discussion of Zen patrons and why they supported the new creed.

Covell, Jon and Yamada Sōbin. *Zen at Daitoku-ji*. Tokyo, New York, and San Francisco: Kodansha International, 1974.
A tour through the history and art of a major Zen temple complex.

Fukuyama Toshio. *Heian Temples: Byodo-in and Chuson-ji*. Trans. Ronald K. Jones. Heibonsha Survey of Japanese Art, vol. 9. New York and Tokyo: Weatherhill/Heibonsha, 1976.
Treats the architecture of the Pure Land (Jōdo) sect. Primarily historical.

Kidder, Edward. *Japanese Temples*. Tokyo: Bijutsu Shuppansha, 1966.
A deluxe treatment of select temples, with elegant photographs and accompanying commentary.

Kobayashi, Takeshi. *Nara Buddhist Art: Todaiji*. Trans. Richard L. Gage. Heibonsha Survey of Japanese Art, vol. 5. New York and Tokyo: Weatherhill/Heibonsha, 1975.
Focuses mostly on sculpture, but includes a short section on Tōdaiji architecture.

Machida Kōichi. "A Historical Survey of the Controversy as to Whether the Hōryū-ji Was Rebuilt or Not." In *Acta Asiatica*, 15 (1968), pp. 87–114.
An exhaustive account, of primary interest with regard to the history and nature of Japanese architectural scholarship. Valuable bibliography.

Mizuno, Seiichi. *Asuka Buddhist Art: Horyu-ji*. Trans. Richard L. Gage. Heibonsha Survey of Japanese Art, vol. 4. New York and Tokyo: Weatherhill/Heibonsha, 1974.
Concentrates on sculpture, but includes brief remarks on the Hōryūji complex.

Ōdate, Toshio. *Japanese Woodworking Tools: Their Tradition, Spirit, and Use*. Newtown, Conn.: Taunton Press, 1984.

A practical guide to the basics of Japanese carpentry.

Okawa, Naomi. *Edo Architecture: Katsura and Nikko*. Trans. Alan Woodhull and Akito Miyamoto. Heibonsha Survey of Japanese Art, vol. 20. New York and Tokyo: Weatherhill/Heibonsha, 1975.

A historical and appreciative account of Nikkō and Katsura, with good photos of detail.

Ooka, Minoru. *Temples of Nara and Their Art*. Trans. Dennis Lishka. Heibonsha Survey of Japanese Art, vol. 7. New York and Tokyo: Weatherhill/Heibonsha, 1973.

A well-illustrated overview of Buddhist architecture not only in Nara but Kyōto and elsewhere. Includes helpful schematic foldouts of details and plans.

Parent, Mary Neighbor. *The Roof in Japanese Buddhist Architecture*. New York and Tokyo: Weatherhill/Kajima, 1983.

An exhaustive treatment of roofing systems in Buddhist temples from the Asuka through the Muromachi periods. With copious tables, glossary, and bibliography.

Suzuki Kakichi. *Early Buddhist Architecture in Japan*. Trans. Mary N. Parent and Nancy S. Steinhardt. Japanese Arts Library, vol. 9. Tokyo, New York, and San Francisco: Kodansha International and Shibundō, 1980.

A superb study of Buddhist architecture from the Asuka through the Heian periods. With a technical introduction by Mary N. Parent, glossary, and bibliography.

Watanabe, Yasutada. *Shinto Art: Ise and Izumo Shrines*. Trans. Robert Ricketts. Heibonsha Survey of Japanese Art, vol. 3. New York and Tokyo: Weatherhill/Heibonsha, 1974.

Good introduction to the beginnings of Japanese architecture, with an overview of the main shrine types.

DAILY LIFE

Engel, Heinrich. *The Japanese House: A Tradition for Contemporary Architecture*. Tokyo and Rutland, Vermont: Tuttle, 1964.

The most detailed treatment of the traditional Japanese house in English. Illustrated with many line drawings and photographs.

Fujioka, Michio. *Japanese Residences and Gardens: A Tradition of Integration*. Photographs by Tsunenari Kazunori. Trans. H. Mack Horton. Great Japanese Art series. Tokyo, New York, and San Francisco: Kodansha International, 1982.

Fine photographs and concise commentary of select masterpieces of Japanese building art.

Hashimoto, Fumio. *Architecture in the Shoin Style*. Trans. and adapted, with an introduction, by H. Mack Horton. Japanese Arts Library, vol. 10. Tokyo, New York, and San Francisco: Kodansha International, 1981.

An in-depth study of the Shoin style and its antecedents and Sukiya variations. With glossary, plans, and bibliography.

Ito, Teiji. *The Elegant Japanese House: Traditional Sukiya Architecture*. New York and Tokyo: Walker and Weatherhill, 1969.

An impressionistic survey of select modern and premodern Sukiya dwellings. Splendid plates.

———. *Traditional Domestic Architecture of Japan*. Trans. and adapted by Richard L. Gage. Heibonsha Survey of Japanese Art, vol. 21. New York and Tokyo: Weatherhill/Heibonsha, 1972.

An overview of *minka*, with a discussion of the standard building techniques and regional variations.

——— and Futagawa Yukio. *Traditional Japanese Houses*. Trans. Richard L. Gage. New York: Rizzoli International, 1983.

A deluxe presentation of select examples of *minka* architecture.

———, with Novograd, Paul. "The Development of Shoin-style Architecture." In *Japan in the Muromachi Age*. Ed. John W. Hall and Toyoda Takeshi. Berkeley, Los Angeles, and London: University of California Press, 1977.

A very helpful article on the shift from the Shinden to the Shoin style.

Kitao Harumichi. *Shoin Architecture in Detailed Illustrations*. Tokyo: Shōkokusha, 1956.

Line drawings and photographs of Shoin structures, with special attention given to detailing. Useful on terminology.

Morse, Edward. *Japanese Homes and Their Surroundings*. 1896. Reprint. Tokyo and Rutland, Vermont: Tuttle, 1972.

A classic investigation of Japanese dwellings by a pioneer in the field of Japanese studies.

Yagi, Koji. *A Japanese Touch for Your Home*. Photographs by Hata Ryo. Trans. Mark Williams. Tokyo, New York, and San Francisco: Kodansha International, 1982.

Shows how traditional architecture continues to influence moderns and provide lessons for contemporary design. Well illustrated.

WAR

Coaldrake, William. "Edo Architecture and Tokugawa Law." *Monumenta Nipponica*, 36, no. 3 (Autumn 1981), pp. 235–84.

Discusses cosmological theory behind the layout of Edo, political rationale for urban design, and sumptuary regulations.

Hirai Kiyoshi. *Feudal Architecture of Japan*. Trans. and adapted by Hiroaki Sato and Jeannine Ciliotta. Heibonsha Survey of Japanese Art. vol. 13. New York and Tokyo: Weatherhill/Heibonsha, 1974.

Covers castles as well as Shoin structures. Includes helpful foldouts of plans and castle details.

Kirby, John B. *From Castle to Teahouse: Japanese Architecture of the Momoyama Period*. Tokyo and Rutland, Vermont: Tuttle, 1962.

A good introduction to the architecture of the Momoyama and early Edo periods.

McClain, James L. *Kanazawa: A Seventeenth-Century Japanese Castle Town*. New Haven and London: Yale University Press, 1982.

A detailed study of the development of a well-preserved

castle town. Covers urban planning, economic life, and political system.

Okumura Yoshitarō, ed. *Photo Collection: Castles of Japan.* Tokyo: Mainichi Newspapers, 1970.

Good photographs of a large number of Japanese castles, with a short text and captions in Japanese and English. Added information on Himeji Castle and its mechanisms for defense.

ENTERTAINMENT

Brandon, James; Malm, William; and Shively, Donald. *Studies in Kabuki: Its Acting, Music, and Historical Context.* Honolulu: The University of Hawaii Press, 1978.

A full treatment of the Kabuki drama by three foremost Western experts.

Bring, Mitchell, and Wayembergh, Josse. *Japanese Gardens: Design and Meaning.* New York: McGraw-Hill, 1981.

A thorough introduction to the principles of Japanese garden art.

Fujioka, Michio. *Kyoto Country Retreats: The Shugakuin and Katsura Palaces.* Photographs by Okamoto Shigeo. Trans. Bruce A. Coats. Great Japanese Art series. Tokyo, New York, and San Francisco: Kodansha International, 1983.

Fine photographs with short explanatory text.

Hayakawa Masao. *The Garden Art of Japan.* Trans. Richard L. Gage. Heibonsha Survey of Japanese Art, vol. 28. New York and Tokyo: Weatherhill/Heibonsha, 1973.

An introduction to Japanese gardens, presented with emphasis on historical development.

Hayashiya Tatsusaburo; Nakamura, Masao; and Hayashiya, Seizo. *Japanese Arts and the Tea Ceremony.* Trans. and adapted by James P. Macadam. Heibonsha Survey of Japanese Art, vol. 15. New York and Tokyo: Weatherhill/Heibonsha, 1974.

A guide to the architecture, gardens, and utensils used in the tea ceremony.

Ito, Teiji. *The Japanese Garden: An Approach to Nature.* Photographs by Takeji Iwamiya. Trans. Donald Richie. New Haven and London: Yale University Press, 1972.

A concise summary of the main types of Japanese gardens, supported by good plates.

————. *Space and Illusion in the Japanese Garden.* Photographs by Sosei Kusunishi. Trans. and adapted by Ralph Friedrich and Masajiro Shimamura. New York and Tokyo: Weatherhill/Tankosha, 1973.

Compares the design characteristics of enclosed courtyards and open gardens.

Keene, Donald. *Nō: The Classical Theatre of Japan.* Rev. ed. Tokyo and Palo Alto: Kodansha International, 1973.

Introduction to the music, dance, and literature of the Nō drama.

Naito Akira. *Katsura: A Princely Retreat.* Photography by Takeshi Nishikawa. Trans. Charles S. Terry. Tokyo, New York, and San Francisco: Kodansha International, 1977.

A deluxe treatment of Katsura, the quintessence of Japanese traditional domestic architecture.

Shigemori Kanto. *Japanese Gardens: Islands of Serenity.* Tokyo: Japan Publications, 1971.

A general introduction of major garden types, together with a short historical discussion by one of the great experts of Japanese garden art.

INDEX

定価3,300円
in Japan

WEST	JAPANESE PERIODS	JAPAN
	Jōmon 10000 B.C.	
		1st pit dwellings (c. 5000–c. 3500)
Great Sphinx at Giza (c. 2530)		
Stonehedge (c. 1800)		
Parthenon (447–432)		
Colossus of Rhodes (292–280)		
	Yayoi 200 B.C.	
Temple of the Sibyl, Tivoli (1st c. B.C.)		
	1 A.D.	
Pont du Gard, Nîmes (c. 14)		
Colosseum, Rome (72–80)		
Pompeii destroyed (79)		
Pantheon, Rome (120–24)		Toro site (100–300)
	Tumulus 250 A.D.	
Basilica of Constantine (310-20)		
Hagia Sophia (532–37)		
S. Apollinare in Classe, Ravenna (533–49)		
	Asuka 552	Buddhism to Japan (538 or 552)
		temple carpenter arrives from Paekche, Korea (577)
		Asukadera (588)
		orig. Hōryūji (607)
		Hōryūji rebuilt (c. 670)
		Hokkiji pagoda (685)
		Fujiwara Captial (694)
	Nara 710	Heijō Capital (710)
		Yakushiji pagoda (730)
		Hōryūji east precinct (739)
		Tōdaiji orig. Great Buddha Hall (760)

WEST	JAPANESE PERIODS	JAPAN
	Heian 784	Nagaoka Capital (784)
Palace Chapel of Charlemagne (792–805)		
		Heian Capital (794)
Santa Maria de Naranco, Oviedo (c. 848)		
		Daigoji pagoda (952)
St. Michael's, Hildesheim (1001–33)		
Cathedral of St. Sophia, Novgorod (1045–52)		Byōdōin Phoenix Ha[ll] (1053)
St. Mark's, Venice (begun 1063)		Hōshōji (1075)
Tower of London (1078–97)		
Durham Cathedral (1093–1130)		Ishiyamadera Main Hall (1096)
		Chūsonji Golden Hall (1126)
Chartres Cathedral (begun 1145)		
Notre-Dame, Paris (begun 1163)		
Leaning Tower of Pisa (begun 1174)		
Canterbury Cathedral (begun 1175)		
		Tōdaiji & Kōfukuji destroyed (1180)
		destruction of Heik[e] clan (1185)
	Kamakura 1185	Kamakura shoguna[te] (1192)
		Jōdoji Jōdodō (1192)
		Ishiyamadera *tahōtō* (1194)
		reconstruction of Tōdaiji Great Buddha Hall (1195)
		reconstruction of Tōdaiji Nandaimon gate (1199)
		Kenninji (1202)
Reims Cathedral (begun 1211)		
Amiens Cathedral (begun 1220)		
Salisbury Cathedral (1220–70)		